Latin American Integration

MAP OF LATIN AMERICA

LATIN AMERICAN INTEGRATION

Vasant Kumar Bawa

HUMANITIES PRESS
ATLANTIC HIGHLANDS, N.J.

First Published 1980 in the United States of America by
Humanities Press Inc.
Atlantic Highlands
N. J. 07716

ISBN 0-391-01899-X

Printed in India

Dedicated
to
my mother
and the memory of my father

CONTENTS

LIST OF TABLES

PREFACE

In recent years the study of problems of economic development has been focused on the developing countries of Asia, Africa and Latin America, which are often referred to as the "Third World" or the South. These countries, however, often maintain closer ties with metropolitan countries or with Communist countries than with one another. The models of development which they seek to follow are usually those of the industrialised countries. In fact even the concepts of the "developing countries" and the "Third World" appear to owe a good deal to writers, policy-makers, and educators from the industrialised countries who have sought to compare conditions in different developing countries.

It may be argued that the developing countries have nothing to learn from one another, as they are all approximately at the same level of backwardness, and that they should emulate the countries which have given up their traditional ways, and modernize their social and economic systems.

This study, by an Asian political scientist, is based on the opposite supposition, viz. that the developing countries not only can, but should, learn from one another. This learning process need not be confined to their successes; it may also extend to the mistakes which have been committed.

Since World War II the developing countries have been coming closer together, at least in economic matters. The United Nations Conference on Trade and Development is one of the results of this joint action in the economic sphere, based on the Prebisch thesis, which challenged some of the established principles of classical international trade theory and asserted the necessity of the industrialisation of the peripheral countries.

Reports of political struggles and revolutions give us a

confused picture of Latin America. There is inadequate knowledge in Asia of Latin American economic and political traditions and its long experience of economic and political confrontation with the metropolitan countries. Integration of Latin America has been taken up as the focus of this study because of its economic and political significance, and its link with major political, economic and strategic factors concerned with world developments in the twentieth century.

Among the complex changes which humanity has undergone in the twentieth century, two major trends appear to be of particular significance for the international scene today.

The first is the search for identity, the trend toward smaller groupings which allow the individual enough room for his cultural and political development, in a unit where he has a sense of belonging. This trend is seen in the rise of separatist movements, based on language and culture, which are found even in old established countries like Great Britain (the Welsh, Scots and Irish) and Belgium, and was seen in the creation of Bangladesh in 1972.

A second important trend, to some extent contradicting the first, is that toward major state groupings based on a merger of many and varied nationalities. The emergence of the United States, the Soviet Union, and China as major world powers has an obvious connection with changes in technology and the art of warfare, as well as with the decline of smaller countries like Britain and France after the disappearance of their overseas empires.

The emergence of a United Europe, which was the dream of many thinkers for centuries, is still a remote prospect, but a union of Western Europe based on economic institutions and something approaching a common foreign policy, seems a possible achievement in the future.

Economic integration acquires greater significance in the light of these major developments, which indicate a close link between world political and economic movements. Neither economics nor political science by itself can provide an adequate framework for analysis of a multidimensional problem like integration. It appears essential to allow for an interplay of the two aspects so as to provide a proper understanding of the process.

The Latin American integration movement now seems to be sufficiently well advanced in years to justify a wider treatment in the context of its history as well as its political framework.

Economists and political scientists have examined the Latin American experience in relation to Western Europe, and the Central American Common Market in relation to East Africa. However, a consideration of the Latin American experience from an Asian point of view is of particular significance because of the increasingly close contacts among the Third World countries and the movement toward common policy of the developing countries to the industrialised countries in the world today. In Asia, the words "economic cooperation" are preferred to "economic integration."

Most of the existing studies on Latin American integration deal with the subject from an economic point of view. Historical accounts of the developments and some political analysis are usually added, so as to place the economic analysis in context.

In a comparative framework, it is necessary to realise how complex is the process of economic integration and how difficult it is to exclude non-economic factors. The best laid plans of economists may go astray, if political and social forces are given inadequate attention. On the other hand, it may be possible to utilise those political and social factors which may appear to be inimical to integration in a constructive fashion. This can only be done, however, if both the similarities and differences between the areas under discussion are taken into account.

The study of integration must take into account the *ambiente* in which it operates. The Latin American scene is very different from the European. Even the alleged unity of Latin America has to be established; and geographic, cultural, social and political aspects of the Latin American situation have to be taken into account.

The working definition which I propose to adopt is therefore one which provides for both an economic and a political content. It has to be distinguished from international economic cooperation. Whereas cooperation refers to "the process of collaboration between independent sovereign states," each retaining its right "to participate or not in any project that is submitted for consideration," integration implies the gradual emergence of interdependent economies, based on removal of discrimination between national economies.

The study is intended not only to assess the Latin American experience with integration, but also to bring out the policy implications of the findings, based on a long view of the integration process. The findings are more directly applicable to Latin America because of the detailed examination of the situation in that region, based on a study of the literature in the field as well as on interviews, discussions and participation in meetings in Washington, D.C., New York, and Mexico City. However, an attempt is made in the concluding chapter to draw lessons from the Latin American experience for Asian developing countries.

The objects of the study are (i) to take an overview of the Latin American integration movement, taking into account political as well as economic factors with special reference to the first development decade of the United Nations; (ii) to analyse, for the benefit of other developing areas, the complexity of the integration process in Latin America, and thus enable policy-makers to learn from the successes as well as the failures of the formative period of the Latin American integration process; and (iii) to arrive at tentative findings to help shape the process of integration in developing areas generally.

In order to place the Latin American integration process in the context of developments in the United Nations and the Third World generally, the first chapter describes the international framework in which the integration movement operated. Chapter II describes the economic, social and political background of the movement and analyses the Prebisch thesis which played an important role in the movement. Chapter III discusses the events leading upto the first treaties of 1960, while Chapter IV analyses the actual integration process from 1961 to 1973. Chapters V and VI discuss the US role in the integration process and the politics of Latin American integration respectively. Chapter VII assesses the developments in Latin America upto the early seventies. The eighth chapter describes the Asian movement towards economic cooperation and the relevance of the Latin American integration experience to Asia.

By the early seventies the integration movement in Latin America appeared to have reached a dead end. The Western

European model, combined with the Prebisch approach to economic development, had not yielded the expected results. The reasons for this have been analysed in Chapter VII, which assesses the position as it existed in the early seventies. The later developments have been summarised in Chapter IX, both for Latin America and Asia. The Latin American section not only describes the developments in Latin America and the Andean group, but also discusses the new emphasis on the building up of infrastructure (especially in the major river valley projects), the emergence of a new stress on mobilising regional resources through SELA, and the evolution of a functional approach to the problems of the region.

Similarly the Asian experience upto the early seventies has been described in Chapter VIII and the later developments upto 1979-80 have been covered in Chapter IX in regard to regional cooperation in the ESCAP region as well as sub-regional cooperation in the ASEAN area. Chapter X provides a general conclusion to the work.

The text is preceded by a political map of Latin America which will help the reader in understanding the text. It is followed by a series of statistical tables which include Country Profiles of the Latin American countries, data on their imports and exports within the region as well as for the world, and a statement of leading export commodities.

The developments in the English-speaking Caribbean countries have not been examined in detail because of their ties with the British Commonwealth, and the special access accorded to them, along with many African and Asian countries, to the European Economic Community in direct competition with Latin American producers, in February 1975. Although some of them have later joined the Economic System of Latin America (SELA), this is a fairly recent development.

The Caribbean Free Trade Association (CARIFTA) was set up in 1968 to foster the development of member-countries through the expansion of inter-regional trade. Subsequently it converted itself into the Caribbean Community (CARICOM). Its membership includes Barbados, Belize, Guyana, Jamaica, Trinidad and Tobago, as well as some of the smaller islands.

Developments in the Caribbean region have been covered in some detail in the Monthly Report on Latin American Integration which appears in the Mexican journal *Comercio Exterior*.

My interest in Latin America dates back to the early 1950's when, as a student at the School of Foreign Services of Georgetown University, I specialised in Latin American studies and studied Spanish and French. The subject of my master's thesis at Georgetown University in 1953 was "Pacific Settlement and Security Procedures in the Organisation of American States."

The Late Dr. Kalman H Silvert was largely responsible for my decision to study at Tulane University, where I worked for my Ph.D. in Political Science with a minor in Latin American Studies from 1952 to 1954.

In the early seventies I was fortunate to have the opportunity of revisiting North America on leave and to take up the present study. During the period (1970-1972) I was in contact with people involved in the Latin American integration movement, and had access to much unpublished information on the subject.

I owe a debt of gratitude to a number of scholars, diplomats, and officials of North and South America, and officials of international organisations who spared their time to discuss with me the problems of international economic integration with special reference to Latin America and Asia. Some of them also took the trouble to read my manuscript at various stages of its preparation and offered comments on it.

It would be difficult to list all those who have helped me by their discussions and comments in arriving at a clearer picture of the integration process in Latin America. I would, however, like to mention in particular Messrs. Raul Rey Alvarez and Luis Ratinoff of the Inter-American Development Bank, Mrs. Elba Kybal and Mr. Manuel Trucco of the Organisation of American States, Mr. Jose Guerra of the World Bank, and Messrs. Diego Cordovez and David Pollock of the United Nations. I also benefited greatly from participation in meetings addressed by Raul Prebisch, Felipe Herrera, Fernando Belaunde Terry, and other distinguished Latin Americans who played a key role in the integration movement.

I had valuable discussions with Philippe Schmitter of the University of Chicago. While in Mexico I had the benefit of discussions with a number of scholars and officials working in the field, including Professor Victor Urquidi, Messrs Enrique

Angulo, Jorge Eduardo Navarrete, Miguel Wionczek, Sergio de la Pena and Edelberto Torres.

Dr Victor Urquidi of El Colegio de Mexico and Dr William V O'Brien of the Institute of World Polity, Georgetown University, were of great assistance in facilitating my research. I am grateful to them, and also to Sri and Srimati G.V. Shukla, and Sri and Srimati Sunil K Roy, formerly of the Indian Foreign Service for their hospitality and assistance in many ways. Among those who have read parts of the manuscript or commented on the study, I am especially grateful to Sri K.B. Lall and Sri K.L. Mehta, both formerly of the Indian Civil Service, to Prof Rajni Kothari, Prof N.V. Sovani and Prof S.V. Bokil of the Gokhale Institute of Politics and Economics, Pune.

I thank the Indian Council of Social Science Research for having made this publication possible, especially Prof Rajni Kothari, Dr T.N. Madan and Sri Kashmiri Singh. The publishers have taken great pains to comment on the manuscript and seen to its early publication.

Lastly, to the many friends and relations who have helped me in completing this work, and whom I am unable to mention by name, I offer my thanks.

Gokhale Institute of Politics
and Economics
Pune-411004

VASANT KUMAR BAWA

LIST OF ABBREVIATIONS

ACU	Asian Clearing Union
ADB	Asian Development Bank
AFP (ALPRO)	Alliance for Progress
AMU	Asian Monetary Unit
APRA	Alianza Popular Revolucionaria Americana (a Peruuan political party)
ARB	Asian Reserve Bank
ASEAN	Association of South-East Asian Nations
CABEI	Central American Bank for Economic Integration
CACM	Central American Common Market
CARICOM	Caribbean Common Market and Community
CARIFTA	Caribbean Free Trade Association (now CARICOM)
CECLA	Special Commission for Latin American Coordination
CEESI	Committee to Study the restructuring of the Inter-American System
CENTO	Central Treaty Organisation
CIAP	(Inter-American) Committee of the Alliance for Progress
ECA	Economic Commission for Africa
ECAFE	Economic Commission for Asia and the Far East (now ESCAP)
ECC	Economic Cooperation Committee
ECE	Economic Commission for Europe
ECLA	Economic Commission for Latin America
ECOSOC	(United Nations) Economic and Social Council.
EEC	European Economic Community

EFTA	European Free Trade Association
ESCAP	Economic and Social Commission for Asia and Pacific (formerly ECAFE)
FSO	Fund for Special Operations
GATT	General Agreement on Tariffs and Trade
IA-ECOSOC	Inter-American Economic and Social Council
IBRD	International Bank for Reconstruction and Development (World Bank)
IDB (IADB)	Inter-American Development Bank
ILPES	Latin American Institute for Economic and Social Planning
IMF	International Monetary Fund
INTAL	Institute for Latin American Integration
LACM	Latin American Common Market
LAFTA	Latin American Free Trade Association (in Spanish, ALALC)
LDC	Less Developed Countries
Multifert	Multinational Company for Marketing of Fertilizers
NIEO	New International Economic Order
OAS	Organisation of American States
ODECA	Organisation of Central American States
OLADE	Latin American Energy Organisation
OPEC	Organisation of Petroleum Exporting Countries
PEC	Permanent Executive Committee
PRI	Partido Revolucionaria Institucional of Mexico
PTA	Preferential Trading Agreement
RCD	Regional Cooperation for Development
ROCAP	Regional Office for Central America and Panama
SDR	Special Drawing Rights
SEATO	South-East Asia Treaty Organisation
SELA	Latin American Economic System
SPTF	Social Progress Trust Fund
USAID	United States Agency for International Development

UNCTAD	United Nations Conference on Trade and Development
UNDP	United Nations Development Programme
UNESCO	United Nations Educational, Scientific, and Cultural Organisation
UNIDO	United Nations Industrial Development Organisation
UNRRA	United Nations Relief and Rehabilitation Administration

GLOSSARY

Commercialista-exportadora	commercial exporting
desarrollismo	"developmentalism"
desarrollista-integracionista	developmental-integrationist
tecnicos	literally technocrats. In Latin America engineers or economists who have technical competence.
zollverein	customs union in 19th century Germany which preceded the German unification.

CHAPTER I

THE INTERNATIONAL FRAMEWORK

One of the remarkable features of the post-war period has been the emergence of an international climate of opinion in the sphere of economic development, especially as regards the developing areas of the world. Economists and academicians specialising in the study of developmental problems and specialists in the United Nations and specialized agencies have primarily contributed to this phenomenon.

The existence of such a climate of opinion does not imply that all countries or even all international agencies are agreed on a particular developmental strategy. There are also wide differences in regard to the solutions to be applied to developmental problems among specialists in different international organizations, as well as among the representatives of different countries. Nevertheless, the clash of opposing views at international conferences, the creation of new international organizations, and the necessity of arriving at agreed solutions to be embodied in international agreements—all these have led to the gradual emergence of a body of ideas which is now fairly widely accepted. The recommendations of the Pearsons Commission, for example, reflect in many respects the demands of the developing countries, as embodied in the proposals of the two UNCTAD (United Nations Conference on Trade and Development) conferences held at Geneva in 1964 and at New Delhi in 1968.[1]

IMITATION IN INTERNATIONAL ORGANISATION

The phenomenon of an international climate of opinion has been related to the tendency to adapt institutional structures from one part of the world to another. This tendency, which may be described as "imitation" in international organization, has been made possible by the improvements in communications, and the growth of a class of experts who function in international organisations at the global or regional levels, or with national governments as officials or consultants in various parts of the world. It is surprising to note the readiness with which an institution which has worked successfully in one culture area and in one set of circumstances is sought to be adapted to another culture area and in rather different conditions. The example of the Inter-American Development Bank, for example, clearly had an influence on the creation of the Asian and African Development Banks.[2]

An early example of what we have described as 'imitation' occurred in the late 1950's, when the comparative success of the Western European experiment in economic integration, led to integration being proposed as a solution to the problems of developing countries. These countries often found it difficult to develop industry without a large internal market. Perhaps, the earliest attempt to adapt the Western European experience was in Latin America. The institutions established in that area in turn gave rise to the demand for the establishment of economic institutions of a similar type in Africa, the Middle East and Asia. Considerable effort was expended in drawing up schemes in this regard, although the practical results have not been commensurate with expectations. In fact, most of the economic unions have failed to get off the ground.[3]

The imitation of the Western European experiment in Latin America was based, as we will see in the succeeding chapters of this study, on an inadequate appreciation of the situation prevalent in Latin America. It was assumed that the successes of the European Economic Community could be reproduced on the broader canvas of the Latin American region, notwithstanding the great variations in the territories extending from the Rio Grande, on the borders of Texas, to the Tierra del Fuego, at the southern-most tip of South America.

The arguments for the establishment of a common market for Latin America and for a free trade area as a stage toward this goal, were based on the view that intra-regional trade could be increased substantially, and that the economies of scale would operate in the Latin American region. These assumptions could only operate in a fairly well-defined and compact region, without any major obstacle to the movement of goods and services.

Such a region would also have to have a fairly high level of communication, at least among the elites, in order to be comparable to Western Europe. These elites should not only be able to communicate with one another but should also have a motive for coming together in an economic or political arrangement.

The situation in Western Europe during the late 1940's and 1950's was characterised by a number of special features. In the first place, there was a common fear of an outside Power, viz. the Soviet Union. Secondly, there was the incentive of massive aid from the United States, and the benefits expected to be derived from the more rapid industrialisation of the Western European region by the establishment of a common market. Thirdly, there was an affinity among the Western European countries due to the existence of a common tradition of democratic government, and a movement for the unification of Europe. Lastly, there was the need to integrate Germany into an economic and political system along with other countries so that in would not be a threat to the peace of the area for a third time in the twentieth century.

If the Western European experiment is taken as a model, it should be clear that for a successful integration to take place, a combination of political and economic motivations is essential, because the existence of economic conditions favourable to integration without the "will to integrate" is no guarantee that integration will indeed take place. It is not necessary, however, that all the original factors must be present in every case of successful integration. It is possible that "functional equivalents" may be found which may take the place of some of the original variables.[4] Any attempt to apply the lessons of one region to another must be approached with great caution because of the danger of seeing similarities where they do not exist, and the possibility that inherent differences in the background or in the situation may produce a very different result.

Nevertheless, the Economic Commission for Asia and the Far East (ECAFE) has, over a period of several years, been urging the member-states to take up measures of regional economic cooperation. At the Ministerial Conference on Asian Economic Cooperation held at Manila in December 1963, the Executive Secretary of ECAFE said that ". . . we cannot afford to stand still. In a world in which every region is moving forward, the ECAFE region must move forward too, and we are determined to do so."[5] Later the Japanese economist and former official of the ECAFE, Hiroshi Kitamura, urged in an article that the countries of the ECAFE region should coordinate their economic policies in order to tackle urgent economic problems (such as the falling prices of agricultural products on the international market), as well as to enter into joint industrial ventures. He mentioned the lessons to be learnt from the Latin American Free Trade Association (LAFTA), and urged that economists should perform the crucial role of advocates of economic union, as was done by Monnet and his adherents in Europe.[6]

The Regional Economic Commissions and the Special Role of ECLA

The United Nations Charter was drawn up on the assumption that the organization would play a crucial role in world affairs. No specific provision was made for the establishment of regional organs of the United Nations and the regional economic commission had therefore to be set up under the provisions of Article 68 of the Charter, which enabled the Economic and Social Council (ECOSOC) to set up subsidiary bodies.

The development of underdeveloped areas did not receive a high priority in the United Nations during its early years. Although the creation of the Economic Commission for Europe (ECE) was considered essential in order to take over the rehabilitation of refugees and the post-war reconstruction of Europe from the United Nations Relief and Rehabilitation Administration (UNRRA) after the end of 1946, there was opposition to the creation of ECAFE and the Economic Commission for Latin America (ECLA). These two regional organisations were evidently the subject of the behind-the-scenes agreement between the Chinese and Chilean representatives. As a result of this early example of Asian-Latin American cooperation, ECAFE came into being along with ECE in March 1947, and ECLA in February 1948.[7] The United States considered ECLA to be encroaching on the preserves of the Organisation of American States (OAS); however, the Latin American delegations were determined to have such an organisation under the United Nations. Its jurisdiction was limited to the Latin American countries, although its membership included the United States as well as Canada, France, the Netherlands, and the United Kingdom.[8]

The representatives of Asian countries in ECAFE regarded it as the most appropriate instrument for Asian economic development, and particularly for the channeling of aid from the industrialised countries. During the first few years of its existence, however, ECAFE had to face obstructions due to the negative attitude of the representatives of Western countries. The Economic Commission for Africa (ECA), created much later, in 1958, also faced a similar situation in regard to some colonial countries.[9]

The problem of Western obstructionism does not seem to have been a major one for ECLA. While all the regional economic commissions have sought to play a role more or less connected with the aspirations of their respective regions, ECLA is the only one to have played a substantial role in the region's economic integration.

ECE'S original function of aiding the reconstruction of Europe would have made it a logical medium for the distribution of Marshall Aid. The onset of the Cold War, and the refusal of US aid by the Soviet Union and Eastern Europe left ECE with the more limited role of maintaining the continuity of a minimal economic relationship between Eastern and Western Europe. This it could do by maintaining its non-political character.[10] ECAFE pressed the demand for industrialisation, plan coordination and foreign aid, and ECA worked for African unity and anti-colonialism. Neither of them has made a substantial impact in solving the problems of the region, partly due to the attitude of extra-regional members and partly due to the conflicts among countries of the region themselves, apart from the general reluctance of new states to surrender any part of their sovereignty or their capacity to take economic decisions.[11]

ECLA alone seems to have overcome its initial difficulties to become the focus of the integration movement in Latin America. The region which it covered was clearly defined. It had a long tradition of diplomatic contact at the multilateral level in the OAS, and also some common cultural traditions, with the Spanish language serving as a kind of *lingua franca* for the area. The acceptance of the English-speaking Caribbean countries into ECLA indicates that geographical unity sometimes supersedes cultural differences and may even create contacts which provide the basis of potitical collaboration. The ECLA area had other advantages, perhaps the most important being the existence of an outside power, viz. the United States, whose dominant position in the continent was a factor that affected all countries and helped to unite them against the common prospect political and economic dependency. Another important factor was the absence of major Cold War issues. When the United States sought to introduce such issues, as in Guatemala (1954) and Cuba (1958 onwards), public opinion in Latin America tended to coalesce in an anti-US posture, even when the governments supported the US stand in the OAS.[12]

The Chilean sociologist, Gustavo Lagos. has in a series of articles put forth the view that regional economic organisations in the Americas play a political role which is closely connected with the Latin Americans' view of their own position in the world today. He argues that the national political systems of Latin America constitute "open or boundless systems" which operate under the influence of external factors which are sometimes beyond their control.[13] Integration in Western Europe, according to Lagos, is the result of the "partial atimia" of the countries like France after the Second World War. This situation is produced when a nation does not have the technological and economic strength to take part in the race for technical progress, which is a prerequisite for the attainment of maximum military power. Similarly, integration of Latin America is the response of Latin American countries to the condition of "generalised atimia" which is an indication of their economic and technological weakness, which has kept their productivity low and prevented their social development.[14]

A striking example of the political role played by regional economic organisations in Latin America is the formulation of Latin America's integration programme, which Lagos takes up as a case-study of the politics of economic organisations. He points to the successes and failures of the regional organisations in furthering economic policies, and shows that a "permanent dialogue," is in progress between the regional organisations and nation states. Instances are not lacking of the States rejecting the proposals of the regional organisations. An important instance of this was the unwillingness of Latin American participants in the Punta del Este conference in April 1967 to set up strong regional institutions like those in the EEC to guide Latin America's integration process.[15]

The crucial difference between ECLA and the other regional economic organisations of the United Nations appears to lie therefore not in the different circumstances of the regions, the absence of Cold War disputes in Latin America, and the long-standing mutual awareness of Latin American countries; but in the willingness of the regional economic organisations themselves to play a "political," as against the "economic" role marked out for bodies of this kind. A regional organ of the United States could have played one of three possible roles. The first was the minimal role visualised for the regional commissions by the UN Secretariat, as a disseminator of information providing training and undertaking research and study. A second possible role was the establishment of a regional centre of authority by the setting up of subsidiary organs and the taking up of direct administrative responsibilities. This was the role taken up by ECE and in a different way by ECAFE, which administers the Mekong Project and the Asian Highway directly. The third possible role which a regional organisation could have taken would be that taken by ECLA, the role of a cataylst, launching experiments and supplying creative leadership, but keeping away from direct adminstrative responsibility. That ECLA did take this role is perhaps due more to the personality of its second executive secretary, Raul Prebisch, than to any other single factor.

REFERENCES

[1] David H. Pollock, "Pearson and UNCTAD: A Comparison," *International Development Review*, XII, No. 4 (1970/4), pp. 14-21.

[2] John White, *Regional Development Banks: A Study of Institutional Style* (London, 1970), p. 41 and *passim*.

[3] A discussion of the status and prospects of the economic integration movements in developing countries will be found in Miguel S. Wionczek, ed., *Economic Cooperation in Latin America, Africa and Asia: A Handbook of Documents* (Cambridge, Mass., 1969), pp. 1-29.

[4] Haas and Schmitter propounded the view that "functional equivalents" will be found for some variables which may be absent in Latin America, and by a process of "reform-mongering" (using a phrase by A.O. Hirschman), Latin American integration will make progress, provided certain conditions are met. See their article "Economics and Differential Patterns of Political Integration: Projections about Unity in Latin America," *International Organization* (New York) (Autumn 1964).

[5] Statement by U. Nyun, United Nations, ECAFE, *Regional Cooperation in Asia and the Far East: Report of the Ministerial Conference on Asian Economic Cooperation* (E/CN/11/641), 1964, p. 13.

[6] Hiroshi Kitamura, "Economic Development and Regional Planning in Southeast Asia," *Economic Bulletin for Asia and the Far East* (September 1969), pp. 1-8.

[7] David Wightman, *Toward Economic Cooperation in Asia: The United Nations Economic Commission for Asia and the Far East* (New Haven, 1963), pp. 12-8.

[8] Gordon Connell-Smith, *The Inter-American System* (London, 1966), pp. 151-4.

[9] See Wightman n. 7, pp. 37-52, and James S. Magee, "ECA and the Paradox of African Cooperation," *International Conciliation*. No 580 (New York) (November 1970), p. 11.

[10] David Wightman, *Economic Cooperation in Europe: A Study of the United Nations Economic Commission for Europe* (New York), pp. 48-51.

[11] The work of the three regional commissions in the developing areas is summarised in regard to the integration activities of Robert W. Gregg, "The United Nations Regional Economic Commissions and Integration in the Underdeveloped Regions," *International Organisation* (Spring 1966), pp. 208-32. For the work of the ECE, see Wightman, n. 10.

[12] Connell-Smith, n. 8, pp. 161-70, 229-37, and 240ff.

[13] Gustavo Lagos, "Factores externos e internos en la political latinoamericana," *Institutiones v Desarrollo Politico de America Latina* (Buenos Aires, 1966), cited in Lagos, "The Political Role of the Regional Economic Organisations in Latin America," *Journal of Common Market Studies* (*JCMS*) (June 1968), p. 291.

[14] Gustavo Lagos, "La Integracion de America Latina y su influencia en el sistema internacional," in Lagos, ed., *La Integracion Latinoamericana: Situacion y perspectivas* (Buenos Aires, 1965), pp. 162-7. These concepts are spelt out in detail in Gustavo Lagos, *International Stratification and Underdeveloped Countries* (Chapel Hill, 1963), pp. 23-30.

[15] Lagos, n. 13, pp. 302-8.

CHAPTER II

THE BACKGROUND OF INTEGRATION IN LATIN AMERICA

Economic, Social, and Political Changes Since World War II

(i) *Economic aspects*

Spanish and Portuguese rule in Latin America brought about a fundamental change in the economic pattern of the continent. A monopolistic pattern of trade with the mother-country was established. New cities were founded on the coast, geared to the export trade and based on mines rather than on internal agricultural production. The old Indian roads fell into disuse and communication patterns within the region were altered by the new orientation of trade with the Iberian Peninsula, carried on by sea.[1] The Latin American situation was in contrast to that in the North American colonies of England, where the initial settlements on the coast were followed by a movement of trade towards the interior, and an increasing drive for the integration of trade among the colonies.

As a result of the severing of ties by the Latin American countries with Spain and Portugal in the 1820's they entered the world markets and began to trade with Western Europe and the United States. The new export markets brought great prosperity to the elites, but the economies of the countries continued to be oriented to exports rather than to the development of the local economy. It was not till the depression of the 1930's that some steps were taken to encourage domestic industry and to develop import substitution. These steps were given a further impetus by the Second World War, when there was a growth of national industry to compensate for the shortage of imported manufactured goods. The close of the war saw a reversion to the earlier pattern of increased imports of consumer items and of heavy industrial equipment.[2] The economies of the Latin American countries continued to be characterised by a high degree of dependence on imports and on the production of primary products for export.

It is sometimes stated that Latin American countries are characterised by dual societies in which the "modern" (or capitalist) sector is based on a rational and utilitarian approach, while the "feudal" or "archaic" sector is dominated by conservative social and economic groups representing the old oligarchy, local political strongmen, etc. It would be more accurate to describe the economy of most Latin American countries as controlled by an alliance of the traditional landed classes (which control the production of primary products for export with the help of cheap labour) with the export-oriented mercantile-capitalist class. These two groups continued to dominate the economies of these countries during the post-independence period, and in many cases continue to do so today.[3]

The dependence and foreign markets and the close ties between local ruling classes and foreign economic interests enabled foreign capital to gain control of public services and the main sources of export production of many Latin American countries.[4] The main feature of the economic relations between Latin America and the United States was the dominant role played by American private economic interests. The pattern of United States investment in Latin America might be categorised into two types of situations. The first situation was one in which the key points in the economic structure, such as copper in Chile, or oil in Venezuela, and essential services like railways, were under foreign control. In the second situation the secondary or tertiary sectors, such as the industrial sector and service industries, were characterised by foreign investment.[5] In the recent past a demand was expressed by economists and intellectuals that foreign investment should be restricted to certain sectors where they could not dominate the economy, where local capital was not forthcoming, and where they would contribute to national goals and assist in the building up of national industry.[6]

Foreign investment in Latin America has taken different shapes. Although the United States investor often raises a hue and cry at home when a country nationalises an extractive industry, or excludes foreign capital from a particular sector it frequently happens that there is a shift of investment to some other sector of the economy.[7]

A basic characteristic of the economies of Latin American countries, which has remained unchanged despite marginal developments in the field of industry, is their dependence on exports of raw materials for their survival. The world markets for primary commodities are controlled by the industrialised countries. The predominance of raw materials in the exports of Latin American countries makes them extremely vulnerable to changes in prices on the world market. To add to their difficulties, most of the Latin American countries are dependent on one or two major exports which constitute a very high proportion of their total exports.[8]

In 1959, 58 per cent of Brazil's and 77 per cent of Colombia's export earnings were derived from coffee. El Salvador, Guatemala and Costa Rica were heavily dependent on coffee; Cuba and the Dominican Republic on sugar; and Ecuador, Honduras and Panama on bananas. Chile derived 66 per cent of her export earnings from copper, Bolivia 62 per cent from tin, and Venezuela derived 92 per cent from oil.[9]

An examination of the general trends and fluctuations of the international trade in primary commodities since the Second World War throws a good deal of light on the economic situation in Latin America, which caused the countries of the area to consider economic integration as a feasible policy in the late 1950's.[10] Primary commodities experienced a boom during the period from mid-1945, when the war ended, till mid-1948. This temporary boom was ascribed to a number of fortuitous factors like the failure of harvests in Europe in 1947, the decline in imports from Indonesia due to the political disturbances which led to its independence, and the greatly increased demand for raw materials in the United States. This boom had, however, run itself out by the middle of 1948, and the following year, there was a marked downward trend. The Korean War, which broke out in July 1950 caught the world's commodity markets unawares, and there was a remarkable increase in the prices of certain raw materials. The price of wool increased four times, that of rubber trebled, and tin, jute, and sisal doubled in one year. Other commodities also registered substantial increases. Although the initial scramble had spent itself by mid-1951, the commodities which had registered heavy increases in prices fell heavily, while others which had risen least, such as wheat, sugar, coffee, and cotton, fell less fast during the next year or so till September 1952. From late 1952 till 1956 they were drifting slowly downwards although there were some large fluctuations in the prices of particular commodities.[11] In fact, according to Row,

> the course of commodity prices since the end of the sellers' market in 1948-49 should be viewed as a single period of transition to the essentially buyers' market of 1956, interrupted generally by the Korean War, and interrupted for certain commodities by the development of special temporary situations in those industries individually . . . It is not suggested that readjustment was completed by 1956 but rather that by then the unusual readjustments required by six years of world war were in the main accomplished. The process was becoming one of normal adaptation to the more usual sort of changing world.
>
> During the year 1956, however, a new phase of the downward movement of prices began. Until then world consumption of most primary commodities had been increasing, but in 1956 and 1957, many showed no increase, and some a reduction, while market absorption tended to contract still further, because in some cases stocks at the consuming end were reduced to the bare minimum of convenience . . . .[12]

At the same time that prices of primary commodities were registering a general decline (although there was a temporary rise in prices in certain specific commodities) the total quantum of exports of raw materials from Latin America registered a continuous increase. The following table gives a general picture of the pattern as it emerged during the 1950's.

The picture becomes still clearer when we look at the export figures of individual Latin American countries. While the figures of volume of exports registers a general increase, the figures indicating the price levels indicates a general decline; 1954 or 1956 being the book year for most of the countries covered.[13]

TABLE 1

World Trade, Index Numbers by Regions

Exports 1953=100

Regions	1938	1948	1951	1952	1954	1955	1956	1957	1958	1959	1960
Quantum Index											
Latin America	86	95	95	90	98	106	116	118	121	131	134
LA excluding petroleum	99	99	95	87	95	102	111	111	115	127	129
Unit Value Price Index (in United States dollars)											
Latin America	26	90	107	102	106	99	98	96	89	83	85
LA excluding petroleum	25	89	109	104	105	97	96	93	84	78	80

Source : *United Nations Statistical Yearbook, 1961*, Table No. 152, p. 427.

(ii) Social and political aspects

An understanding of the social background of Latin America is necessary in order to appreciate the economic system which operates in the region as well as to assess the political aspects of the economic integration movement. An influential study which appeared in 1958 argued that the "middle sectors" had taken over the affairs of state in some Latin American countries (Uruguay in 1903; Chile, Argentina, Mexico, and Brazil between 1916 and 1940) and that they could be expected to play a more substantial role in regard to development and technological changes because of the progressive spirit which the embodied.[14]

This somewhat optimistic view of the role of the middle classes was challenged in later years. Claudio Veliz argued that unlike in Europe, urbanization preceded industrialisation in Latin America. Although the middle class was in power for three or four decades, depending on the country—it had generally succeeded only in maintaining or strengthening the trade structure and in "leading some of the major countries into a situation of institutional stability and economic stagnation." This was done by "defending their present interests and future prospects." Instead of carrying out agrarian or fiscal reforms, they tried to identify themselves with the aristocracy.[15] The "demonstration effect" of the mass consumption of consumer goods and aspirations of the affluent society affected not only the oligarchies but also the middle class and even part of the working class. The middle class thus became a conservative force rather than an instrument of dynamism and change.[16]

The form of government, expected to become an instrument fot the political and economic development of the Latin American countries, was a subject of much discussion. The possibility of the military becoming a progressive force and an instrument of change was being increasingly put forward. In a well-reasoned article, examining the Brazilian and Argentine cases, Jose Nun argued that the middle class in Latin America had not become a bourgeoisie (a bourgeoisie being defined as a dominant group controlling industry and not taking second place to an aristocracy or oligarchy). While it did not succeed in working out a stable political compromise with the oligarchy, it was already facing what Disraeli called "the working class question." Although Nun did not think that the army in Latin America could be a progressive force in the sense that Nasserism was in Egypt, because of the more sophisticated nature of Latin American politics and the participation of the working class in political life, the then military regime of Peru appeared to contradict his thesis. By its devotion to the cause of state socialism, its restrictions on foreign investment, and its active role in the Andean Pact, the regime indicated its devotion to what Nun described as Nasserism, or "progressive Caesarism."[17] It could, however, be said that such a solution might face greater obstacles in a country like Argentina or Chile, where the working class was better organised than in Peru.

The political relationship between the United States and the Latin American Republics had reached perhaps its highest point of amicability during the Good Neighbour Policy of the Roosevelt Era. The earlier period of United States intervention in the Caribbean was superseded by an acceptance of the principle of non-intervention at the Seventh International American Conference held at Montevideo in December 1933 only a few months after Franklin Deleno Roosevelt took office as President of the United States.[18]

In the course of its long history since 1889, the Inter-American system served several distinct purposes: (1) the maintenance of Western hemisphere security against extra-continental aggression; (2) the settlement of disputes among Latin American countries themselves; (3) facilitating cooperation among Latin American countries for achievement of their economic, social and political aspirations; and (4) protecting the security and promoting the interests of the Latin American countries in their relations with the United States.[19]

In regard to the first of these items, both the United States and Latin American nations tend to use the Inter-American system for their own purposes. "The United States looks to the OAS for endorsement of its policies; Latin Americans see it as an instrument to use, if possible, to persuade their powerful neighbour to modify its policies",[20] as well as to maintain the peace of the continent.[21] A series of conferences were held since 1889, and by the end of World War II the Inter-American system had become so accepted among the Latin American countries that they expressed considerable doubts as to the effectiveness of the United Nations in handling matters of international peace, particularly in the light of the great power veto. They wanted the peace and security provisions of the Inter-American system to be given preference, the United Nations intervening only if more than one region were concerned.[22] As a result of the pressure exerted by the Latin American nations at the San Francisco meeting through the United States, not only were the provisions for the existence of regional organisations (which had been included in the Dumbarton Oaks Proposals) retained under Chapter VIII of the Charter; but Article 51, which recognised the right of "individual and collective self defence," was inserted in the Charter.[23]

Relations between the Latin American countries and the United States deteriorated considerably during the post-war period. The massive United States aid to Europe under the Marshall Plan had raised expectations that similar assistance would be made to Latin America and the failure to do so caused great disappointment, in view of the "special relationship" which had existed between the United States and Latin America. The arguments put forth by Secretary of State,

Marshall at the Special Inter-American Conference for the Maintenance of Continental Peace and Security in Rio in 1947 and at the Ninth International Conference of American States at Bogota in 1948 indicated not only that the United States had decided to give priority to European recovery as against Latin American development, but also that a crucial role was visualised for capital in the southern continent. The Latin Americans were urged to attract US investments by according it fair and equitable treatment.[24]

The relations between Latin America and the United States during the period between the close of the Second World War and the signature of the economic integration agreements in 1960 were characterised by a continuous concern about economic issues on the part of the Latin American countries, and an equally insistent harping on security matters on the part of the United States at the various Inter-American conferences. The demand for a separate economic institution to assist in the solution of the serious economic problems facing the Latin American countries led to the creation of ECLA under the auspices of the United Nations in February 1948, in the teeth of US opposition.[25]

Two major issues which arose in the Inter-American system at this time were the questions of what was described as the Communist-dominated government of Arbenz in Guatemala which was discussed in the Tenth International American Conference at Caracas in 1954, and the Castro regime which gained power in Cuba early in 1959. In each of these cases, there seemed to have been a combination of strategic and economic motivations for intervention by the United States and for the overthrow of the existing regimes. In both cases, the regimes had expropriated US companies which exercised considerable influence on the United States Government. In the Guatemalan case, Secretary of State John Foster Dulles was able to secure a condemnation of the regime at the Caracas Conference in March 1954 with the support of a number of Latin American dictators.[26] This was followed by Mutual Security Treaties entered into by the United States with Guatemala's neighbours, Nicaragua and Honduras, and an invasion of Guatemala on 19 June 1954, from Honduras by troops led by Colonel Castillo Armas, an exiled Guatemalan officer, with

United States support. The fears of the Latin American States that the anti-Communist resolution was a prelude to United States intervention for the overthrow of the Guatemalan Government of Arbenz were thus confirmed. Action by the Inter-American Peace Committee of the OAS was delayed till the Arbenz Government had been overthrown, and the United Nations was prevented from taking action.[27]

Although the Cuban situation was, as previously stated, comparable in many respects to the Guatemalan case, and the reaction in the United States was also not dissimilar, there had been a remarkable change in atmosphere in Latin America between 1954 and 1959, and the events of Guatemala could not be repeated in Cuba in spite of the pressures operating in the United States in that direction.

Any general statement about an area as complex as Latin America in which the states are extremely diverse in size, population, industrial growth, urbanisation and degree of political sophistication, is necessarily subject to many reservations. It may be useful, however, to assess the mood of Latin America at the end of the 1950's when the integration movement was beginning to take active shape.

The comparative isolation of the Latin American countries from the currents of the Cold War and their weak economic position led to a resentment of the United States economic presence on the one hand, and a continued acceptance of United States leadership in political matters on the other. The acceptance of United States leadership in the Organisation of American States (OAS) and the United Nations seemed to be due partly to a habit formed over a period of decades in the Inter-American system, but was also a reflection of the economic dependency of the Latin American States in relation to the United States.

During the second half of the 1950's, however, there seemed to be a change of mood. A number of new leaders, oriented to constitutionalism and to the modernisation of the economies of Latin America, came to the fore. These included Frondizi in Argentina (1958-62), Kubitschek in Brazil (1954-59), Lleras Camargo in Colombia (1957-62), and Betancourt in Venezuela (1958-64). This combination of Liberal regimes coincided with a period when the United States appeared to be willing to change its stand on a number of important economic questions, such as the establishment of an Inter-American Bank, giving large-scale aid, and the acceptance of Latin American integration. Although these hopes were not all fulfilled, it did appear as if the Western hemisphere was entering into a new pattern of relationship which would show the way to other developing areas.

The new climate of opinion in Latin America was not a sudden development. This situation had been emerging since the Second World War. Three important features of the changed climate may be noted here. First of all, there was an increasing focus in Latin America on the economic as against the political problems of the region and a great resentment of the region's state of dependence on the United States economy. Secondly, there was a demand that the United States give massive aid to the Latin American countries as it had done to Europe. Thirdly, the period was characterised by the gradual rise to power of a middle class which had a sense of self-confidence symbolised by the new leaders who came into power in the late fifties and early sixties.

The ambivalent relationship of Latin America to the United States, to which we have referred, was accentuated by the changing class structure of Latin America during this period. The acceptance of United States influence in the 1950's by some of the revolutionary figures of the 1930's (such as the leaders of Accion Democratica Party in Venezuela and the Aprista Party in Peru) stood in striking contrast to the situation in the 1960's, characterised by Castro's rejection of United States influence, which seemed to have been feared by him as a "kiss of death." This change in attitude was also seen in the then military regime in Peru, whose first major act was to nationalise the International Petroleum Company; thus indicating publicly its independence of United States influence. This change was evidently a result of the new pressures on the middle class to obtain mass support, the masses being easily rallied with anti-American sentiments. Dr. Castro, on his way back from Chile to Cuba, stopped at Lima, Peru, on 4 December 1971, and had a talk for over four hours with President Velasco Alvarado of Peru. He said afterwards that if he were a revolutionary in Peru, he would support President Velasco and not fight against him.[28] Thus Latin America appeared to be approaching a new type of political system, qualitatively different from the middle class politics described by Johnson and others, and likely to have far-reaching effects on international relations in the continent.

ECLA and the Prebisch Thesis

In an essay entitled "Ideologies of Economic Development in Latin America," Albert O. Hirschman sought to apply to the Latin American scene the dictum of Keynes that "the world is ruled by little else than by the ideas, both the right and wrong ones, of economists and political philosophers." While not accepting this view in toto, Hirschman sought to trace the economic ideas of political thinkers during different periods in post-independence Latin American history. He found that from independence to the First World War Latin American writers were preoccupied with the political, rather than with the economic, causes of the backwardness of Latin America. They tended to blame the situation on the Latin American character, which many of them felt, needed a complete transformation. Economic doctrines were still linked with British free trade and non-interventionist ideas. A transformation of Latin American character by imitating the United States was suggested by two Argentinians, Sarmiento and Alberdi, in the middle and late nineteenth century.[29]

In the inter-war period, the impact of Marxism and the desire to adapt these ideas to conditions in Latin America led to the stress on the collectivist traditions of the village community, called the *ayllu* in Peru and the *ejido* in Mexico. On the other hand, imperialism in Latin America was seen as the first experience which the Latin Americans had with capitalism, and the revolution in Latin America was therefore expected to be undertaken not by the proletariat but by the intellectuals and middle classes with control over the state machinery: "*The capitalist stage must therefore unfold under the leadership of the anti-imperialist state.*"[30] This combination of statism with a revival of indigenous cultural values was in contrast to the free-enterprise-oriented ideas which were dominant before the First World War.

During the 1930's the new generation of Latin American

intellectuals began to give up the traditional *laissez-faire* economics in favour of a Keynesian analysis, focusing on investment as the key to devlopment and recognising the multiplier effects of foreign trade. Central banks and develepment banks came into fashion.

The period after the Second World War saw the emergence of a coherent body of economic ideas which sought to analyse the economic situation of Latin America, find out the reasons for its continued backwardness, and made recommendations for changing the situation drastically. The most important figure in this movement was Argentine economist Raul Prebisch.

During the Peron regime (1943-55), Prebisch taught at the University of Buenos Aires, and at this time he sought to apply the Keynesian anlaysis to the Latin American economic scene. Like Keynes in his *General Theory of Employment, Interest and Money*, Prebisch took his point of departure from classical economic theory.[31] In the opening statement of his first important work, *The Economic Development of Latin America and Its Principal Problems*,[32] he posed the problem which has subsequently dominated the debate between the developing and the developed countries of the world:

> In Latin America, reality is undermining the outdated scheme of the international division of labor, which achieved great importance in the nineteenth century and as a theoretical concept, continued to exert considerable influence until very recently. Under that schema, the specific task that fell to Latin America, as part of the periphery of the world economic system, was that of producing food and raw materials for the great industrial centres.
>
> There was no place within it for the industrialization of the new countries. It is nevertheless being forced upon them by events. Two world wars in a single generation and a great economic crisis between them have shown the Latin American countries their opportunities, clearly pointing the way to industrial activity.

Prebisch went on to point out that the assumption that the benefits of the technological progress tend to be distributed alike over the whole community was not borne out by facts if the countries constituting the "periphery of the world economy" were to be included in the "community". He concluded that the disequilibrium between the standards of living of the masses in the periphery and the centre "destroys the basic premise underlying the scheme of the international division of labour."[33]

The millitant tone in which the propositions were stated characterised the document as a whole. Within a short time of its issue, Prebisch, then an Adviser to the United Nations Economic Commission for Latin America (ECLA), was appointed by Mr. Trygve Lie, Secretary-General of the United Nations, as its Executive Secretary, reportedly at the request of several Latin American delegations.[34]

Unlike other international organisations, the ECLA possessed "a cohesive personality which evokes loyalty from the staff, and a set of distinctive beliefs, principles and attitudes; in brief an ideology which is highly influential among Latin American intellectuals and policy-makers."[35] This achievement was to a large extent due to Prebisch.

Prebisch's formulation of the doctrine that the gains from trade are uneqnally divided between the centre and the periphery, and the terms of trade are constantly moving against the primary producing countries, is not entirely original. Similar arguments were put forth by the American colonies to protest against the suppression of their industries by manufacturers from Great Britain.[36] There are some parallels between the Prebisch thesis and the "drain theory" proposed by the Indian statesman, Dadabhai Naoroji, in the late nineteenth century, which argued that Btitish rule was draining away the wealth of India.[37]

The main contribution of Prebisch and of the ECLA school of economists has been to place the whole question in the context of classical economic theory and bring it into the mainstream of the economic debate in the post-Second World War period. By challenging the basic assumption that the developing countries would have to go through the same stages of development as the advanced countries, by asserting the uniqueness of the developmental process in the developing countries, and by raising to the status of a general rule the need for protection (which till then had been admitted only as an exception to the general rule of free trade), Prebisch was able to "inspire a whole new generation of economists, particularly in less developed countries," to challenge the established doctrines.[38] In bringing this issue to the forefront of the debate in economics, he forced the leading economists of the West into a confrontation, enabled the creation of a new international organisation to serve the interests of the developing countries in trade and development matters, and laid the foundations for a process of re-thinking in which the developing countries came closer to wresting major concessions from the developed countries in trade and other economic issues. The focus of Prebisch's arguments was on the asymmetry in the relationship between the "centre" and "periphery". This was interpreted in several different ways. The first, known as the Prebisch-Singer thesis, propounded the view already stated about the unequal distribution of gains from trade. Subsequent publications of ECLA focused attention on income inelasticity of the demand for imports by the periphery from the centre compared to that of the centre for goods from the periphery. ECLA also pointed out the different roles played in the centre and the periphery by protection and import restrictions.[39] The whole thrust of the argument was (1) to focus attention on the international trading system as the basic cause of Latin America's backwardness and (2) to urge that public policy be altered to correct the faults of the international trade system, and to promote industry through protection and import controls. The attention of ECLA was therefore directed towards two somewhat dissimilar goals: constructing the international trade pattern on the one hand, and altering government policies in the direction of planning long-range economic development on the other. Hirschman found that the first of these two policies tended to fit in with the alleged Latin American tendency to blame an outside agency—usually the United States—for its ills. The second objective seemed Utopian in the context of unpredictable policy-makers and the reversal of policies by individuals.[40]

The Prebisch thesis in its pristine from, i.e. the declining terms of trade for the countries in the periphery, was supported by a report of the General Agreement on Tariffs and Trade (GATT).

While some expansion in the volume of imports of primary

> products is implicit in the future growth of manufacturing production in the industrial countries (where about nine-tenths of the world's total industrial capacity is at present located) it is equally certain in the light of experiences of the 1950's, that such imports would not rise proportionately with the advance of the industrial economies. Thus, the paradox facing the low-income countries is that, while they cannot raise their output and real incomes without a substantial growth in imports from industrial countries, the industrial countries have been able to raise output and incomes with a diminishing proportion of imports from primary producing countries.[41]

Criticism of Prebisch's theory by economists has tended to focus either on the validity of the historical evidence put forth by him in regard to the declining terms of trade,[42] or on the importance of the challenge to the classical theory of international trade.[43] A careful examination of the theory, however, leads to the realization that there are three different problems which are posed by Prebisch, viz. (1) the deterioration in the terms of trade and the accompanying decline in the real income of the periphery; (2) the fluctuations in total earnings from exports which present peripheral countries with cyclical balance of payment crises; and (3) the singular decline of earnings from exports relating to desired expenditures on imports, which create long-run balance of payment problems.[44]

In order to understand the significance of the Prebisch thesis and the role it has played in the confrontation of the advanced countries with the developing countries, it is necessary to see it as a part of development theory rather than of international trade theory, as has been done by many of his critics. In the context of development theory, the ideas and proposals of Prebisch and ECLA have evolved over the years. While some of the early publications do contain the seeds of arguments developed later, the emphasis has changed, and some new concepts have been developed. Thus, the main emphasis on *The Economic Development of Latin America and its Principal Problems* was the need for industrialization. In an article published in 1951 in Brazil,[45] Prebisch developed the theme that the only way in which countries in the periphery could assimilate modern technology was by the protection of industry. In 1958 he presented a paper for discussion at the American

Economic Association in which he argued that a common market was necessary for the countries of Latin America to benefit from protectionism, in order to correct "the splitting of the industrialization process into as many watertight compartments as there are countries, without the advantages of specialization and the economies of scale."[46]

The major writings of Prebisch from 1963 onward appear to focus more and more on internal and inter-regional factors affecting the developmental process in Latin America. The first two parts of a report published in 1963 deal with the structural reforms necessary to clear the way for development, such as changes in social structure, the role played in the "dynamic weakness of Latin America's development" by surplus manpower and the need for capital formation. It goes on to discuss land as an obstacle to development, problems of distribution, inflation, foreign capital, and planning.[47] The third part of the report (which was written when Prebisch was turning his attention from the regional to the world scene as the Secretary General of the first UNCTAD Conference held in Geneva in 1964) focusses on the effects of the world trade pattern and other factors obstructing the Latin American Common Market and urges a continuous series of cordinated efforts arising out of measures adopted at the national and international level.

During the period from 1964 to early 1969, Prebisch functioned on the world stage as Secretary General of UNCTAD. His report to the first UNCTAD conference,[48] summarises his view in regard to world trade at that stage in his career.

In an article published in 1969, Prebisch stressed the need to do away with distributional privilege as a disincentive to economic activity, the harmful social consequences of inflation, and discussed the role of foreign capital and of State planning in Latin American development.[49]

The publications of ECLA continued the trend of stressing internal factors in development.[50] Prebisch's later work, *Change and Development: Latin America's Great Task*,[51] focusses on the need for the mobilization of internal resources for the development of Latin America and urges a rate of growth of at least eight per cent per year, which involves a higher investment rate. He stresses that external investment, both public and private, can play a comparatively minor role in Latin American development.

Analysing some types of Latin American development strategies, Anderson finds three main approaches to the problem: (1) the "conventional approaches" which regards development as an "elaboration of the existing modern sector," (2) the "democratic reform approach," which seems to accommodate demands present in the system, and (3) the "revolutionary approach" which regards the modern sector as an obstacle to development.[52] According to this analysis, the early Prebisch-ECLA school was a programme of adjustment and "system maintenance" by original intent, and acquired an ideology of development only as a by-product. The introduction of a social welfare component, which appears to be extraneous to the propositions originally propounded by Prebisch, would thus seem to be motivated by a desire to make the conventional approach more palatable to the new social forces in Latin America.[53]

The views of Prebisch and ECLA have been criticised, however, both from the right and the left. His concept of the State as the instrument of economic and social change has to confront the strong mistrust of the State's capabilities in Latin America, especially in business circles. There is also a group of enonomists, the most prominent being the Brazilian Roberto de Oliviera Campos, who disagree with parts of the ECLA analysis and its policy implications, especially with the stress on the State as the instrument of change, and on industrial development as against agriculture.[54] Some of the economists who are most optimistic about the rapid economic growth of Brazil and Mexico have been influenced by the ECLA school of thought. Capitalism to them is a form of national assertion involving a "conquest of decision centres" which were previously in foreign hands, and a gradual shedding of the "peripheral" character of the nation, in all spheres—economic, political, and intellectual.[55]

A criticism which has been voiced by a number of academic observers of the Latin American scene is that the Prebisch thesis lays undue stress on the relationships between the periphery and the centre in global terms and neglects the major imbalances between the major industrial cities and urban centres on the one hand and the rural and poverty-stricken agricultural areas on the other. Thus Frankenhoff cites a Brazilian article entitled ' Imperialismo Paulista" which underlines the enormous stake of the state of Sao Paolo, with one third of the national product and only 17 per cent of its population. The "capitalist mentality" of the city people with its Italian and German immigrants, is resented by the people in other parts of Brazil.[56] It has been urged that regional planning should be undertaken on a comprehensive basis in order to counter the tendency towards the concentration of development in limited pockets or enclaves, as otherwise the gap between the rich and poor within a country will become greater.[57]

A more trenchant critique of the Prebisch thesis will be found in the writings of a group of Latin American social scientists who have developed what has come to be known as the Dependency Model to describe the situation of the countries of Latin America, whose economies are "conditioned by the development and expansion of another economy to which their own [economy] is subjected . . ."[58] The criticism to which the writers on dependency have subjected the ECLA model is based on the following set of arguments:

1) ECLA's explanation of why Latin America has been at such a disadvantage in the world market relies mainly on the nature of traditional Latin America exports and does not give importance to the conscious policies and needs of developed nations.

2) ECLA lays the blame for retarded industrialization on the "traditional" or "feudal" oligarchies of Latin America, whereas the Latin American society has been geared to the international capitalist market since the sixteenth century. The assumption that the industrial bourgeoisie would be oriented to development, nationalism and progress requires re-examination.

3) The development of industry as a result of import-substitution in some countries (e.g. Chile, Argentina, Brazil) has led to economic stagnation, increased dependence on imports of capital goods etc. from the advanced countries, and greater foreign ownership and control of industry. Thus the hopes of decision-making being transferred to Latin America have been belied by events. Regional economic integration cannot solve these problems without basic structural changes involving drastic social reforms, policies to counter unemployment, and strict control of foreign investment.

4) ECLA's recommendation of increasing foreign investment and aid would lead to a greater outflow of capital and increased dependence on the metropolitan powers.[59]

Although the Prebisch thesis has been criticised from the left as being inadequate as an explanation of the relations between Latin America and the United States, it has received the compliment of being adapted and used by social scientists other than economists. Not only the "dependency" model of Dos Santos, Sunkel and others, but the "centre-periphery model" which was put forth by some Latin American political scientists to explain the variations in the internal political development of a country at a United Nations Economic and Social Commission (UNESCO) meeting in 1970 would seem to owe their origin to the Prebisch thesis.[60]

Despite all the criticism that has been levelled against it on pragmatic as well as theoretical grounds, the Prebisch thesis has the merit of having brought the underdeveloped countries into the forefront of a theory of economic development. It has a flexibility which enables it to be adapted to the needs of a changing world. Although Prebisch was personally convinced that free enterprise and foreign investment should be encouraged, the thesis could be adapted to a different kind of situation in which socialist policies, state enterprise and restrictions on foreign capital could accompany a policy of integrated economic development.[61]

REFERENCES

1 Donald W. Baerrensen, Martin Carnoy and Joseph Grunwald, *Latin American Trade Patterns* (Washington, D.C., 1965), pp. 7-13. Felipe Herrera, "Disunity as an Obstacle to Progress," in Claudio Veliz, ed., *Obstacles to Change in Latin America* (London, 1965), pp. 231-3. The Peruvian writer and ideologue, Jose Carlos Mariategui, a founder of the APRA Movement which sought to restore the Indian to his rightful place in Latin America, stressed the importance of the change from inward to outward orientation of trade patterns in his book, *Siete Ensayos de Interpretacion de la Realided Peruane* (La Habana, 1963), pp. 1-4.

2 Baerrensen, n. 1, pp. 13-29.

3 For an exposition of this point of view see Rodolfo Stavenhagen, "Seven Erroneous Theses about Latin America," in Irving Louis Horwitz, Josue de Castro and John Gerassi, eds., *Latin American Radicalism: A Document Report on Left and Nationalist Movements* (New York, 1969), pp. 102-6.

[4] Herrera, n. 1, p. 238.

[5] Antibal Pinto, "Political Aspects of Economic Development in Latin America," in Veliz, ed., n. 1, pp. 41-2.

[6] For a discussion of these and related points see, for example, Victor L. Urquidi, "Implications of Foreign Investment in Latin America," in Veliz, ed., n. 1, pp. 114-5. It is of interest to note that many of these principles have been accepted and enforced by the Government of India in regard to foreign investment in a series of decisions commencing with the Industrial Policy Resolution of 1948. United States entrepreneurs in Latin America have only recently been confronted with restrictions which have been taken for granted in many developing countries of Asia and Africa, although Mexico was a partial exception.

[7] See for example, an account of the shift of investment by International Telephone and Telegraph Corporation (ITT) from telephones to hotels after the Peruvian Government took over the telephone system, in *AFR Weekly Newsletter*, 31 May 1971, (Washington, D.C.), p. 1. See also the item "Freeman Pleads for New Attitudes," in ibid., p. 2, in which the former United States Secretary of Agriculture is quoted as urging US business to adapt to the new circumstances in Latin America and to benefit from the expanding markets there.

[8] See Appendices, Table II. F. *A Statement of Leading Export Commodities for the year 1967*, and also the Table II. A on Total Exports.

[9] See John Gerassi, *The Great Fear: The Reconquest of Latin America by Latin Americans* (New York, 1963), p. 20.

[10] The account which follows is based on the analysis of J.W.F. Rowe, *Primary Commodities in International Trade* (Cambridge, 1965), pp. 96-104.

[11] Ibid., p. 104.

[12] Ibid., pp. 105-6.

[13] Appendices, Table II. E., *World Trade: Index Numbers by Regions and Countries.*

[14] John J. Johnsons, *Political Change in Latin America: The Emergence of the Middle Sectors* (Stanford, Calif., 1959), especially pp. 180-95.

In a review of the book in *Review of Politics* (October 1959), pp. 727-8, Frederick B. Pike expressed the view that the United States found it easier to deal with the old elites who were not interested in economic nationalism, industrialisation and the common good of their countries. This may partially explain the US coolness toward the populist regimes of Getulio Vargas in Brazil (1930-45; 1951-54), and of Juan Peron in Argentina (1946-55).

[15] Claudio Veliz, "Introduction," in Veliz, n. 1, pp. 2-8.

[16] Pinto, n. 5, pp. 44-5. For a careful summary of the two alternative hypotheses regarding the role of the middle sectors, see Luis Ratinoff, "The New Urban Groups: The Middle Classes," in Seymour Martin Lipset and Aldo Solari, eds., *Elites in Latin America* (London, 1967), pp. 61-93.

[17] Jose Nun, "The Middle Class Military Coup," in Claudio Veliz,, ed.,

The Politics of Conformity in Latin America (London, 1967), pp. 112-8.

[18] Charles G. Fenwick, *The Inter-American Regional System* (New York, 1949), pp. 43-5. The Roosevelt era was characterised by a considerable increase in US trade with Latin American countries, the encouragement of private US investment in Latin America and large public loans which made Latin American countries more dependent on the United States. However, when Mexico expropriated US oil companies in 1938, the United States did not intervene. Gordon Connell-Smith, *The Inter-American System* (London, 1966), pp. 31, 104.

For the text of the Additional Protocol on Non-Intervention, see *International Conferences of American States: First Supplement 1933-40* (Washington, D.C., 1940), pp. 191-2.

[19] John C. Dreier, "The Special Nature of Western Hemisphere Experience with International Organization," in Robert W. Gregg, ed., *International Organization in the Western Hemisphere* (Syracuse, 1968), p. 21.

[20] Gordon Connell-Smith, "Political Problems of Latin American Integration," in Claudio Veliz, ed., *Latin America and the Caribbean: A Handbook of Documents* (New York, 1968), p. 399.

[21] Alice Felt Tyler, *The Foreign Policy of James G. Blaine* (Minneapolis, 1927), p. 174.

[22] Dana G. Munro, "The Mexico City Conference and the Inter-American System," *Department of State Bulletin*, (1945), pp. 529-30.

[23] Arthur H. Vandenberg, Jr., ed,, *The Private Papers of Senator Vandenberg* (Cambridge, Mass, 1952) pp. 187-93, 366.

[24] Connell-Smith, n. 18, pp. 151-4.

An Economic Agreement which was approved at the Bogota Conference and constituted a compromise between opposing views on foreign investment but "the basic disagreement had not been disposed of." Charles G. Fenwick, "The Ninth International Conference of American States," *American Journal of International Law* (July 1968), pp. 561-2. See also Josef L. Kunz, "The Bogota Charter of the OAS," in ibid., p. 573. The text of the agreement will be found in *International Conference of American States: Second Supplement 1942-54* (Washington, D.C., 1958), pp. 213-29.

[25] The United States was afraid that the work of the Inter-American Economic and Social Council would be duplicated, and wanted the matter brought before the Ninth International Conference of American States. That Conference was presented with a *fait accompli* and appointed a Committee to recommend a division of functions between IA-ECOSOC and ECLA. Connell-Smith, n. 18, pp. 152, 218.

[26] Rojas Pinilla in Colombia (1953-57), Batista in Cuba (1952-59), Trujillo in the Dominican Republic (1930-61), Somoza in Nicaragua (1947-56), Stroessner in Paraguay (1954-). Odria in Peru (1948-56), and Perez Jimenez in Venezuela (1952-58). These have been described as "some of the most vicious and bloody dictators Latin America has ever known." John Gerassi, *The Great Fear in Latin America* (New York,

1966, 2nd edition), pp. 241-2.

The text of the Resolution will be found in *The International Conferences of the American States, Second Supplement, 1942-54*, pp. 433-5.

27 Connell-Smith, n. 18, pp. 161-4, 232-7.

28 *Keesing's Contemporary Archives*, 22-29 January 1972, p. 25067.

29 A.O. Hirschman, "Ideologies of Economic Development in Latin America," in A.O. Hirschman, ed., *Latin American Issues: Essays and Comments* (New York, 1969) pp. 4-8.

30 Haya de la Torre, *El anti imperlalismo yel APRA* (Santiago, 1936), p. 159. The translation follows Hirscnman, n. 29, p. 11.

31 Charles A. Frankenhoff, S.J., "The Prebisch Thesis: A Theory of Industrialism for Latin America," *Journal of Inter-American Studies* (*JIAS*) (April 1962), p. 181.

32 (New York, ECLA, 1950), p. 1.

33 Ibid., pp. 1-2.

34 Frankenhoff, n. 31, p. 187. Brief summaries of Prebisch's career will be found in *Who's Who in America, with World Notables* (Chicago, Ill., 1970-71), p. 1825 and *Quien es Quien en la Argentina: Biografias Contemporaneas* (Buenos Aires, 8th edition, 1963), p. 794. The former, however, states incorrectly that Prebisch became Executive Secretary of ECLA in 1948.

35 Hirschman, n. 29, p. 13.

36 Sidney Dell, *Trade Blocs and Common Markets* (New York, 1963), pp. 207-8.

37 Dadabhai Naoroji, *Poverty and Un-British Rule in India*, 1st Indian ed. (Delhi, 1962).

38 Isaiah Frank, "Aid, Trade and Economic Development: Issues Before the UN Conference," *Affair* (January 1964), p. 214.

39 A convenient summary of the most important publications of ECLA will be found in *Development Problems in Latin America: An Analysis by the UN Economic Commission for Latin America* (Austin, 1970). This volume covers the following topics in relation to Latin American development: (1) foreign trade, (2) industrialisation, (3) planning concepts and experiences, (4) financing and foreign investment, (5) economic integration, (6), inflation and growth, (7) social conditions and effects of economic development, (8) world trade policies and problems, and (9) toward a dynamic development policy for Latin America. The Spanish text is *El Pensamiento de la CEPAL* (Santigo de Chile, 1969). The volume should be read keeping in mind the dates when the various articles were prepared.

Although most of the documents in this volume owe a great deal to the ideas of Raul Prebisch, it is necessary to distinguish between his writings, especially those of a theoretical nature, and the official publications of ECLA.

40 "ECLA's detailed projections where all economic sectors are made to mesh harmoniously are in a sense the 20th century equivalent of Latin America's 19th century constitutions—and are as far removed from the

real world. They are a protest, both pathetic and subtle, against a reality where politicians relying on brilliant or drastic improvisations hold sway, where decisions are taken under multiple pressures rather than in advance of a crisis and emergency situations, and where conflicts are resolved on the basis of personal considerations after the contending parties have revealed their strength in more or less open battle rather than in accordance with objective principles and scientific criteria." Hirchman, n. 29, p. 22.

41 General Agreement on Tariff and Trade, *Internal Trade 1959* (Geneva, 1960), p. 38, Quoted in Werner Baer, "The Economics of Prebisch and ECLA", in Charles T. Nisbet, ed., *Latin America: Problems in Economic Development* (New York, 1969), p. 214.

42 For brief accounts of the debate on the subject, see Hirschman, n. 29, p. 38, and Werner Baer, in Nisbet, n. 41, pp. 210-7. See also the article by Gottfried Haberler and the discussion in Howard S. Ellis, ed., *Economic Development for Latin America* (New York, 1961), pp. 275-307. In a dissertation by Jaqueline Lou Hodgson entitled, "An Evaluation of the Prebisch Thesis" (Doctoral Dissertation, University of Wisconsin, Department of Economics, 1965-66), the writer reviewed Prebisch's major works from 1949 to 1964, analysed his arguments and assumptions regarding the terms of trade, and examined in detail the figures for India and New Zealand in order to test the validity of the Prebisch thesis. Her findings did not support the Prebisch theory that the terms of trade were deteriorating. Prebisch's argument that the dynamic weakness of the periphery is due to surplus labour seemed to her incorrect, but he may have discovered an important fact that the "economic man" of Adam Smith could not function in an environment where he could not hope to compete and enjoy a higher standard of living. Hence foreligners benefit from pockets of growth in the less developed countries. "His conclusions were right, but for the wrong reasons". *Dissertation Abstracts 28 A. July-August, 1967*, p. 381 A, Order No. 6609921.

43 It has been argued by Jacob Viner and others that even if the Prebisch thesis has some validity it is not a challenge to the (classical) theory of international trade as the need for the protection of infant industries has been argued since the days of List and Carey. See Werner Baer, in Nisbet, n. 41, p. 217.

44 M. June Flanders, "The Economics of Prebisch and ECLA: A Comment," in *Economic Development and Cultural Change* (EDCC) (April 1964), p. 312. In another article entitled "Prebisch on Protectionism: An Evaluation," in the *The Economic Journal* (June 1964), pp. 323-4, the same writer argues that the basic Prebisch thesis consists of "two components": (1) a "balance of payment" problem, with demand for imports in P (a country in the Periphery) tending to grow faster than import demand in C (a country in the Centre), so that equilibrium can be achieved only if P grows more slowly than C. This problem arises from C's inelastic demand (for imports from P) in respect to *income* (italics in original); (2) a "real income" problem. This is frequently

stated as C's price-inelastic demand for imports from P, but more correctly should be attributed to P's monopolistic position in the world market, which causes the demand for her exports to be less than infinitely elastic with respect to price. The result of this is that the "free market," responding to existing relative prices, misallocates resources in P between export industries and import-competing industries, so that aggregate real income in P is not maximised. (It should be remembered, however, that this misallocation is the result of two assumptions about market structure, both of whlch are necessary: (1) the monopolistic position of P in the world market, *and* either (2) perfect competition among producers of the export goods in each P country or (3) perfectly competitive behaviour on the part of decision-makers in each P country, each assuming that output of its export good remains constant in the other countries of the periphery).

This highly sophisticated argument does not appear to take account of several factors which have arisen in regard to the production of primary commodities in developing countries: (1) the practical difficulty of shifting from an established line of raw material production to a new line of production, even after the colonial restraints on such a shift have been removed; (2) competition among different countries in the periphery producing the same commodity; (3) the discovery of oil and other natural resources in countries in the centre; and (4) the production by countries in the centre of substitutes for the raw materials imported from the periphery.

45 Raul Prebisch, "Interpretacao do Processo de Desenvolvimento Economico," *Revista Brasileisa de Economia* (March 1951), 7-117. (Summary in English, 117-27), cited in Frankenhoff, n. 31 (April 1962), p. 196. The analysis here is that of Frankenhoff.

46 Raul Prebisch, "International Trade and Payments in an Era of Coexistence: Commerical Policy in the Underdeveloped Countries," *The American Economic Review* (May 1959), Papers and proceedings of the Seventy-first Annual Meeting of the American Economic Association, Chicago, Illinois, 27-29 December 1958, p. 268. For a brief and stimulating defense of this view by Prebisch see his comments in Gunnar Myrdal's paper "Toward a More Closely Integrated Free-World Economy," in Robert Lekachman, ed., *National Policy for Economic Welfare at Home and Abroad* (New York, 1961), pp. 277-80. Prebisch's comment begins as follows:

> Is it not a paradox to recognise the merits of industrial protection in underdeveloped countries as Dr. Myrdal does and advocate simultaneously the need for international economic integration? Yet it is not a paradox: it is bold thinking indeed; and we economic heretics of the underdeveloped countries feel today very fortunate in securing in such a way the full support of an eminent economist of the Old World.

Prebisch also summarised his views at this stage in an article "Joint Responsibilities for Latin American Progress," *Foreign Affairs* (July 1961), pp. 622-33.

47 *Towards a Dynamic Development Policy for Latin America*, United Nations Document E/CN-12/680/Rev. 7. (New York, December 1963).

48 *Towards a New Commercial Policy for Development*, United Nations Document E/CONF/46/3 (New York, 1964).

49 "The system and the Social Structure of Latin America," in Horowitz, et al (eds.), *Latin American Radicalism* (New York, 1969), pp. 39-52.

50 *Education, Human Resources and Development in Latin America*, U. N. Document E/CN-12/800 (New York, 1968) discusses the role of education, and especially University education as a human resource in development.

51 Report submitted to the Inter-American Development Bank, (New York, 1971).

52 Charles W. Anderson, *Politics and Economic Change in Latin America: The Governing of Restless Nations*, (Princeton, N.J., 1967), pp. 163-96.

53 This explanation fits in with Anderson's basic thesis that politics in Latin America is characterised by "imperfect consensus on the nature of political regime" and that "power contenders" acquire access to political power merely by virtue of demonstrating their "power capability," and not by actually *exercising* political power or armed force. Only in a few revolutionary situations, viz. Mexico in 1910, Bolivia in 1952, Cuba in 1959 and Guatemala (temporarily from 1945 to 1956) has this situation been altered, by the elimination of some power contenders or some types of power capabilities from political participation. Anderson, n. 52, pp. 89-98; 108-9.

54 Hirschman, n. 29, pp. 23-9.

55 Ibid., pp. 29-35

56 Frankenhoff, n. 31, p. 204-5.

57 Donald Solar, "The Case Against Latin American Integration: Economic and Political Factors," in Ronald Hilton (ed.), *The Movement Toward Latin American Unity*, p. 115-127. Harold Wood, "The Regional Implication of Economic Integration," Ibid., pp. 141-7. Peter Odell, "Economic Integration and Spatial Patterns of Economic Development in Latin America," *Journal of Common Market Studies* (*JCMS*) (March 1968), p. 267.

58 Theotonio Dos Santos, "Crisis de la Teoria del Desarollo y las Relaciones de Dependencia en America Latina" *Reprint from Boletin de CESO*, October-November 1968, pp. 26, 29, quoted in Susanne Bodenheimer, "Dependency and Imperialism: The Roots of Latin American Underdevelopment," *Readings in US Imperialism*, (Boston, 1971), p. 158.

59 Bodenheimer, in ibid., pp. 166-7. This critique of the ECLA thesis, which is based on the views of a number of Latin American writers, regards Dependency and Imperialism as two different aspects of the same process. It is admitted, however, that the ECLA thesis was valuable in pointing out the link between Latin American underdevelopment and the international economic system. It would appear that the dependency model is a peculiarly Latin American development, born out

of a merger of the Prebisch thesis with a more radical line of thought, somewhat akin to Lenin's theory of imperialism. Another essay which summarises the thinking of this school of writers is Antonio Murga, F., "Dependency: A Latin American View," *NACLA Newsletter*, No. 10, (New York, February 1971), pp. 1-13. See also the report on the "Conference of the Pacific" held at Vina del Mar, Chile from 27 September to 3 October 1970, in H.W. Arndt, "Latin America turns to the Pacific?" *International Development Review* (1971/1), pp. 41-3, in which the writer takes a rather skeptical view of the arguments of Osvaldo Sunkel and others on the dangers of dependence to the United States. The views of Andre Gunder Frank on the relations between metropolis and satellite are somewhat akin to those of the writers on dependency. See for example A.G. Frank "The Development of Underdevelopment" in Robert I. Rhodes (ed.), *Imperialism and Underdevelopment: A Reader* (New York, 1970), pp. 4-17.

60 Rajni Kothari, "Variations and Uniformities in National Building: Report on a UNESCO Meeting of Experts" (UNESCO meeting of Experts on Problems of State Formation and Nation Building, held at Ceriby la Salle from 7 to, 14 August 1970 mimeographed, pp. 9-15.

61 See Frankenhoff, n. 31, pp. 202-3 for a discussion of this point.

CHAPTER III

THE PROCESS OF INTEGRATION IN LATIN AMERICA, 1948-1961

INTRODUCTION

In earlier parts of this study we have referred to the changed climate of opinion which was emerging in Latin America after the close of the Second World War. The reorganisation of the Inter-American system had been completed and the main juridical and political problems appeared to have been solved by the signing of the Charter of Bogota and the establishment of the Organisation of American States. The discussions at the organisation acquired an increasingly economic content as Latin American spokesmen began to realise the importance of economic factors in their international relations. The main stress at the meetings of the inter-American system, which has been described as "a framework for the containment of anti-Americanism within the bounds of seemliness,"[1] was on the granting of economic concessions in matters of trade as well as on increased aid from the United States.[2]

The demand of the Latin Americans for a separate economic institution under the auspices of the United Nations is significant. In the field of security, they had the confidence that legal principles and political traditions had been established so that the United States would not intervene unilaterally in the region, as she had done in the 1920's before the Good Neighbour Policy. However, in the economic sphere, the Latin American countries did not have confidence in the United States.

The attitude of indifference in the United States to the economic demands of the Latin Americans had two major causes. In the first place, United States policy in Latin America was dictated, probably to a greater extent than anywhere else in the world, by US companies, which constituted a powerful lobby in Washington. Secondly, there was no sense of urgency on the part of the United States Government in giving aid to Latin American countries because there was no immediate threat of communism there. These two factors of security and economics seem to have reinforced each other, with the result that Latin America received little attention in the economic sphere from the United States Government.

Most existing studies of the Latin American integration process rightly give credit to ECLA and Prebisch for originating the concept of Latin American integration[3] and some also for asserting the position of the Latin American countries *vis-a-vis* the United States.[4] The economic ideas spread by ECLA were an important source of a series of developments in the Latin America area, including the acceptance of the OAS of integration as a desirable goal, the change of United States policy in regard to the establishment of the Inter-American Development Bank, and the development of the United Nations Conference on Trade and Development as an instrument of the developing countries. It should be noted, however, that ECLA could not have played the role it did if it were not for the fact that the atmosphere was favourable for it. There is some evidence, in fact, that the OAS itself served for some time as one of the instruments of the Latin American countries not only in asserting their position *vis-a-vis* the United States in economic matters, but also in building up the economic integration movement.[5]

ECLA and Latin American Economic Development, 1948-1953

During the first phase of its activity from 1948 to 1953, ECLA was preoccupied with the formulation of an economic ideology, the collection of basic data regarding the economic situation of Latin American countries, and determining the relationship between ideology and data, theory, and fact.[6] Its basic ideology was stated, as we have seen, in Prebisch's manifesto, prepared while he was still an Adviser to ECLA, and published by the United Nations in 1950. During this formative period of ECLA's activity, the view was propounded that industrialisation, which was regarded as the key to the development of Latin

America, should be promoted through the protection of internal markets, import controls and import substitution. However, the efforts of ECLA to persuade member countries to launch social and economic reforms for the rational allocation of resources, or even to adopt autarchic national production policies, were not successful.[7]

This was not surprising, as the Latin American economies were at this time still enjoying the advantages of the post-war boom in international commodity markets which tapered off only after the end of the Korean War. This boom had led to some important Latin American countries (Argentina, Brazil, Chile, Mexico, and to some extent Colombia) establishing consumer goods industries. The ECLA reports of the period pointed out that the prosperity it brought was illusory, and urged the need for structural reforms, as well as for increased United States aid to Latin America.[8] The countries of the region were, however, unwilling to accept the advice of ECLA, and continued to improvise their domestic economic policies. It should be remembered that many of the Latin American countries were under authoritarian or populist regimes[9] which were unsympathetic to ideas of state planning, particularly if it involved control of government expenditure in the fields of defence and welfare. Few Latin American Governments were equipped to handle intricate economic problems. Moreover, orthodox financial policies were insisted upon by the United States and by international organisations, especially the World Bank and the IMF. The pleadings of ECLA therefore fell too often on deaf ears.[10]

In one area, however, the ideas of ECLA were having considerable influence at this time. This was in the five states of Central America, which between them occupy the narrow strip between the Isthmus of Panama and Mexico. Covering a small area of 207,456 square miles and a population in the early 1950's of less than ten million people, these small countries had been united for three centuries under colonial rule. From January 1822 to March 1823, they were officially a part of Mexico. In November 1824, the five provinces of Central America promulgated a constitution for a Federal Republic of Central America, which broke down finally in 1838.[11] Panama, which was separated from Colombia in 1903 by a manoeuvre of the United States in order to ensure the building of the Panama Canal usually kept aloof from the other States of the Isthmus.

Geography and economics alike seemed to demand a single unit for the Central American countries; politics kept them apart. The comparative lack of geographical barriers, the proximity of the states to one another, and the similarity of their economic problems, make it difficult to understand why they had not been united. Numerous attempts at unification were made over a period of 135 years, under different forms of government, and all "failed unconditionally, even though they apparently possess more bonds of similarity, than any other small group of nations in the world . . . ."[12] In spite of these discouragements, a Unionist Party (*Partido Unionista*) founded by a group of Guatemalan students, provided the impetus for the spread of the idea of political and economic union from 1920 to the 1950's. This political group, which cut across national lines, was identified with opposition to the dictatorial regimes and to colonialism. The fall of dictatorial regimes in Guatemala and El Salvador in 1945 led to a brief revival of the spirit of unity in an announcement of complete political merger, which other Central American countries were invited to join. The plans for a confederation were, however, set aside in the wake of political tension among the Central American countries.[13]

The basic urge of the Central American countries for unity was revived at meetings held at San Salvador in October 1951 to discuss "mutual problems." These talks led to the emergence of the Organisation of Central American States (ODECA) based on a Charter which stated in the preamble that the five republics were disintegrated portions of a single nation attempting to coordinate their efforts for the re-establishment of the old unity and to break down the artificial barriers holding the people apart. The Charter declared, *inter alia*, the intention of the members to carry on consultations to promote and maintain peaceful relations and help solve Central American problems, and the acceptance of the five Foreign Ministers as the main body of the Organization, meeting at least once a year and functioning by unanimous decision.[14] The Ministers of Economy of the Central American republics formed the Central Economic

Cooperation Committee (ECC) which originally met under the auspices of ECLA to coordinate studies undertaken in Central America by that organization, but eventually acquired greater influence than the foreign ministers' organisation. The strength of the economic organisation seems to have been its non-political character, which enabled it to carry on its activities outside the glare of publicity. Political spokesmen were able to dissociate themselves from the "technical" nature of the work of the economic ministers, many of whom were themselves young technicos who had been exposed to modern education in the United States or to the training courses of ECLA.[15]

The ECC, better than any other organisation, served as a liaison between ODECA's policies and the economic philosophy and programmes of ECLA. ECC prepared the draft for the basic treaties that were later signed and put into operation. It played an important role in the long drawn-out negotiations on effective multilateral agreements and economic integration in Latin America and helped to establish the institutional framework of a common market itself.[16]

A number of bilateral treaties for the promotion of free trade were signed between Central American countries. But the main thrust of the integration process was yet to come. The period till 1953 was mainly important for the studies which were undertaken under the auspices of the ECLA and the impetus given to the idea of Central American economic integration by the establishment of the Central American School of Public Administration and the Central American Institute of Research and Industrial Technology.[17]

LATIN AMERICA AND THE COMMON MARKET IDEA, 1953-1961

During the second phase of its activity after 1953, ECLA began to give attention to country by country analyses and to the principle of programming. A limited working dialogue was established with the governments, but there was little influence on the planning organisations. ECLA was stil seen as propounding dangerous "socialistic" doctrines. This period, however, saw the emergence of ECLA's influential training programme. This process gradually began to affect the acceptance of ECLA's ideas in the various Latin American governments.

A pamphlet issued by ECLA in 1966 states that in 1952 a programme of advisory services and training of professional staff in planning and programming techniques was initiated in response to requests from member governments. As part of that work ECLA sent advisory groups to set up machinery for formulating development policy at the government level and launched professional training programmes for economists, engineers, agronomists, government officials, and other professional personnel. Many of those who underwent that training either in basic courses given in Santiago or in intensive courses in various countries of the region later occupied responsible positions in the Latin American economies.

The training functions of ECLA were taken over by the Latin American Institute for Economic and Social Planning (ILPES) in 1962. By 1966, about 5,000 professionals had been trained under the ECLA program.[18]

It was not only the *fact* that training courses were held for Latin America as a whole, but the *content* of the courses, as well as the sense of commitment communicated to the trainees, that constituted the essential element in the building up of a sense of regional solidarity. Dell comments:

> Dr. Prebisch and his staff did have one great asset—their intimate contact with the member-governments of ECLA. There was hardly a government in Latin America that did not have at least one prominent member, often at Cabinet level, who had served a term on the ECLA staff or in an ECLA training course. Thus the ideas of ECLA were known and understood by government officials who had become acquainted with them as insiders. And ECLA commanded a respect all over Latin America that was quite unrivalled.[19]

Although a reference had been made in Prebisch's "manifesto" of 1949 to the need for removing "the present division of markets with its constant inefficiency" which was a limitation to industrial growth, this point was not pursued for Latin America as a whole till the late fifties. According to Wionczek, until 1956, no one, including the ECLA group, had any notion of how regional economic cooperation should be implemented as there were no precedents available except the *zollverein* and Benelux. The appearance of the concept in ECLA's Trade

Committee in its meetings in 1956-57 and the signature of the Treaty of Rome in March 1957 seem to have resulted in a change in the situation, and led to a gradual acceptance of the need for a Latin American Common Market, as an answer to the stagnation of Latin America's economic growth as indicated by the passing of a resolution by the Buenos Aires Conference of the OAS.[20]

Another grouping in some ways similar to the Central American experiment began to develop at this time; Venezuela, Colombia and Ecuador which had constituted the old viceroyalty of Nueva Granada under Spanish rule and later for a few years the Republic of Gran Colombia, explored the possibility of economic cooperation. Their efforts led only to the setting up of a common merchant marine for Gran Colombia.[21]

These two groupings of states were, in a sense, movements of an irredentist nature, harking back to a political unity which was lost in the early nineteenth century. But the movement for closer economic ties among the countries of the Cono del Sur (Southern Cone), viz. Argentina, Uruguay, Brazil, and Chile, was based primarily on commercial motivations. These four countries were comparatively more industrialised than the other Latin American countries and there was a tradition of inter-regional trade among them which dated back to before the Second World War. At the time of ratifying their adherence to the General Agreement on Tariffs and Trade (GATT), a number of bilateral arrangements among the countries were preserved. The trade relations of these countries naturally complemented one another and by 1960, 70 per cent of the Inter-Latin American trade was between them.[22]

At the sixth session of ECLA in August-September 1955, a Trade Committee was set up to intensify inter-regional trade and facilitate trade negotiations. This Trade Committee in turn set up subsidiary groups. At the seventh session of ECLA in 1957, the governments reaffirmed their support for regional economic integration, but wanted that the special problems of landlocked countries, economies lacking even fundamental diversification, and variances in size, population, and levels of economic development should be borne in mind.[23] In September 1957, the long-awaited Economic Conference of the OAS held at Buenos Aires, passed a resolution declaring "the advisability of establishing gradually and progressively, in multilateral and competitive form, a Latin American Regional Market," and recommened to IA-ECOSOC that it cooperate with ECLA in "studies and activities leading to its creation."[24]

Early in 1958 the steps taken towards a Latin American Common Market began to take a more decisive shape. The Trade Committee set up a Working Group of Experts under Galo Plaza Lasso, former President of Ecuador, to draw up a plan for a LAFTA and regional free trade areas or customs union. This Working Group held two meetings in February 1958 and February 1959 and presented its proposals to the Eighth Session of ECLA at Panama in May 1959.

Meanwhile, experts from the four Southern Cone countries held meetings with the initial help of ECLA at Santiago in August-September 1958 and April 1959. They developed proposals for a sub-regional free trade area agreement embracing these four countries. These proposals were also placed before the Panama session of ECLA.[25]

"The simultaneous appearance of two concrete, but competitive, proposals forced upon ECLA and the Latin American Governments the necessity to define speedily their respective positions and the course to be followed."[26] The recommendations of the Trade Committee were ambitious and broad in scope. They distinguished between primary goods, products of industry and light manufactures. It was proposed to make the most rapid steps toward integration in respect of heavy industry and raw materials in which field there was least opposition, as against light manufactures in which there were established vested interests who would oppose integration. The Draft Agreement drawn up by the Southern Zone countries for a free trade area, on the other hand, was weaker in scope, and favoured the more developed nations as against the less advanced ones. It had no provision for "reciprocity", made only passing reference to special concessions for the lesser developed countries, and did not provide for special treatment for agriculture.[27]

The discussions at the Panama Conference indicated a questioning of the concept of sub-regionalism on which the draft of the southern zone was based. It was felt that if a southern zone were allowed to come into being, there might be a tendency to put off altogether the integration of Latin America, just as Western European unity stood in the way of the integration of Europe as a whole. The ECLA Secretariat and leading Latin American economists and policy-makers were therefore looking for some way in which the two projects could be reconciled.[28] As a result of discussions at conferences held from June to September 1959, the southern zone countries decided to modify their proposal and to accept certain features of the Trade Committee proposal. Bolivia, Paraguay, and Peru were invited to join the free trade zone and the formal diplomatic conference was convened at Montevideo in February 1969 by Argentina, Brazil, Chile, Mexico, Paraguay, Peru, and Uruguay. Colombia and Ecuador joined in 1961, Venezuela in 1966 and Bolivia in 1967.[29]

It is not yet clear whether Prebisch and ECLA worked for a LAFTA covering almost the whole of Latin America, or whether the idea emerged as a compromise proposal. Mikesell, who was a member of the second session of the Working Group of Experts, states that the adherence of Mexico to the Treaty "which came as something of a surprise, eliminated the regional character of the Association and undoubtedly doomed ECLA's plans for a Latin America-wide agreement which would encompass [sub-] regional trade association. . ."[30] However, there are also indications that Prebisch was anxious to ensure some kind of basic commitment to a Latin America-wide agreement, and did not approve of sub-regional agreements at that stage.[31]

Apart from the diplomatic role performed by Prebisch and the officials of ECLA, there is strong reason to believe that Mexico played an important role in the decision to create a wider union including the important Latin American countries outside the Cono del Sur. A group of *tecnicos*, who exercised high-level influence in the Mexican Government, had come to the conclusion that, both for economic and political reasons, the entry of Mexico into a common market with Latin America was a desirable course. The most important economic factor was the need to counter the stagnation in Mexican industrial development by an expansion of trade towards the southern continent, as against the traditional direction of Mexican trade, viz. the United States.[32]

While the economic agreements were used to convince the reluctant Mexican industrialists of the necessity for entry into LAFTA, the basic motivations of the *tecnicos* seem to have been political and ideological. Personal contacts with Prebisch, who had come to Mexico in exile in 1944, had accustomed many Mexican economists to think in terms of reducing dependence on the US. Moreover, Mexico's revolutionary past and her autonomous cultural tradition made it appropriate for her to consider herself a leader in Latin America. It was easier for her to maintain such a position by entering into an economic arrangement with other Latin American countries than by taking any step which might be considered a political challenge to the United States. Lastly, a sub-regional economic arrangement which included the two most powerful countries of Latin America, Brazil and Argentina, and excluded Mexico, would be highly undesirable, both from the economic and the political points of view. Thus it was during his southern tour in January 1960, President Lopez Matoes of Mexico announced that his country would adhere to the Treaty of Montevideo.[33]

The Treaty of Montevideo has been criticised for being "deliberately general, not binding and full of traditional Latin American loopholes which leave the member countries free to choose any course of action at any stage of negotiations and after any agreement." It is contrasted with the Treaty of Rome which set up the European Common Market and which is described as "precise, clear, decisive, and 'involving.'"[34]

Unlike the Treaty of Rome and the treaty setting up the Central American Common Market, the Montevideo Treaty merely formed an association of nations, which could not speak with one voice. It was "a commercial instrument conceived as a substitute for the old bilateral trade and payment agreements set up among several Lalin American countries." There were no automatic across-the-board provisions for moving towards the complete elimination of trade barriers. It provided a mechanism for conducting reciprocal negotiations for the reduction of tariffs, and was intended to facilitate freer trade in the region rather than provide for the automatic freeing of trade.

The reasons for these weaknesses of the Treaty are to be found in the desire for the integration of Latin America as a whole, rather than for the few countries which might have agreed to more substantial reductions of trade barriers.[35]

The Treaty, which contained sixty-five articles grouped under twelve chapters, mentioned in the Preamble, *inter alia*, the need for expansion of national markets to accelerate economic development of Latin America, the need to compensate countries at a relatively less advanced stage of economic development, and the intention to "establish, gradually and progressively, a Latin American Common Market."

Thus it accepted the basic premises of the ECLA proposal of a regional market for continued economic growth, and of a Latin American Free Trade Area as a step towards a common market for Latin America as well as the protection of the interests of lesser developed contries in the region.

The Treaty vistualised the gradual establishment of national schedules of bilaterally negotiated products and a common schedule of products on which duties, charges and restriction would be eliminated by 1973. The Treaty had special concession schedules for less developed nations and made provision for complementary and reciprocity agreements under which the advantages of integration were sought to be equalised. It also looked towards cordinated and harmonised policies of industrial and agricultural development. The Treaty set up two supreme organs, the conference and the standing Executive Committee.[36]

Wionczek points out that there is "a certain disproportion" between the provisions for a free trade area and the the broader aims as defined in the Preamble in Chapter Three on "expansion of trade and economic complementarity." The treaty established in its main operative sections

> a fairly modest machanism calling for a very slow and gradual expansion of intra-regional trade with the emphasis on existing trade. . . Even in this respect, the scope of the Treaty was closely circumscribed by a special regime for agriculture, escape clauses, and a possiblity of renegotiating the composition of the national schedules in the light of the subsequent experience of the member countries.[37]

On the other hand, according to the sponsors and authors and most Latin American economists, the free trade area was intended to be "a major vehicle for regional economic cooperation and integration." This leads to the following conclusion:

Clearly the Montevideo Treaty, in spirit if not in letter, aims at establishing something potentially larger than a free trade zone but, at the same time, much less ambitious than a common market. On the other hand, it leaves open, presumably for future negotiation, not only all the basic measures needed to implement regional integration objectives but also certain important issues that are of critical importance to the adequate functioning of a free trade zone in a region characterised by a very uneven and still incipient overall economic development.

These issues include the key question of an intra-regional payments system and the practical measures necessary for enabling lesser developed countries to benefit fully from participation.[38]

The movement for the economic integration of Central America, which had received an impetus between 1951 and 1953, suffered a setback as a result of the tense situation created by El Salvador's anti-communist resolution which caused the leftist Guatemalan Government to withdraw from ODECA in April 1953. Although the conservative government of Carlos Castillo Armas brought Guatemala back to ODECA in 1955, most of its efforts during the latter part of the decade were devoted to the settlement of intra-regional disputes.[39]

In the economic sphere, however, there was considerable progress, partly because economic matters were treated as technical and non-controversial. Bilateral treaties for the freezing of trade between countries of the sub-region, continued to be signed, culminating in the multilateral treaty on Free Trade and Central American Economic Integration and an Agreement on the Regime for Central American Integration Industries, both signed at Tegucigalpa, Honduras, on 10 June 1958.

Unlike the Montevideo Treaty which provided for the liberalisation of existing trade, the Multilateral Treaty provided for the freeing of trade in 200 commodities which were proposed to be manufactured in the region. The stress was therefore on the creation of new industries rather than the increase of competition among existing industries. The special agreement on industrial integration was intended to ensure that every country would benefit from industrial development and to discourage new industries gravitating toward existing industrial centres.[40]

El Salvador, Guatemala, and Honduras signed a tripartite Treaty in February 1960 which presented the other two states, viz. Costa Rica and Nicaragua, with a *fait accompli*, and forced them to negotiate for a fresh treaty.[41] The new General Treaty on Central American Economic Integration was signed at Managua in December 1960. It provided for immediate free trade in all products originating in the region, except for those specifically listed. This resulted in nearly fifty per cent of intra-regional trade being freed. Trade in other products was to be freed within five years, and the signatories undertook to adopt a common external tariff in an unspecified period. A Central American Bank for Economic Integration was set up to finance and promote "regionally balanced, integrated economic growth" with an initial capital of $16 million. A Central American Economic Council, composed of the Ministers of Economic Affairs, an Executive Council, and a Secretariat was established.

The Treaty came into force in June 1961 after ratification by the four signatories—El Salvador, Guatemala, Honduras, and Nicaragua. Costa Rica joined in July 1962.[42] Important features of this treaty were a common external tariff instead of merely a a free trade zone, the automatic reduction of tariffs instead of item by item reduction, and the provision of a regional development fund.[43] In all these respects, the treaty constituted a definite advance over the Treaty of Montevideo.

There was a remarkable extension of Central America's regional trade from 1956 onwards. Unlike LEFTA, the Central American integration programme did not depend on annual negotiations for the elimination of obstacles to trade and hence "took off" at an early stage.

Intra-regional trade increased from 1950 to 1959 by more then three times from $8.3 million to $28 million, and rose from 3 per cent to 6.5 per cent of the total exports of the countries.[44] However, the economy as a whole did not expand proportionately. The expansion of the then small sector of intra-regional trade could not offset the effect of the deterioration in terms of trade during this period.[45]

REFERENCES

1 John White, *Regional Development Banks: A Study of Institutional Style* (London, 1970), p. 150.

2 See *supra*, Ch. II (a) (ii).

3 See for example, Sidney Dell, *A Latin American Common Market?* (*A LACM?*) (London, 1966), p. 25.

4 This is implied, though not precisely stated, in Gustavo Lagos, "The Political Role of Regional Economic Organisations in Latin America," *Journal of Common Market Studies* (June 1968), *passim.*

There was some rivalry betweet the OAS and ECLA. Whereas the former was widely known as a US-dominated institution, the latter was an instrument of Latin American regional "nationalism" (to use the term used by Felipe Herrera). "Regional pride in ECLA and a disposition to listen when ECLA prescribes for the region's ills may be inversely related to regional acceptance of the OAS machinery."

Richard B. Gregg, "The UN Regional Economic Commission and Integration in the Underdeveloped Regions," *International Organisation* (New York) (Spring 1966), pp. 219-20.

5 Jose A. Mora, *From Panama to Punta del Este: Past Experience and Future Prospects* (Washington, D.C.), pp. vii-viii; 3-36.

6 Dennis J. Vodarsik, "Building the Latin American Community: The Meaning and Politics of Latin American Integration," Ph.D. Dissertation (Georgetown University, 1969), pp. 150-2.

7 Miguel S. Wionczek, "LAFTA," *International Conciliation* (January 1965), p. 8.

8 For a discussion of the developments during this period, see Miguel S. Wionczek, "A History of the Montevideo Treaty," in Wionczek (ed.), *Latin American Economic Integration: Experiences and Prospects* (New York, 1966), pp. 73-6.

9 Vargas in Brazil (1930-45; 1951-54), Peron in Argentina (1946-55), Trujillo in the Dominican Republic (1930-61), Odria in Peru (1948-56), and Perez Jimenes in Venezuela (1952-58).

10 Wionczek, n. 8, p. 74.

11 Thomas L. Karnes, *The Failure of Union, Central America, 1824-1960* (Chapel Hill, 1961), pp. 24, 29, 243.

12 Ibid., p. 3.

13 Nino Maritano, *A Latin American Economic Community: History, Policies and Problems* (Notre Dame, 1970), pp. 23-4.

14 Karnes, n. 11, pp. 238-39.

15 For a discussion of the political and economic factors in Central American economic integration, see Joseph S. Nye, "Central American Regional Integration," in J.S. Nye, Jr. (ed.), *International Regionalism: Readings* (Boston, 1968), p. 388.

16 Maritano, n. 13, p. 28.

17 Nye, n. 15, p. 388.

18 United Nations, Office of Public Information, *UN Economic Commission*

for Latin America (*ECLA*) (OPI/227-18828, August 1966-1 CM), p. 3.

19 Dell, n. 3, p. 25.

20 Wionczek, n. 8. References regarding the early activities of ECLA in regard to integration will be found in A.O. Hirschman (ed.), *Latin American Issues: Essays and Comments* (New York, 1969), p. 19, and Romulo Almedida's essay, "Origen, estructura, funcionamiento y problemas de la ALALC," in Gustavo Lagos (ed.), *La Integracion Lationoamerica: Situacion y Perspectivas* (Buenos Aires, 1965), p. 17.

21 Almeida, n. 20, p. 18. These three countries are sometimes referred to as the Bolivarian Republics.

22 A Resolution was brought forth contemplating a special accord among the countries of the Southern Zone but was not approved, evidently because of disapproval of the Argentine regime (of Peron) at the time, ibid., p. 17.
Wionczek remarks: "Since the only commercial exchange worth mentioning, with the exception of the four southernmost countries (Argentina, Brazil, Chile and Uruguay), the early efforts under ECLA auspices were directed to the solution of the trade problems within the southern zone of Latin America and were not truly regional arrangements." Wionczek, n. 8, p. 75.

23 United Nations, ECLA, *The Economic Development of Latin America and its Principal Problems* (New York, 1950), p. 16, cited in Vodarsik, n. 6, p. 159.

24 Resolution XL of the Final Act, Economic Conference of the OAS, *Annals, OAS,* no. 4 (1954), pp. 258-89, cited in Godon Connell-Smith, *Inter-American System* (London, 1966), pp. 165-269.

25 Christopher Mitchell, "Role of Technocrats in Latin American Integration," *Inter-American Economic Affairs* (IAEA) (Summer 1967), pp. 15-8. See also Wionczek, n. 8, pp. 73-6, 81. The documents relating to the Panama Conference including the reports of the working groups and the addresses of Raul Prebisch and Dag Hammarskjold, Secretary General of the UN, will be found in *The Latin American Common Market* (UN, New York, Department of Economic and Social Affairs, 1959E/CN. 12/523-31).

26 Wionczek, n. 8, p. 83.

27 Mitchell, n. 25.

28 Wionczek, n. 8, pp. 76-84.

29 Inter-American Institute of International Legal Studies (IILS), *Instruments Relating to the Economic Integration of Latin Amercia* (Dobbs Ferry, N.Y., 1968), pp. 221-2.

30 Raymond F. Mikesell, "The Movement toward Regional Trading Groups in Latin America," in Hirschman (ed.), n. 20, pp. 129-30.

31 Wionczek, n. 8, pp. 16-8. Prebisch's reluctance to accept sub-regional integration at the period under discussion was confirmed to me during a personal interview by an official of the Inter-American Development Bank, Senor Raul Rey Alvarez, who was at that time an official of ECLA.

32 Philippe C. Schmitter and Ernst B. Haas, *Mexico and Latin American Economic Integration* (Berkeley, Calif , 1964), pp. 7-17.

33 Interview with Professor Victor Urquidi, President, El Colegio de Mexico, Mexico City, 9 November 1971. Urquidi was a Mexican Delegate to the Panama Conference and one of the leading *tecnicos of* of the period. See the account of these events in ibid., pp. 18-21.

34 Maritano, n. 13, p. 65.

35 Ibid., pp. 65-6.

36 For the text of the Treaty and the Protocols, see IIILS, n. 29, pp. 207-29.

Analyses of the Treaty will be found in Wionczek, n. 7, pp. 19-22, and Maritano, n. 13, pp. 59-65.

37 Wionczek, n. 8, p. 71.

38 Ibid., pp. 71-2.

39 Nye, n. 15, p. 387.

40 Dell, n. 3, pp. 53-5. In September 1959 a Central American Agreement on the Equalisation of Import Duties and Charges was signed by the five countries. Ibid., p. 55.

41 Ibid., p. 56.

42 Ibid., pp. 55-8. A more detailed account of these developments will be found in Victor Urquidi, *Free Trade and Economic Integration in Latin America: The Evolution of a Common Market Policy* (Berkeley and Los Angeles, 1962), pp. 97-101. Urquidi was for several years Head of the Mexico Branch Office of ECLA, which handled Central American Integration.

For the text of the treaties and agreement, see IIILS, n. 29, pp. 3-34.

43 See Aaron Segal, "The Integration of Developing Countries: Some Thoughts on East Africa and Central America." *JCMS* (March 1967), p. 267, f.n. 29, for a discussion of these points in relation to the Tripartite Treaty of February 1960.

44 See Table in Dell, n. 3, p. 59.

Also refer Table II. D. at the Appendices for Intra-LAFTA Trade from 1965-70.

45 "From 1950 to 1957, the total output of the area rose at an average annual rate of 4.6 per cent, but from 1957 to 1960, the rate dropped to 2.8 per cent, less than the rate of increase in population." A major cause for the decline was the decline in the terms of trade. The purchasing power of exports declined at the rate of 2.1 per cent per annum, whereas export volume was advancing at the rate of 7.1 per cent per annum. Ibid., p. 62.

CHAPTER IV

THE PROCESS OF INTEGRATION IN LATIN AMERICA, 1961-1973

The Rise and Decline of Central American Integration

A major experiment in the integration of developing countries was launched with the coming into force of the General Treaty on Central American Economic Integration in June 1961, involving the establishment of a common external tariff, the breaking down of internal tariff barriers, and the establishment of the Central American Bank for Economic Integration.[1]

The combination of provisions regarding trade liberalisation and financial assistance for industry in the same instrument underlined the close link visualised between trade and industry in Central America. This link was not present in the Montevideo Treaty which set up LAFTA.

In July 1961 a clearing house for handling payments within the region was set up. The success of the clearing house is indicated by the signing of a clearing agreement between Banco de Mexico and the Central American Clearing House in 1963, the establishment of a Central American Monetary Council of representatives of Central Banks to work towards a standardised currency and a Central American Compensation Common Fund to provide mutual assistance in time of balance of payment difficulties.[2]

These developments had consequences in three major fields, viz. (1) intra-regional trade, (2) the external trade of the region, and (3) the establishment of industry.

The "most immediate and spectacular results" of the economic integration of five Central American countries were the liberalisation and growth in intra-Central American trade. In

December 1963, the customs procedures were unified and customs barriers were almost totally eliminated. Intra-regional trade increased from $32.6 million in 1960 to $176 2 million in 1966. The ten-fold increase in inter-Central American trade in ten years "can only be compared to that of the European Economic Community."[3]

According to an agreement on the Equalisation of Import Duties and Charges in force since 1960, a uniform external tariff was fixed on imports from outside Central America. Both imports and exports increased rapidly from 1960 onwards. Although exports began to experience reverses in 1967 and 1968, these were partly compensated by a pick-up of inter-Central American trade.[4]

The rate of increase of total output also recovered between 1960 and 1964 from a low 2.8 per cent to an average of over 5 per cent. Industrial production advanced at the rate of over 7 per cent per annum. The trade among Central American countries began to show indications of including some manufactures, in contrast to the LAFTA area, whose intra-regional trade consisted overwhelmingly of primary commodities.[5] However, the programme for joint industrial development in Central America languished in the 1960's. The "integrated industries" scheme became controversial, partly due to its alleged tendency to create monopolies.[6]

By 1967 it was clear to one observer of the African and Central American scene that Central America had also encountered, although in less acute form, the same three problems that beset East African integration:

1) The gap between political and economic integration had "impeded the formation of regional policies to take maximum advantage of the common market." National development plans had not been regionally coordinated. Central America, like the East Africa, "competed bitterly. . .over such matters as the allocation of quotas under international coffee and sugar agreements."[7]

2) Non-locals, viz. American, European and Japanese firms were quicker to take advantage of the new trading and industrial possibilities offered by the Central American Common Market. Several Central American firms were bought by foreign firms and then expanded to serve the regional market.

3) The benefits of integration tended to be concentrated in "certain growth poles" while others claimed that they did not benefit from integration. Honduras complained that it had failed to benefit from integration and that El Salvador was the major beneficiary. A similar complaint had been made by Tanganyika against Kenya in East Africa. In both cases the countries threatened to revert to national economic policies.[8]

However, in Central America, two external factors played a major role in providing the viability of Central American economic integration. According to Segal, US aid was the first. "Not only does the US maintain a special high office for Central America and Panama (ROCAP) to coordinate its regional aid policies, but American financial support has been instrumental in shaping the General Treaty of Integration and in accelerating the integration process."[9]

The second major external factor was the role of ECLA in championing integration, providing technical assistance by preparing studies, assisting in the drafting of documents etc. On the other hand, in East Africa, US and other foreign assistance played a negligible role, and ECA, instead of helping to salvage East Africa Economic Union, appeared to have "chided East Africans for narrowly concentrating on their region rather than seeking to establish a pan African Market."[10]

It is necessary to examine these propositions a little more closely in the light of the developments in Central American integration. The original proposals of ECLA for Central American integration stressed the need for "balanced economic development." The term refers to an equitable spread of industrialisation in the region, but the Central American region has been characterised by continuous complaints from lesser developed countries, Honduras and Nicaragua, that they have not gained from the Union proportionately to the others and that they were, "through their increased industrial imports from the other three, supporting the expansion of manufacturing activity in those countries, while receiving few of the benefits of industrialisation at home. They insisted on special treatment to encourage continued adherence to the Common Market."[11]

While it was generally agreed that the Central American Common Market and the CABEI had many substantial achievements to their credit, there was considerable evidence that much of the industrial development was "of the traditional and easy kind," not involving new production techniques, or much capital investment.[12] The CABEI was criticised for its failure to encourage new types of industries and for following a conservative policy on loans.[13] Miguel Wionczek argued that

> . . . the economic integration scheme in the area, despite all its limited success, proved, firstly, unprepared to face the fundamental issue of the equal distribution of gains; secondly, impotent to bring about any tangible degree of political integration of the five minute republics; and thirdly, unable to foster social modernisation in this particularly backward part of Latin America.[14]

He also pointed out that if the CACM appeared to be an unqualified success in contrast to LAFTA it was because the achievements of the organisation were judged mainly by the growth of trade within their respective areas.[15] Although the sub-regional agencies had worked with relative efficiency, the "coordination of major economic policies, particularly in respect to the siting of new industries and the common treatment of foreign investment, has proved very difficult" due to the absence of national economic planning machinery and the "opposition of powerful external political and economic interests. . ."[16] It was estimated that "of the roughly 7 per cent per year growth in regional GNP in Central America from mid-1962 through 1965, around 4 per cent was due to minimum normal growth, 2 per cent to the increase in export receipts and 1 per cent to the expansionary effect of the CACM and related forces.[17]

This factor by itself would not be a cause for alarms but much of the industrialisation which did take place in Central America appeared to have consisted largely of 'final-touch' industries. Most of these industries were concentrated in the more advanced countries, viz. Guatemala, El Salvador and Costa Rica, which became the principal exporters of manufactured goods to the area. Early in 1969, Nicaragua found her balance of payments position *vis-a-vis* the outside world to be acute, and unilaterally imposed custom duties on imports from Central America, contrary to the original treaty. This step was successful in forcing the other members to ratify pending regional protocols, one of which was intended to counter "the initial free for all to attract foreign industrial investment."[18]

In July 1969, there occurred the four-day 'Football War' between El Salvador and Honduras. This was a consequence of the land reforms initiated in Honduras which was directed against the influx of labour from its overcrowded neighbour, El Salvador, which had the smallest area of the five republics (8,200 sq. miles) as against Nicaragua (57,000 sq. miles), the second largest population (2.8 million as against Guatemala's 4.3 million) and a population density of 332 per sq. mile as against 27 per sq. mile in Nicaragua. It had, however, a per capita income of $272 per annum as against $207 per annum in Honduras. (These two are the lowest of the five republics, the highest being Costa Rica with $365).[19]

Economists who examined the Central American experiment in economic integration pointed to the basic economic issues which had to be faced if the integration experiment was to succeed.

Sidney Dell pointed out in 1966 that although concessions were made to attract foreign capital, the progress in investment was not rapid, and many of the new manufacturing activities consisted of assembly plants, putting the finishing touches on almost completed goods. The growth of regional trade and of increased manufacture had therefore to be seen in the context of the contribution it made to the overall development of the area, and not merely to the increase in trade and manufacturing activities.[20]

In a study published in 1967, Hansen argued that the main problem in Central America was one of reforming the agricultural system. Quoting a study by ECLA of 1963, he stated

> So long as the productivity and therefore the purchasing power of the trade agricultural sector in Central America remains low and relatively stagnant, it will represent a major bottleneck to the present policy of industrialisation in the area. . .[21]

Hansen argued for land reform, based on efficiency rather than the size of the farm, in order to increase the purchasing power of the rural people.[22]

Hansen felt that the second major factor was the role the Government could play in economic development. He stressed the need for political stability, administrative capacity, and changes in fiscal policy.

> In the long run, the political questions cannot be avoided. For when plans for economic integration move from the blueprint stage to that of implementation, individual and group interests are immediately affected, and 'economics' very quickly becomes 'politics' . . . [23]

Dell was of the same opinion:

> No integration program, however well conceived, can do much for under-developed countries in the long run unless it forms part of an overall strategy for development. Experience suggests that without the requisite measures of land reform, without really purposeful national and regional planning, and without the many other measures needed for harnessing the region's human and material resources, no sustained progress or development will be possible.[24]

THE DISAPPOINTMENTS OF LAFTA : ATTEMPTS TO SALVAGE LATIN AMERICAN INTEGRATION

An examination of the work of LAFTA indicates that the fears of those who anticipated that it would not achieve its targets were not exaggerated. The experience of the Association has shown that an emphasis on reduction of trade barriers in the expectation that intra-regional trade will increase and industrialisation will follow is over-optimistic. Three major criticisms of the achievements of LAFTA in the field of trade and industrialisation can be made. These relate to the slow rate of negotiations for the reduction of tariff barriers, the decline in intra-area trade after 1967, and the failure of the provisions for complementary industries to contribute to industrial development.

In the first place, the negotiations among members of LAFTA for drawing up of bilateral national schedules between members, and the negotiation of a common schedule constituting at least 50 per cent of intra-area trade, made slow progress. Although a "maze of 9000 concessions on individual trade items was negotiated in five successive annual rounds" by 1968, it was difficult to say what part of the intra-zonal trade had been freed, or "what is the equivalent of trade preferences mutually granted in terms of protection against third countries."[25] ECLA pointed out in 1969 that "the states members of the Association are in arrears as regards compliance with the terms of article 7 of the Treaty, respecting the establishment of the Common Schedule . . . and they have not yet decided how to remedy this state of affairs." Moreover, with regard to the drawing up of National Schedules, it commented: "Whereas in the first two rounds of negotiations tariff concessions were agreed upon for a large number of products, as from the third round a considerable falling-off is observable . . . "[26] ECLA examined in the same report the proposals for overcoming these difficulties, and found them unsatisfactory. The first was a proposal to eliminate the Common Schedule. which would have meant the abandonment of the idea of a Free Trade Area altogether, and a reversion to the pattern of bilateral preferences. The second suggestion, to defer the time limits, would "do no more than put off the task of solving the basic problem."[27]

The fundamental reason for the situation which has been described is that "*the conflicting purposes of member governments* served to deflect the course of regional integration from the optimal pattern implicit in the ECLA doctrine. Rather than mirroring identical commitments based on similar national economic purposes, the final draft represents a convergence upon the lowest common denominator among generally conflicting aims."[28]

The second major failure of LAFTA was that the increase in intra-area trade which was shown until 1967 began to decline after that date, and even so was confined mainly to certain countries.[29] Although the figures of intra-area trade indicated an increase upto 1964, and this increase did not compare unfavourably with that in the European Economic Community and the European Free Trade Association (EFTA), it must be noted that the base year of 1961 was a record low year in intra-LAFTA trade and that by 1963, zonal commerce had merely regained the importance which it had in 1952 (8.4 per cent). The very low figure of zonal trade as a percentage of total foreign trade indicates clearly the marginal function which the trade among countries of the region played as compared with trade in the EEC and EFTA areas.[30]

As regards the composition of trade, in the early years it consisted mainly of traditional items like cereals, wood, coffee, live animals, fruits, copper, cotton and sugar.[31] This pattern however underwent some change and by 1969 ECLA found that "the system has generated steadily increasing flows of industrial products, many of them highly processed."[32]

The main beneficiaries of the increased trade were the bigger countries of South America, some of whom had conceived of LAFTA as an instrument for the stabilisation of their existing trade,[33] while Mexico entered the scene as a newcomer with a very low share of the intra-regional trade, but moved rapidly to a position where its high industrial capacity enabled it to benefit from the newly opened up markets in the south, without providing for complementarity and reciprocal trade to any large extent. Mexico, having achieved short-range gains did not stand to gain from a further acceleration of the integration process, and became a conservative force in the free trade area.[34] One indication of the importance of trade between the major countries is that a major factor in the decline in the overall growth rate of intra-LAFTA trade was "the fluctuation in the trade of Argentina and Brazil, which in the aggregate accounts for almost 60 per cent of total intra-area trade."[35]

The third important factor which contributed to the disillusionment with LAFTA, particularly on the part of the lesser developed countries, was the failure of the provision for complementary industries. This provision was a reflection of one of the cardinal principles of ECLA's doctrine of integration, based on the combination of import substitution with the widening of industrial markets. The treaty visualised the state playing a role in the negotiation of "mutual agreements on complementary economies by industrial sectors," as well as in promoting the coordination of industrialisation policies and the sponsoring of "agreements among representatives of the economic sectors concerned."[36]

Attempts to enter into complementarity agreements in Latin America have run into serious problems owing to the reluctance of governments to coordinate the planning of their industrial development—a problem which had been sought to be tackled by ECLA during the 1950's, without success, and which was aggravated by the fact that few Latin American countries had taken even to national planning by the early sixties.[37] Added to this were the serious problems created by the fact that benefits derived from such agreements are hardly ever uniform, and that national and international lending agencies were unenthusiastic about investing large funds in projects of this kind, on grounds that they might encourage the creation of monopolies.[38]

The main obstacles to the success of complementarity agreements coming into effect were the reluctance of member countries to coordinate their policies, and the fact that only foreign enterprise appeared to have the necessary initiative, organisation and financial resources to benefit from the provisions in the treaty and the rules laid down by LAFTA in regard to such agreements.[39] A more fundamental factor however would seem to have been the coexistence in LAFTA of a number of countries at widely varying levels of economic development, a situation, which required the introduction of a complex series of checks and balances which tend to discourage the evolution of an integrated pattern of economy for the region as a whole.

Among the major factors involved in the reluctance of member states of LAFTA to enter into agreements for the freeing of intra-regional trade were the fears of damaging competition on the one hand and of imbalance in intra-regional trade and payments on the other. The reluctance of the members to enter into agreements which granted substantial concessions prompted them to take advantage of a loophole in the wording of the Treaty of Montevideo which made it possible for them to free only their existing trade, and thus defeat the spirit of the treaty by maintaining restrictions on items on which no trade exists with other LAFTA members.[40]

In spite of the existence in the Montevideo Treaty of provisions which were intended to protect the interests of the least developed countries in the region, these countries were not satisfied with the benefits they derived from LAFTA. Paraguay and Ecuador attracted very little capital or other factors of production. Bolivia joined only much later. An attempt in 1964 to provide for financial aid and technical assistance from the more advanced countries and support in requests for aid from the industrialised countries came to nothing, due to the reluctance of the latter to forego assistance which they could receive, in favour of the less developed countries.[41]

To this group of backward economies which were unable to benefit from LAFTA there were added four additional dissatisfied clients, Chile, Colombia, Peru and Uruguay. Although at least two of them Colombia and Uruguay, were suffering the economic consequences of a lack of internal policy, all four tended to blame their trade deficits on the other LAFTA members. Thus six out of the nine original members were deeply dissatisfied, and the veto exercised by each member resulted in the conversion of the "process of bargaining and mutual accommodation" in the LAFTA negotiations to one of "blackmail."[42]

The countries which were members of LAFTA may thus be divided into three groups: (1) Brazil, Argentina and Mexico, whose industries seemed to be gaining ground and who were willing to grant concessions to others desirous of reciprocity, (2) the middle countries, which claimed to be suffering adversely from the policies of other LAFTA members, (3) the lesser developed countries, like Ecuador and Paraguay, which had gained practically nothing from LAFTA.[43]

Countries were not however the only actors in the Latin American stage. Three international organisations emerged as pressure groups operating in order to save LAFTA from collapse. These were (1) the ECLA Secretariat, (2) the Inter-American Development Bank (IDB), and (3) the LAFTA Secretariat and its Permanent Executive Committee (PEC). Of these organisations ECLA tried to maintain a certain aloofness from the details of the integration process, in order to propose changes in the organisation, convinced as it was that revisions would be necessary in institutional structure and powers of LAFTA.

The crisis of the show-down in tariff cuts and rising use of escape clauses was sought to be used to bring about a "spillover" from the existing pattern to new measures of policy harmonization and new powers for LAFTA. The IDB, under the leadership of Felipe Herrera, became a spokesman for integration but the Alliance for Progress appears to have played only a minor role in the process.

The LAFTA Secretariat attempted to play a more substantial role in integration than the "purely technical" function which seemed to have been assigned to them, by exercising influence through national representatives, organising a program of "sectoral meetings" among LAFTA industrialists and a series of "Advisory Commissions" created by the conference for agricultural affairs, monetary and fiscal policy, transport, etc., in which national representatives, often drawn from semi-private organisations, exchanged information and advised the PEC.[44] The LAFTA Secretariat was however considerably overshadowed in its role as the spokesman for integration not only by the existence of other organisations but the presence of personalities who sought to build a niche for themseleves as spokesmen with the Third World (Raul Prebisch became Secretary General of UNCTAD in 1964) the European Economic Community (Jose A. Mora, Secretary General of OAS) and for Latin American integration generally (Felipe Herrera, President, IDB).[45]

The initiative for accelerated economic integration came from Chile, the only member country which was sufficiently dissatisfied with LAFTA and at the same time hopeful of an altered set of relationships to move for a change.

Somewhat isolated geographically with a small population of about eight million and a highly literate and talented elite with inadequate scope for employment in the country, Chile was the strongest force moving for integration since the nineteenth century.[46]

In April 1963 Presidents Goulart of Brazil and Alessandri of Chile expressed dissatisfaction with the progress of LAFTA in a joint declaration which called for a special conference of LAFTA Foreign Ministers to establish a high level permanent consultative body for all integration matters.[47]

Raul Prebisch, who was about to leave his post of Executive Secretary of ECLA, published a study in 1964 which was openly critical of the achievements of LAFTA. He argued that the instruments established under the Treaty required important policy decisions before their "efficacy can be reflected in concrete achievements capable of withstanding whatever factors may make for stagnation in the near future." To counter the stagnation of LAFTA, Prebisch proposed a number of concrete measures involving the drastic reduction of all tariff duties and other trade restrictions, complementarity agreements in basic and dynamic industries, the redefinition of the reciprocity principle, and establishment of a new financing institution for regional industrial projects and trade flows. He also urged close links between the allocation of resources under national plans and the measures establishing the Common Market.[48]

At the request of President Frei of Chile, four leading Latin American experts on problems of economic integration, Raul Prebisch, Felipe Herrera, Jose Antonio Mayobre, the new Executive Secretary of ECLA, and Carlos Sanz de Santamaria, Chairman of the Inter-American Committee for the Alliance for Progress submitted a report on the economic integration of Latin America in the spring of 1965. The "Report of the Four," as it is widely known in Latin America, proposed the establishment of a regional common market by 1975 through annual accross-the-board tariff cuts. The leaders of the integration movement now clearly asserted that "what is needed more than technical studies, is a definition of major objectives and the adoption of political decisions at the highest level." They proposed a number of policy changes which implied greater central guidance for the organisation, viz. a common external tariff, a multilateral regional payments scheme and a unified investment-allocation policy. They also proposed the creation of a Council of Ministers, to meet twice a year, having "the supreme power of decision," the establishment of a Latin American Parliament with the existing Parliament in Lima as a nucleus, an organ to promote regional planning and investment, and an executive board of four to six members appointed by the Council of Ministers and representing "not the governments . . , but the Community itself." It was to be given sweeping powers for the implementation of the Treaty.[49]

Although the recommendations were accepted at a conference of LAFTA Foreign Ministers in December 1964, and two meetings of Foreign Ministers were held subsequently, in November 1965 and December 1966, these meetings failed to come up with clear recommendations in favour of the Report of the Four. The technocrats had been able, however, to obtain resolutions from government representatives, at a far higher level than in 1959-60, in favour of the "abstract concept of policy harmonization."[50] They were exploring new possibilities of support among businessmen of the region.[51] Moreover United States policy toward integration was undergoing a change at this time.[52]

THE SUMMIT OF PUNTA DEL ESTE, 1967

From the first official expression of discontent with the shortcomings of LAFTA in Apirl 1963, it took four years to hold a summit meeting of the Latin American Presidents at Punta del Este. At this conference the recommendations in the Report of the Four for "political decisions at the highest level" was carried out, more in form than in substance. The initiative for the summit meeting was taken by President Arturo Illia of Argentina (as a result of discussions he had held with President Eduardo Frei of Chile) at a meeting of IA ECOSOC in Buenos Aires in April 1966. The Secretary General of the OAS was entrusted with consulting the governments and preparing the ground for the conference. Ministerial level conferences were held at Washington, Buenos Aires and Montevideo between January and April 1967, which prepared the Declaration of the Presidents of America approved at the summit conference.[53]

The Declaration consisted of six chapters, the first and most important of which dealt with economic integration. Accepting the proposal of the four, the Latin American Presidents undertook "to create progressively, beginning in 1970, the Latin American Common Market, which shall be substantially in operation in a period of no more than fifteen years." This was to be achieved through the "complete development and progressive convergence of the Latin American Free Trade Area and of the Central American Common Market taking into account the interests of the Latin American countries not yet affiliated with these systems."

The LAFTA states agreed to initiate a progressive elimination of duties and a harmonization of tariffs "in order to establish progressively a common external tariff at levels that will promote efficiency and productivity, as well as the expansion of trade."[54] National economic policies and laws were also to be harmonised to the extent required for integration. Sectoral agreements for industrial complementation in order to obtain the participation of less developed countries were provided for. For the first time a provision was made recognising the need for sub-regional integration, although this was to be promoted only on a "temporary" basis. The agreements were to contain "provision for reducing tariffs in their sub-regions and harmonising treatments towards third nations more rapidly than in the general agreements, in keeping with the objectives of regional integration."[55]

Members of the CACM undertook to strengthen their integrative measures by establishing a monetary union and by fostering closer ties with Panama and the Caribbean states. The Latin American states undertook to bring together LAFTA and CACM machineries into a Latin American Common Market by the negotiation of a general treaty or the necessary protocols.[56]

For its part, the United States as one of the member states of the OAS undertook to "mobilize financial and technical resources within and without the hemisphere to contribute to the solution of problems in connection with the balance of payments, industrial readjustments" etc., as well as to provide additional export credits. The IDB and the organs of both existing integration systems were to participate in the mobilization of such resources. The members of the OAS also committed themselves to mobilise resources for industrial development and to provide technical and financial resources for studies connected with the conversion of LAFTA into a Latin American Common Market (LACM).[57] Other parts of the Declaration dealt with multi-national infrastructure projects; improvement of international trade conditions for Latin America; rural modernization and productivity; education, technology, scientific development, and health programs; and elimination of unnecessary military expenditures.

The great significance of the Punta del Este conference lay not in the commitments which were undertaken by the member states of LAFTA, but in the association of the United States with the integration of Latin America. There was no commitment on the part of the Latin American signatories to abide by the terms of the Declaration, which lacked binding force. However, it recognised the existence of a separate set of relationships among the Latin American states, thus justifying the conception of a Latin sphere of activity in economic matters, which the United States would respect and which it was also expected to assist financially. Thus the Latin American states appeared to have wrested a major concession from the United States at least on paper.[58]

The summit meeting of the Presidents was followed in June the same year by a meeting of the Inter-American Economic and Social Council held at Vina del Mar, Chile, which sought to spell out the steps to be taken in order to implement the Presidents' decisions.[59] A meeting of LAFTA Foreign Ministers was held at Asuncion Paraguay in August-September 1967. A demand by the least developed countries, Paraguay, Ecuador and Bolivia that other members grant them tariff cuts of 100 per eent on selected lists of primary products met with resistance, especially from Mexico, Colombia and Chile. "The tariff freeze, a common external tariff, a gradual reduction of Common List tariffs, and a timetable for tariff advantages to the 'less developed' countries all had to be put off for further study by the LAFTA Permanent Executive Committee . . ."[60]

Meanwhile the trend of thinking had shifted to the desirability of integration at the sub-regional level. In August 1966 the five Andean countries—Colombia, Chile, Ecuador, Peru and Venezuela—had meet at Bogota and proposed "the establishment of differential tariff reduction systems, when complementation agreements arc concerned with general participation, applied according to the differential levels of development and non-reciprocal temporary concessions during the initial stage."[61] These agreements were further elaborated in meetings of the five countries held at Vina del Mar, Quito, and Caracas. The bases for a sub-regional Agreement drawn up by them were approved by the LAFTA Foreign Ministers at their meeting on September 2, 1967. At the same time Norms for Subregional Agreements were drawn up, these were generally expected to conform with the provisions of the Treaty of Montevideo and the Declaration of the Presidents of America. The Subregional Agreements were declared to be "transitory" and as such were required to "fix the date of entry into effect and duration."[62]

The new stress on sub-regionalism and the renewed interest in United States assistance could not however conceal a fact which by the end of the 1960's had become evident, viz., the failure of the Punta del Este summit meeting to inject into the Latin American integration process the necessary degree of dynamism to enable it to overcome the formidable obstacles which threatened to bring it down. Although the Presidents had agreed at Punta del Este to instruct their Ministers of foreign affairs to take the necessary steps for the "convergence" of LAFTA and CACM, the commitment in this regard was couched in extremely vague language. A proposal had been made by the committee of Four to set up an executive board consisting of a President and four to six members. A Latin American Parliament made up of delegates from National legislations was to serve as an advisory group to the Council. The IDB was to be charged with the preparation of surveys and regional investment projects. These proposals were not considered by the Presidents and even a proposal to set up a permanent Council of LAFTA foreign Ministers was dropped because of Chile's unwillingness to sign it at the second Ministerial meeting preparatory to Punta del Este.[63]

Latin American Integration at the End of the 1960's

At the end of the 1960's Latin America found itself in a peculiar position economically. The short-run trends appeared to be favourable. The economy including the annual growth of exports continued to show an upward trend.[64] Nevertheless in relation to other areas the Latin American performance was disappointing. While its overall growth rate was higher than that of Africa and East and Southeast Asia, the per capita income rose to the Alliance for Progress target of 2.5 per cent per annum only in six countries. "Regional exports grew by only 43.4 per cent during the period 1960-1968, less than the increase achieved by the developed countries, the developing countries as a whole, and the Socialist Countries."[65] Exports were not diversified and the terms of trade declined during the 1960's. At the same time indebtedness more than doubled and over 35 per cent of the current value of export of goods and services was represented by "remittances of profits and interest and a mortisation and other payments on foreign capital." Generally there was "profound disquiet regarding the ultimate course of Latin American development, stimulated by the fact that social unrest and conflict have been aggravated and by the new dimensions and characteristics of long standing obstacles to development."[66] Not only was the gap between the developing countries and the Andean countries widening; but Latin America was in some respects worse off than other regions on the periphery. Targets set by regional agencies and national plans had not been achieved and the fundamental problems of Latin American development had not only not been solved, but had worsened. Latin America was declining in economic importance in the world and at the same time becoming increasingly dependent, financially and politically in the international sphere.[67]

A major factor in the inability of Latin America to raise its standard of living was the massive rate of population increase, the declining productivity of agriculture, and the increase in urban population which rose three times as fast as the rural population (4.5 per cent as against 1.5 per cent). The Inter-American Development Bank report for 1970 states that "by 1980 some 218 million people out of a total of 358 million, or about 60 per cent will be urban dwellers."[68] The situation evidently was one requiring drastic solutions in the form of basic structural change.

The achievements and goals of Latin American integration have to be considered in the light of this situation. Considering the pessimistic view which ECLA has taken of the economic situation in Latin America as a whole one would expect a more critical view of the achievements of the integration process in relation to the overall developmental goals laid down for the region. In a review of "Recent Developments in the Latin American Integration Process," ECLA pointed out that the members of LAFTA were in arrears as regards the establishment of a Common Schedule and that during the past few years "the formal content of the regional economic integration process has been considerably expanded but in respect of practical achievements no correlative development has taken place. Neither the objectives scheduled for the interim period established under the said Treaty, nor the decisions incorporated in the Action Program of the Presidents of America, have been fully implemented."[69]

Regarding the proposal to extricate the Free Trade Association from the deadlock in the Common Schedule negotiations either by amending the Treaty or by extending the time limit for implementation of the program, ECLA held that the first suggestion would halt the process of integration at a stage short of a Free Trade area, a situation which would not be in accord with the General Agreement on Tariff and Trade, and would raise several difficulties. The second suggestion would "do no more than put off the task of solving the basic problem" unless it were to be "supplemented by some sort of machinery for programmed liberalisation based on the attainment of a progressive series of targets."[70]

In December 1969 at the Ninth Annual Conference of LAFTA the fears of many pessimists seemed to have been fulfilled. The implementation of the common list of products to be freely traded was postponed until at least 1974, when the negotiations toward a 'new stage' of LAFTA were to begin. The implementation of the decision of the Presidents at Punta del Este to establish a Latin American Common Market within fifteen years by stages beginning in 1970 was considerably delayed, if not altogether abandoned. The establishment of a Free Trade area between eleven Latin American republics was postponed from 1973 to 1980. Instead of tariff cuts of 8 per cent of weighted average of duties applicable to all imports, each LAFTA member was now required to make annual cuts only of 2·9 per cent.

No new target date for setting up a Common Market was fixed. The Caracas Protocol evidently represented a victory for the three major countries of the region, Argentine, Brazil and Mexico,

> who have lost interest in all but the purely commercial aspects of regional economic integration and who assume—perhaps correctly—that the point reached in tariff cuts assures them enough room for export expansion in the area for some time to come without forcing them to undertake any non-commercial commitments toward the less developed LAFTA members.[71]

The legal and technical aspects of the programme laid down at Punta del Este were not neglected. A number of meetings were held in regard to steps to be taken for the convergence of LAFTA and CACM, and preferential treatment for the relatively less developed countries was being worked out. The payments system of LAFTA was being improved and clearing house arrangements were being discussed.

These efforts however fell short of tackling the basic question of the coordination of exchange and monetary policies.[72]

Studies of LAFTA and CACM did not take an optimistic view of the situation. For example, in a study undertaken for the US State Department, Edward Cale pointed to the high cost of production which he considered to be at the root of LAFTA's problems. He did not anticipate that LAFTA would make rapid progress in the trade field, especially as the non-area markets accounted for 90 per cent of the exports, and internal trade could not be expected to play a major role in the development of the region.[73] Although Krause and Mathis were more optimistic about the future of Latin American trade integration, they seemed to assume the acceptance of large-scale foreign investment, a situation which did not appear likely in the then mood of Latin America.[74] Observers of CACM were till recently optimistic about the possibilities of success of the experiment in sub-regional integration.[75] However, after the Honduras-El Salvador War of July 1969, there was considerable rethinking about the Central American Common Market.[76]

The programme for Latin American economic integration was drawn up in continuation of the earlier efforts by ECLA to persuade Latin American countries to adopt policies of import substitution in order to reduce their dependence on imports from advanced countries and to counter the rising balance of payment problems. Prebisch wryly admitted that the position he had taken, combining a defense of import substitution with a proposal for a regional common market, was a highly unorthodox one, and welcomed the support which Myrdal gave to his proposal.[77] The adaptation of the concept of protection of infant industry and of import substitution to the continental scale was found, however, to benefit certain sectors and certain countries, and tended to conflict with ECLA's own concept of "balanced development among the members of an integrated region and the principle of comparative advantage in the promotion of firms oriented toward regional markets." It was true that these "conflicting objectives can be dealt with by means of technical assistance, by giving high priorities for essential infrastructure projects to less-advanced areas, and, perhaps by special tax and other incentives which will attract both regional and external capital to those areas."[78] But all these measures involved a close coordination of policies on the part of the countries in the region, as well as on the part of the aid-giving agencies in the region and outside, conditions which were by no means always available in developing areas.

In the context of this discussion it is helpful to note Viner's distinction between 'customs unions' which are "trade creating" and those which are "trade diverting." Trade creation is defined as "a shift in trade from a high-cost to a low-cost producer, and trade diversion as a shift in the opposite direction." According to Viner, a customs union would have a favourable effect on world welfare and on the welfare of the members if it had a trade-creating rather than a trade-diverting effect. This view has been subjected to a number of criticisms, the most important being that it is a static, short-term analysis, which does not take account of the special circumstances of developing countries. The building up of a customs union among such countries requires a long time to reach fruition, especially since they usually have very little trade among themselves to begin with.[79]

The experience of both LAFTA and CACM would show, however, that the different rates of benefits derived from regional economic integration were an important factor in the political response of these countries to the integration programme. This was true not only of LAFTA, whose members differed so widely in their economic strength and level of development, but even in CACM, where these differences were far less. Honduras, for example, complained that the more advanced countries of the area benefited from selling their higher priced goods in its territory, and it was deprived of the advantage of importing cheaper goods from outside. It is small consolation to be told that these imbalances will be eliminated in the long run, because there are strong economic and political pressures to be faced in the short run. Evidently some more effective measures have to be taken to counter the flow of benefits to manufacturers in certain parts of an integrated area, before the developing areas can successfully adapt the idea of regional economic integration. As Nye has pointed out, an issue which in a developed area might be considered a technical one is often one charged with political content in a developing area, where the pressures for employment and for a share of the benefits of development are so much greater.[80]

Planning Regional Development: The Need for Infrastructure

We have now to consider some long term problems connected with integration. The protagonists of regional economic integration for Latin America based their calculations and arguments on a country-by-country analysis, taking the state as the unit of calculation and assuming that economic disparities between states in a regional customs union or common market would correct themselves in course of time. The assumption was based on the view that customs unions were governed by the traditional economic theory of international trade. The consequence of taking the state as the unit of calculation was that differential rates of growth and development between countries as well as between different parts of the same country tended to be ignored or underestimated. It was pointed out, however, that this view was not applicable even to Western Europe, where the disparities between countries in respect to level of economic development, literacy level, population and other relevant factors were far less than in developing countries. In later years it was being realised that this assumption led to a neglect of some of the fundamental factors which obstructed the economic integration of Latin America.[81]

In the first place, Latin America did not constitute an economic reagion as much as it did a cultural area with certain common tradition and attitudes toward external factors operating within the area. Not only was it large and sparsely populated, but it was divided by formidable physical barriers which obstructed communication within the area. Secondly, during the period of colonial domination by Spain and Portugal the old communication patterns of the American Indian empires were atrophied. New links were established with Puropean countries and with North America, which isolated the countries from one another. Thirdly, there was as yet little communication among the countries, compared to that in Europe, notwithstanding the common language, Spanish, which united many of the countries and served as a lingua franca for the area.

When the LAFTA treaty was signed, intra-regional trade was slow and the basic transport and communication facilities for the development of intra-regional trade were lacking, both in regard to road and sea transport. Because of the control of shipping by foreign interests, and the fixation of rates on the basis of traffic between Latin American ports and specific European or North American ports, it was often cheaper to send goods from one part of Latin America to another via a port in another continent.[82] Until the building of the Pan American Highway, even the five small countries of Central America had difficulty in communicating with one another, and the stepping up of intra-regional trade would have been difficult, if not impossible, of achievement.

The assumption, which was made by supporters of integration, that backward countries within the free trade area would advance rapidly as the relatively more advanced countries in the region, was disproved by developments in LAFTA and CACM, as well as in an often cited example of regional integration in the developing areas, the East African Common Market. A parallel was drawn between the condition created by a common market and a newly unified country, or a country that was in the process of rapid industrialisation; similar results were found in the latter case. Italian unification in the second half of the nineteenth century was followed by a widening gap in industrialisation and income levels between the north and south. Later trends in industrialising countries like Mexico, Yugoslavia, and (most notably) Pakistan, indicated that industrialisation might be concentrated in certain areas and lead to a widening of regional disparities. According to a study undertaken by Williamson, regional inequalities were accentuated in the early stages of development and began to decline only when economic development reached a fairly mature level. "For countries at the Latin American level of development, the net effect of economic integration on regional economic growth might be to increase disparities between member nations, at least unless deliberate off-setting provisions were instituted."[83]

Thus there are two separate but connected tendencies which have to be noted in connection with the spatial aspects of economic development in Latin America. The first is the trend previously mentioned, for industries in the more advanced countries of the region to develop more rapidly and take the lion's share of the benefits derived from regional economic integration. This led to the demand by the middle-level countries for special treatment on the same lines as the most backward countries who were members of LAFTA. It also led to the setting up of the Andean Pact as a subregional trading arrangement among the middle and 'most backward' countries.[84]

The Swedish economist Myrdal noted the tendency for market forces to "increase rather than to decrease, the inequalities between regions" of a country. He went on to say that:

> If things were left to market forces unhampered by any policy interferences, industrial production, commerce, banking, insurance, shipping and, indeed almost all those economic activities which in a developing economy tend to give a bigger than average return. . . would cluster in certain localities and regions, leaving the rest of the country more or less in a backwater.[85]

Secondly, this situation is accentuated in Latin America by the fact that many national economies appear to be characterised by "a developed 'core' area of limited extent, with an important industrial component contributing to its degree of development, and an extensive undeveloped 'periphery' with few secondary economic activities."[86]

That the chief protagonists of the Latin American integration movement were not adequately aware of the problems of location of industry and the spatial pattern of industrial development as late as 1965 is evident from the fact that the Report of the Four, submitted to President Frei of Chile, contains contradictory recommendations on this point. "They comment, first, that industrial expansion should take advantage of 'suitable siting' and secondly, that the regional investment policy for industry should concentrate on the countries that are relatively less developed." Odell remarks that these comments are not only "inadequate but they are also contradictory for it is highly unlikely that the most suitable sites (in terms of the economic advantages of alternative locations) will be found in the relatively less developed countries!"[87]

The danger lies in integrated industries providing "an easy

way out of the economic, political and social dilemmas involved in the process of creating sufficient new domestic demand for the increasing industrial output of the 'core' areas. . ." An integrated Latin America might thus become "little more than a series of interconnected 'core' areas feeding on and having close relations with each other" but at the same time turning "its back on mutually beneficial contact with the remainder of the national territory within which it is situated."[88]

The solution to this problem would seem to lie in the greater utilisation of the techniques of the regional geographer and their application to the geographic regions within a country and to geographic regions cutting across national frontiers.[89] Multinational planning should include the planning of regions within countries and should seek to integrate them in a plan for Latin American development as a whole.[90] Latin American countries were however handicapped by limited resources and inadequate planning machinery and personnel. Planning at the national level was initiated only in later years, and the coordination of planning at the regional level was still a distant goal. It was however interesting to note that an official of the Inter-American Development Bank stressed in an article the need for a series of coordinated agreements for joint planning in different fields of industrial and agricultural production. The program would involve a series of progressive concessions, harmonised among themselves. At the same time there would be subregional accords, so that countries would negotiate on approximately equal terms. Lastly, there would also be agreements for the joint development of frontier areas.[91]

In later years the realisation spread among the leaders of the Latin American integration movement that without an adequate infrastructure, there could not be real economic integration. The Declaration of Presidents of America, entered into at Punta del Este, Uruguay, in April 1967, affirmed that they would "lay the physical foundations for Latin American economic integration through multinational projects." This commitment (which did not, however, constitute a legal obligation), went on to read as follows:

> Economic integration demands a major sustained effort to build a land transportation network and to improve trans-

portation systems of all kinds so as to open the way for the movement of both people and goods throughout the Continent; to establish an adequate and efficient telecommunications system; to install inter-connected power systems; and to develop jointly international river basins, frontier regions and economic areas which include the territory of two or more countries.[92]

This point was stressed by the new President of the Inter-American Development Bank, Antonio Ortiz Mena of Mexico in his inaugural address at the Special Meeting of the Board of Governors of the Bank. Since the development of physical infrastructure in Latin America "was designed to facilitate the outflow of products needed by the metropolis," there was a need to "intensify the programs of our physical infrastructure under a long-term investment plan to include highways, railroad and air transport; river and maritime shipping; construction of ports; power programs; fuels, and telecommunications."[93] He regarded this task of completing and modernising the physical infrastructure as "the cornerstone for any future planning," and felt that the IDB had a special obligation in that matter.[94]

The IDB had already been devoting some attention to the need for building up an adequate infrastructure, stressing transportation, telecommunications, power and port development in order to counter the lack of adequate physical mobility and contacts within the region. In addition, IDB was acting as coordination agent in the preparation of preliminary technical studies for the development of the River Plate Basin, at the request of five countries, Argentina, Bolivia, Brazil, Paraguay and Uruguay. An attempt was being made to coordinate the planning of the development of border areas. The Bank was also furthering the establishment of import-substituting industries at the Latin American level in accordance with the recommendations of ECLA and in coordination with LAFTA.[95] The Preinvestment Fund for Latin American Integration was set up in 1966. It undertook feasibility studies of projects affecting integration, ranging widely from multinational infrastructure works such as highway networks, communications, air, maritime and river transportation to the development of economic regions and the establishment of basic industries on a regional scale.[96]

The activities of the IDB in regard to the building up of an infrastructure for the Latin American area were useful in bringing to bear on the problem of integration some basic data which would provide the framework upon which a program of integration could be built in the future. It must be recognised, however, that building infrastructure is an activity that will only very slowly contribute to the building up of integrated institutions. To the extent that it is based on a comprehensive analysis of national resources and a micro-planning approach, it will provide a valuable basis for the furthering of integration.[97]

The second comment to be made on the contribution of the Bank in this field of activity is that the task which it set itself in this regard was so enormous that it is difficult to visualise the quantum of funds which would be required to accomplish it even to a minimum level of development. To bring Latin American communications for example to the level of those in Western Europe, which, as Ortiz Mena pointed out, "began at the time of the Roman Empire,"[98] would seem to be a hopeless task in the foreseeable future. It would be advisable to draw up a program of priorities, and to link them with financial implications, before taking up a set of targets which are so unlikely to be accomplished. The criteria which could be adopted in order to take up a program of building up infrastructure could most usefully be based on the need for furthering subregional arrangements, subject to other considerations which could be laid down, based on a combination of economic, social and political factors.

REFERENCES

1 A number of additional legal instruments including Protocols, Instruments of Adherence, etc. have been entered into by the Central American States. A list will be found in Nino Maritano, *A Latin American Economic Community: History, Policies and Problems* (Notre Dame, 1970), pp. 104-6.

2 Ibid., p. 98.

3 Ibid., p. 89.

4 Ibid., p. 90.

5 Sidney Dell, *A Latin American Common Market?* (*A LACM*?) (London, 1966), p. 63.

6 See ibid., pp. 64-9 for a qualified defence of the integrated industries. While admitting that integrated industries may tend to become monopolies, Dell points out that the failure to set up such industries may lead to the establishment of monopolies by foreign companies.

7 Aaron Segal, "The Integration of Developing Countries: Some Thoughts on East Africa and Central America," *JCMS* (March 1967), p. 268.

8 Ibid., pp. 268-9.

9 Ibid., p. 270.

10 Ibid., p. 272.

11 Roger D. Hansen, *Central America: Regional Integration and Economic Development*, National Planning Association Studies in Development Progress, No. 1 (Washington, 1967), p. 56. The ECLA ideas are explained and criticised in Chapter II, pp. 21-7. The concept of "balanced economic development" is placed in the context of theories of Gunnar Myrdal of "spread" and "backwash" effects on pp. 56-9.

12 James D. Cochrane, The Politics of Regional Integration: The Central American Case," *Tulane Studies in Political Science*, vol. XII (New Orleans, 1969), p. 129.

13 Ibid., pp. 139-40.

14 Review of the book by Cochrane, *JCMS* (June 1970), p. 356.

15 Miguel S. Wionczek, "The Rise and Decline of Latin American Economic Integration," *JCMS*, no. 1, 1970, pp. 53-4.

16 Ibid., p. 53.

17 Donald H. McClelland, "The Common Market's Contribution to Central American Economic Growth: A First Approximation," in Ronald Hilton (ed.), *The Movement toward Latin American Unity* (New York, 1969), p. 528.

18 Wionczek, n. 15, pp. 55-6.

19 See table in Nye, "Central American Regional Integration," in J.S. Nye, Jr. (ed.), *International Regionalism: Readings* (Boston, 1968), p. 382

20 Dell, n. 5, pp. 63-4.

21 Hansen, n. 11, p. 67.

22 Ibid., pp. 68-77.

23 Ibid., p. 97.

24 Dell, n. 5, p. 63.

25 Miguel S. Wionczek, "Latin American Integration and U.S. Economic Policies," in Robert W. Gregg (ed.), *International Organisation in the Western Hemisphere* (Syracuse, N.Y., 1969), p. 110.

26 United Nations, EBLA, *Economic Bulletin for Latin America*, vol. XIV no. 2 (second half of 1969), p. 112.

27 Ibid., pp. 113-4.

28 Ernst B. Haas and Philippe C. Schmitter, *The Politics of Economics in Latin American Free Trade Area after Four Years of Operation* (Denver, 1965), p. 5.

29 Dell, n. 5, pp. 70-2.

30 The figure for zonal trade as a percentage of total foreign trade in

LAFTA was only 8.2 as against 10.3 in the CACM, 21.6 in EFTA and 39.5 in EEC for the same year. Haas and Schmitter, n. 28, p. 10. Also see Appendices, Table II. D on *Intra-Lafta Trade.*

31 Ibid., p. 11.

32 *Economic Bulletin for Latin America,* (EBLA) vol. XIV, no. 2, p. 113.

33 The reference is to the southern zone countries, Argentina, Brazil and Chile. Haas and Schmitter, n. 28, p. 5.

34 Ibid., p. 5. A more detailed study of Mexico's role will be found in Philippe C. Schmitter and Ernst B. Haas, *Mexico and Latin American Economic Integration* (Berkeley, Calif., 1964). See especially Chapter VII.

35 The applicating escape clauses also contributed to the decline. See *EBLA*, n. 32. p. 112.

36 Article 16 of the Treaty. See also Mikesell "The Movement toward Regional Trading Groups in Latin America," in Hirschman (ed.), *Latin American Issues: Essays and Comments* (New York, 1969), p. 141.

37 Dell, n. 5, pp. 135-8.

38 Hass and Schmitter, n. 28, p. 24. See also Dell, n. 5, pp. 129-31.

39 Ibid., p. 175. For a discussion of the rules governing complementarity agreements, see pp. 127-8.

40 Sidney Dell, "The Early Years of LAFTA's Experiences," in Miguel S. Wionczek (ed.), *Latin American Economic Integration: Experiences and Prospects* (New York, 1966), p. 108.

41 Wionczek, n. 25, pp. 117-8.

42 Ibid., p. 118.

43 This classification is based on that of Wionczek, n. 15, pp. 59-60. See, however, a different classification by Haas and Schmitter, n. 28, pp. 54-8. Earlier in the monograph they also classify the countries on the basis of the expectations they had from LAFTA, p. 5.

44 Christopher Mitchell, "Role of Technocrats in Latin American Integration," *Inter-American Economic Affairs* (Summer 1967), pp. 21-4. Mitchell also mentions two institutions created in support of integration, the Latin American Parliament and the Institute of Latin American Integration (INTAL). These are discussed elsewhere in this volume.

45 Haas and Schmitter, n. 28, p. 44.

46 The President of Chile from 1958 to 1964 was Alessandri. He was succeeded from 1964 to 1970 by Eduardo Frei, the Christian Democrat who was described as the "last best hope" of Chile. He was followed by Dr. Allende in 1970. An account of the earlier movements for Latin American integration will be found in Dennis Vodarsik, "Building the Latin American Community: The Meaning and Value of Latin American Integration" (unpublished Ph. D. dissertation, Department of Government, Georgetown University, 1970).

47 Declaration conjunta de los Presidentes de Brasil y Chile (Santiago, 24 April 1963) *Comercio Exterior* (May 1963), p. 326-7. Cited in Wionczek, n. 25, p. 119.

48 *Towards a Dynamic Development Policy for Latin America* (UN Publica-

tion 64 II G4, New York, 1964), p. 89. That members of LAFTA were themselves dissatisfied with the progress of the organisation was clear from the appointment of a Special Commission which submitted its report in September, 1964. See Wionczek, n. 25, p. 121, and Haas and Schmitter. n. 28, pp. 35-9.

49 Summaries of the Report of the Four will be found in Mitchell, n. 44, p. 25, and Wionczek, n. 25, pp. 121-2. An English translation of the Report has been reproduced in "Proposals for the creation of the Latin American Common Market," *JCMS* (September 1966). The original Spanish text with letter of President Frei will be found in *Hacia la Integracion Acelerada de America Latina* (Mexico, 1965).

50 Mitchell, n. 44, p. 27.

51 Ibid.

52 Ibid. See *infra*, Chapter five for an account of the changing policies of the United States towards integration.

53 Jose A. Mora, *From Panama to Punta del Este: Past Experience and Future Prospects* (Washington, D.C., n.d.), p. 31.

54 Inter-American Institute of International Legal Studies, *Instruments Relating to the Economic Integration of Latin America* (Dobbs Ferry, N.Y., 1968), pp. 399-400. For a partial summary of the Declaration see Christopher Mitchell, "Common Market: The Future of a Commitment: Punta del Este and After," *IAEA* (Winter 1967), pp. 79-80.

55 (IILS), *Instruments*, n. 54, p. 400.
It is to be noted that "countries of relatively less economic development will have the right to participate and to obtain preferential conditions in the sub-regional agreements in which they have an interest." The implication was that more advanced countries would not have such a right to integrate economically. Ibid.

56 Ibid., pp. 400-2.

57 Ibid., pp. 402-3.

58 Ibid., pp. 403-14.

59 Action Plan of Vina del Mar. Ibid., pp. 387-91.

60 Mitchell, n. 54, p. 83.

61 "Declaration of Bogota," *IAEA* (Winter 1966), p. 90. Quoted in ibid., p. 83.

62 The documents will be found in Miguel S. Wionczek (ed.), *Economic Cooperation in Latin America, Africa and Asia: A Handbook of Documents* (Cambridge, Mass., 1969), pp. 88-95. The quotation is para 6 of Resolution 202 (CM-II/VI/E), p. 89.

63 An account of these developments will be found in ibid., p. 40.

64 United Nations, Economic and Social Council, "The Latin American Economy in 1969: Highlights from the ECLA Survey." UN Doc. E/CN 12/852— (Mimeographic), pp. 17-27.

65 Ibid., p. 2.

66 Ibid.

67 Ibid., p. 1.

68 Inter-American Development Bank, "Socio-Economic Progress in Latin

America," quoted in a survey of *International Development* (April 1971), p. 3.

69 *Economic Bulletin for Latin America*, n. 32, (Second Half of 1969) pp. 112-3.

70 Ibid., p. 113.

71 Wionczek, n. 15, p. 59.

72 *Economic Bulletin for Latin America*, n. 32, pp. 111-2.

73 Edward G. Cale, *LAFTA: Progress, Problems, Prospects* (Washington, D.C., US Department of State Publication No. 8448, Inter-American Series 96, 1969), p. 4.

74 Walter Krause and F. John Mathis, *Latin America and Economic Integration: Regional Planning for Development* (Iowa City, 1970), pp. 48-50.

75 See Jorge Mendez Munevar, "La ALALC y el Mercado Comun Centroamericano: Una Evaluacion Comparativa," in Gustavo Lagos (ed.), *La Integracion Latinoamericana, Situacion y Perspectivas* (Buenos Aires, INTAL, 1965), p. 126. See also Dell n. 5, p. 58; and Wionczek's Introduction in Wionczek (ed.), n. 62, in which he describes the Central American experiment as "the most successful of all."

76 See for example, Wionczek's article, n. 15.

77 Robert Lakachman (ed.), *National Policy for Economic Welfare at Home and Abroad* (New York, 1961), p. 277.

78 Mikesell, "External Financing and Regional Integration," in Miguel S. Wionczek (ed.), *Latin American Integration* (New York, 1966), p. 204.

79 F. Kahnert, P. Richards, E. Stoutjesdijk, P. Thomopoulos, *Economic Integration among Developing Countries* (Paris, 1965), pp. 15-7.

80 "In many underdeveloped areas (and probably among Communist countries), however, much that in the European context would be simple welfare politics becomes tinged with emotive and symbolic content that is usually associated with national security politics." J.S. Nye, "Patterns and Catalysts in Regional Integration," in Nye n. 19, p. 335.

81 Peter R. Odell, "Economic Integration and Special Patterns of Economic Development in Latin America," *JCMS* (March 1968), pp. 267-8. See also Matthew Edel, "Regional Integration and Income Redistribution: Complements or Substitutes ?" in Hilton (ed.), *The Movement towards Latin American Unity*, p. 189.

82 See Enrique Angulo H., "Transportation and Intra-American Trade," in Wionczek (ed.), n. 78, p. 186.

83 Edel, n. 81, pp. 189-90.

84 Ibid., p. 190.

85 Gunnar Myrdal, *Economic Theory and Underdeveloped Regions* (London, 1957), p. 26. This view is based on Myrdal's theory of circular and cumulative causation. Ibid., pp. 11-22.

86 Odell, n. 81, p. 268.

87 Ibid., p. 281. See also Mikesell, n. 78, p. 204.

88 Odell, n. 81, p. 285.

89 The term "geographic region" is here used to distinguish those regions based on clearly defined geographic and economic criteria as distinct

from the more loosely used concepts of "region" and "sub-region" commonly used to designate the Latin American area or sub-groupings of states such as the Andean group and the Caribbean and Central American countries.

90 The argument here follows that of Harold Wood, "The Regional Implications of Economic Integration," in Hilton, n. 81, pp. 14-8.

91 Raul Rey Alvarez, "Planificacion regional e integracion economica on America Latina," in Gustavo Lagos (ed.), n. 75, pp. 138-9.
See also Dell, n. 5, pp. 121-5.

92 IIILS, n. 55, p. 396.

93 Statement by Antonio Ortiz Mena, President of the IDB at the Special Meeting of the Board of Governors, Buenos Aires, 1 March 1971, (Washington, D.C., n.d., mimeographed), pp. 4-5.

94 Ibid., p. 4.

95 International Development Bank, *The Inter-Amercican Development Bank and the Economic Integration of Latin America* (Washington, April 1969) pp. 15-28.

96 Ibid., pp. 29-32.

97 I was given to understand that the bank was conducting comprehensive studies in order to provide a framework for the future development of the South American continent as a whole. Interview with Dr. Jose Cardenas, Integration Advisor to the IDB, Washington, D.C., 4 September 1970.

98 Statement by Antonio Ortiz Mena, n. 93, p. 4.

CHAPTER V

THE UNITED STATES AND LATIN AMERICAN INTEGRATION: AID, TRADE AND INVESTMENT

THE US AS A FACTOR IN LATIN AMERICAN INTEGRATION

The relations between Latin America and the United States provide an essential background for the understanding of the process of integration or the lack of it.

It should be noted that the United States was not always the dominant force in Latin America, either in the strategic or in the economic fields. The United States presence became more noticeable in Latin America when there was a threat to the independence of Latin American countries from Europe. This occurred in the late 1820's when the Monroe Doctrine was promulgated, in the 1860's with the French intervention in Mexico, and as a result of the German threat during the first and second world wars.

It was not till the close of the nineteenth century, at the time of the Spanish-American war of 1899, that the United States emerged as the major power in Latin America. This resulted in a network of relationships between the "paramount" and its "client states," the main purpose of the United States being to prevent the detachment of any client state from its system.[1]

The political dominance of the United States was followed by its emergence as the major source of foreign capital in Latin America. United States assets in Latin America increased from $300 million in 1897 to $7.4 billion in 1960, out of a total of $13.6 billion of all foreign private investment. There was a drastic decline of European investment in Latin America during the depression and it never recovered its position. This led to the emergence of United States investors as a dominant force in Latin America during and after the Second World War.[2]

Towards the end of the 1960's, United States investment in the Latin America had reached a figure of 10 billion dollars, or 70 per cent of the total foreign investment in the area. It was the major trading partner of Latin America, absorbing nearly 40 per cent of the exports and over 40 per cent of the imports of the area. It also supplied a large portion of the external financial aid of the area.[3]

We have noted earlier that the Latin American integration movement is largely a product of a wider movement for the solidarity of Latin America again t the dominance of external factors, particularly the United States The economic terminology of the proponents of integration has to be understood in the context of the political role of the regional economic organisations, especially ECLA.[4] It is not surprising therefore that the original plans drawn up by ECLA for regional economic cooperation were based on the assumption that foreign financial assistance would not be available. However, two factors militated against the success of an integration process based on these assumptions. The first was the reception given to the proposal for a multilateral clearing system when it was promoted by ECLA in 1957. The plan was for the regional trading arrangement to depend not upon tariff negotiations but on a system of intra-regional payments which would have its own dynamic, and would have provided a positive stimuli to trade in the region. It would also have eliminated dollar-earning capacity as a restraint on trade in the region. The strong opposition of the United States and the International Monetary Fund to such an arrangement, and the insistence of the former that the proposed Latin Customs Unions or free trade areas should follow GATT rules, had a negative effect on the development of a viable payments union, which is now generally recognised as an essential accompaniment, if not a pre-requisite, to regional economic integration. "Thus the LAFTA countries were hindered in developing a feeling of responsibility for their regional payments problems, as it was apparent that any solution required the approval of external actors."[5]

Another factor, which directly affected the dependence of

the Latin American integration system on foreign aid, was the somewhat unexpected change which American policy underwent at the end of the Eisenhower administration and at the beginning of the Kennedy administration from 1958 to 1961. A rethinking took place in regard to United States policy concerning aid to Latin America. Till that time the United States had resisted Latin American demands for the introduction of a massive aid program for the region, on the lines of Marshall Aid for Europe. The United States continued to harp on security matters while Latin America was concerned about economic issues.[6]

United States Policy Towards Latin American Integration: The Background

Studies of United States policies towards Latin America indicate that they are primarily a product of pressure groups operating on the political system of that country. Although the political system is based on Presidential authority, there is in fact a strong pluralism. The fragmentation of power and search for an equilibrium of forces in the internal political life of the country leads to a policy of pragmatism and urgency.[7] "It is because of the relentless competitive quest for political support that the American political process is so open and such diverse interests are represented in it . . . Any political goal without a firm extra-political base of support will tend to be deemphasised by policy makers."[8]

First of all, although the main decision-maker in United States policy towards Latin America is theoretically the President, he is assisted and advised by the Departments of State, Defence and Treasury, as well as other agencies of the Federal Government. Secondly, the United States Congress has wide powers to "implement, modify and oppose" policies formulated or proposed by the executive. Thirdly, pressure groups exercise considerable influence on Congress. The most important of these are associations of industrialists and businessmen, such as the Council for Latin America, the Committee for Economlc Development, etc. There are also other pressure groups operating to affect the policies of the United States Government, such as labour unions, the academic community, and the press.[9]

The reconciliation of these different forces operating on government policies is obviously a matter of considerable delicacy. The United States is often considered politically inept and criticised for its failure to anticipate problems and its undue sensitivity to the interests of United States businessmen in Latin America.[10]

According to a study of United States policy toward Latin America from the close of the Second World War to the inauguration of the Alliance for Progress in 1961, there was not much conflict between the objectives of the "main centralising force," i.e. the President, and the interest groups operating in regard to United States economic policies towards Latin America. One possible explanation of this situation would be that the bureaucracy had accepted and internalised views similar to those of private interests. Thus new policies were resisted not because they were contrary to the interest of private groups, but because "they called into question an existing set of formulas . . ."[11]

It must be remembered, however, that apart from the pressure groups operating in the field, US policies are also affected by two additional sets of factors, viz., long-term strategic considerations on the one hand and internal political considerations on the other. Security in the Caribbean and access to the Panama Canal are important strategic factors which affect US policy makers. Among short-term political factors which affect American policy we may mention the importance of American public opinion of an anti-Communist stance, which seems to have been an important factor in President Johnson's intervention in the Dominican Republic in 1965.

There can be little doubt, however, that US business interests in Latin America have played and continued to play a crucial role in US policy-making in the area. As has been mentioned earlier,[12] US investment in Latin America is no longer confined to extractive industries such as copper and oil, or essential services like railways, but has extended to the industrial sector and service industries. In recent years. Latin America appears to be passing into a third stage of economic relation with the industrialised countries, viz., the period of dominance of the multi-national corporations, usually with headquarters in the US and operating in Latin America, through wholly owned subsidiaries. This third stage of economic activity of the foreign interests in Latin America operates on the basis of a stepping up of the industrialisation process in Latin America through international corporations within national economies and under national laws.[13]

This new stage in the economic relations of foreign enterprise in Latin America is a product of an economic system which has developed in recent years in the United States and is described by J.K. Galbraith in his study, *The New Industrial State*.[14] The new pattern had led to the concentration of economic power in the hands of conglomerates which produce a variety of products and carry on activities of various types, from rearing chickens to producing helicopters, in order to provide for constantly changing world market conditions for various products. Secondly, the newly developed techniques which permit the manipulation of information through computers have revolutionised methods of direction and control.[15] The main objection of Latin American economists who have studied this phenomenon is to the fact that the multinational corporation prevents the emergence of the nation state as the main centre of economic decision-making, which is an essential prerequisite for development, more important than the availability of foreign capital for investment.[16]

US investment in Latin America has undergone considerable changes in its composition. However, the attitudes of US businessmen in the area continue to reflect the traditional pattern of nineteenth century advocates of laissez-faire. While American business in other parts of the world, especially in Japan, Sweden, Western Europe and India has aceepted many restrictions imposed by the Governments on foreign investors, the preponderant role of US business in Latin America has enabled its representatives to insist on the observance of a type of economic liberalism which is not followed even in the United States.[17]

In spite of clear indications that the role played by US capital in Latin America was resented and that nationalism in the economic sphere was increasing, US investors continued to increase their role in Latin American economy during the 1950's and 1960's. There was a shift in investments to manufacturing, commerce, and financial services, due to restrictions by Latin American governments on foreign investment in natural resources.[18] A major defect of US investment in Latin America is that it is capital intensive.[19] Since Latin America is characterised by a high rate of population growth, rapid urbanisation, unemployment and social unrest, the importation of advanced American technology is a dubious blessing. Latin American integration was originally intended to strengthen Latin American economies and reduce dependency on the US. The US was at first opposed not only to economic integration but even to the concept of international aid as a means of furthering the region's development. However, within a decade, the US had reversed its position on both these points, and appeared, at least in theory, to be fully committed to the cause of Latin American development and economic integration. In the subsequent sections of this chapter, we propose to consider this phenomenon and to arrive at some conclusions as to the nature of the US support for the Latin American integration movement.

An important factor which appears to have affected the US attitude to Latin American integration was the experience with Western European integration. This experience apparently convinced Americans in policy-making positions that it would be the path of wisdom to accept the demands of leaders of the region rather than to oppose them and that the economic strength of the regional bloc of countries would give them greater stability and security. This would to some extent compensate the US for the loss of influence which would ensue from greater economic independence of the newly integrated region.[20]

A second aspect of major importance was the wave of restlessness which spread in Latin America, strengthened by the emergence of an independent and revolutionary regime in Cuba, and the challenge presented by that regime itself. These developments seem to have affected US policy in the direction of a "policy of prevention"[21] which led to the strengthening in the early sixties, of US relations with liberal regimes devoted to improving economic conditions within a constitutional framework, and the promotion of social reform and economic change, which was laid down as one of the objectives of the Alliance for Progress.

There were, however, other factors affecting US policy toward Latin America. On the one hand, there were strategic and political considerations, and on the other there were the pressures of American business in Latin America, operating primarily through the US Congress, and also directly on the administration. Before long, the basic contradictions in US economic policies toward Latin America became evident.

THE US AND MULTILATERAL AID, 1958-64: THE ALLIANCE FOR PROGRESS

The first major change in American policy came about as a result of two developments which had a great effect on domestic public opinion in the United States, towards the end of Eisenhower's Presidency. The first was the shock engendered by the violent demonstrations against Vice-President Nixon in Lima, Peru and Caracas, Venezuela, during his South American tour in the spring of 1958. The impression of Latin America as "continent in ferment" was then reinforced in a report submitted to President Eisenhower, by his brother Dr. Milton Eisenhower, who urged immediate remedial action.

This report coincided with the second major event which eventually had an even more profound effect on the thinking of policy-makers in the United States. In January 1959, Castro entered Havana at the head of a revolt against the authoritarian regime of Batista.[22]

Dr. Eisenhower points out in his account of the events of this period that the establishment of the Inter-American Development Bank was decided upon and the foundations of the Alliance for Progress were laid prior to the threat of Castro Communism becoming widely known, contrary to the accusation widely made in Latin America. He admits, however, that "subsequent policy changes were hastened by the threat of revolution, for as I have said, we began to see clearly that our constructive efforts were not really getting through to the Latin American people—that they were being bluntly and maliciously misinterpreted."[23]

President Kubitschek of Brazil took the initiative by appealing to President Eisenhower for a revitalisation of the inter-American system. Although the United States responded to these efforts of the Brazilian President, the response was somewhat lacking in enthusiasm. The State Department did not intend to be pushed into a Marshall Plan for Latin America. "Operation Pan America," which was the name given by Kubitschek to his proposal, was considered too grandiose an idea, and a possible "attempt to capitalize on the Nixon debacle and seek conscience money."[24] There was, however, a gradual change of atmosphere in the US Government, as a result of which a decision was taken to establish an Inter-American Development Bank, a long-standing demand of the Latin American countries which had been rejected consistently by the United States till that time.

The OAS Council set up a "Special Committee to Study the Formulation of New Measures of Economic Cooperation," known as the Committee of Twentyone. By April 1959 it had drafted the formal agreement establishing the Inter-American Development Bank, whose authorised capital was fixed at $1 billion, of which $150 million was to be set aside in a Fund for Special Operations for loans to be repaid in local currencies. The US agreed to contribute $350 million of the $850 million regular capital. The balance was to be contributed by other members. The Bank was to operate on a profit-making basis and only the Fund for Special Operations was to be used for 'soft loans.'

The funds provided for development were obviously inadequate. The Cuban leader, Fidel Castro, proposed a $30 billion, ten-year capital loan from the United States for the development of Latin America, while the United States Congress appropriated an amount of $500 million for an Inter-American Social Development Fund. The adoption of the Act of Bogota in September 1960, in the face of Cuban opposition, was significant as being the first comprehensive statement of the need for reform in Latin America, and a precursor of the Alliance for Progress, which was to be introduced by the Kennedy administration the following year.[25]

Although there were changes in policy in regard to aid, there was no change in American policy in regard to the economic integration of Latin America for several years to come. As we have seen, a proposal by ECLA to set up a multilateral clearing system was strongly opposed by the United States. This proposal, which "was, in a sense, a design for Latin America to pull itself up by its own bootstraps dispensing with dollars in the process,"[26] would apparently have gone too far in the opinion of United States officials in permitting the development of an autonomous Latin American economic system. Aid was permissible, but economic independence was not.

It has been pointed out that the United States laid down conditions for support to Latin American integration efforts not due to its Latin American nature, but because of the general belief that the economic interests of the United States and of other countries are best served by global trade liberalisation."[27]

The Alliance for Progress was the product of the combined thinking of many Latin Americans and North Americans who were concerned about the threat of revolutionary change which hung over Latin America. During John F. Kennedy's campaign for the Presidency in 1960, he made a number of speeches in which he elaborated the idea of an "Alianza parael Progreso." His Presidency coincided with the regimes of a number of dynamic leaders in Latin America. The formal announcement of the Alliance for Progress by Kennedy in March 1961 was followed by a conference at Punta del Este, Uruguay. The tension between the United States and Cuba, which led to the abortive Bay of Pigs invasion in April 1961, endangered the Conference and the rhetoric with which the program was launched in the USA gave it the appearance of a United States aid program to "meet overdue promises" rather than a call to action for Latin America, thus diverting attention from the "critical element of self-help and reform."[28]

The Alliance for Progress was inaugurated at an extraordinary meeting of the Inter-American Economic and Social Council which was convened at Punta del Este on 5 August 1961, and resulted in the acceptance by the American States of a series of major reforms involving (1) the economic and social development of Latin America, (2) the economic integration of Latin America, and (3) the expansion of "national" and "international cooperation" measures for the furtherance of regional trade.[29]

The meeting was held on behalf of the OAS, and was characterised by a dramatic confrontation between the chief Cuban delegate, Che Guevara, and the United States' delegation. The Cubans not only rejected the Alliance for Progress, which in their opinion, was bound to fail, but made an eloquent appeal to revolution based on drastic agrarian reform and on "bayonets" instead of long-term loans.

Although the other Latin American delegations rejected the Cuban appeal and approved the Alliance for Progress, there was an element of doubt that the revolutionary challenge set forth by Castro's Cuba would indeed be met by the Alliance for Progress.[30]

Within a year of the inauguration of this ambitious program it was considered to be in crisis. This crisis, as seen by many observers in Latin America, was primarily a matter of lack of adequate aid from the United States. On the other hand, many in the United States saw it as a failure in the utilisation of aid and misdirected policies. A Panel of Nine Members, which came to be known as the Nine Wise Men, had been set up, but did not exercise effective authority.

In the absence of an administrative focus for the work of the Alliance for Progress (ALPRO), which did not even figure in the Washington D.C. telephone directory, decisions regarding the programmes came to be increasingly taken by the United States Agency for International Development (USAID) whose coordinator for Latin American Affairs, Teodoro Moscoso, had come to prominence as an official of "Operation Bootstrap" in Puerto Rico. Thus ALPRO came to be considered as a North American aid program instead of a cooperative endeavour of the United States and Latin America.

In 1962, two eminent Latin Americans, former Presidents Lelras Camargo of Colombia and Kubitscheak of Brazil, were invited to propose a new mechanism for the reform of the machinery of the ALPRO. On the basis of their reports, which coincided with each other in recommending the creation of a permanent, multilateral body, responsible for implementing the APP program of work, an Inter-American Committee on the Alliance for Progress (CIAP) was set up at the second annual review of the Alliance which took place at Sao Paulo, Brazil, in November 1963. This new body was given power "for determining the distribution among the several countries of public funds under the Alliance for Progress. . .,"[31] whereas the Panel of Nine had powers to comment on the program for economic and social development of a country only if the government concerned so desired, and their views were in no way binding on the latter.[32]

CIAP was a consortium in which the donors and recipients of aid worked together. The recipients were full members and discussed their policies and programmes before their peers. It had ten members, elected by groups of countries for two-year terms. It had no budget of its own, and served as a kind of intermediary between the aid giving agencies and the recipients of aid.[33]

Although the United States, by signing the Charter committed itself to giving special attention to the financing of multinational projects, facilitating participation by lesser developed countries of the region, and the channeling of aid through the Latin American countries' "own institutions for financing economic integration," there was considerable dragging of the feet on the part of the United States Government on these points. No special funds were provided for the financing of integration projects, partly because such projects were not available, but also partly because of American suspicion of multilateral aid and multinational projects.

The speed with which the Inter-American Development Bank and the United States Agency for International Development proceeded to set up their activities was far greater than that of the Latin American Free Trade Area. Bilateral aid patterns began to be established between the United States and Latin America as had been done in other parts of the world and the administrative pattern of the Alliance for Progress made it more and more a set of bilateral arrangements between the United States and Latin American countries, contrary to the original intention.[34] This was partly ascribable to the preference of the larger Latin American countries like Argentina and Brazil, which prefered bilateral to multilateral aid.[35]

US Acceptance of Latin American Integration, 1964-67

Another change in the policy of the US toward Latin American economic integration became noticeable in 1964 The location of the Inter-American Economic and Social Council (IA-ECOSOC) and of CIAP in Washington, D.C. evidently facilitated contacts between these agencies and American officials. The change in US policy toward economic integration has been ascribed to three factors: (1) the pressure of political demands at a high level from Chile and other Latin American countries; (2) the desire of President Johnson to "place his own brand on policy toward Latin America," and (3) the high-level influence of two economists, Walt Rostow and Lincoln Gordon, who, like the *tecnicos* of Latin America, were not favourably disposed toward economic integration, but played a major role in this regard.[36]

While each of these factors appears to have played some part in the changed attitude of the US toward integration, we must look more deeply for a fuller explanation of the shift in the US policy.

In the course of our account of the developments in regard to Latin American integration after the signing of the Treaty of Montevideo in 1961, we have indicated that among the actors who played a part in these events were not only countries but also international organisations. The inter-play between these various forces led to the Declaration of the Presidents of America signed at Punta del Este in 1967. From the Declaration itself it would appear that the US was forced to make a major concession to the effect that the latter would not only respect but would financially assist Latin American integration in the economic sphere.[37]

Moreover, the US original intention of offering to consider additional financial aid only in exchange for a multilateral guarantee system for foreign investors was not accepted at the summit meeting. In fact, 'the Action Program' a part of the Declaration of the Presidents, pointedly declared:

> Integration must be fully at the service of Latin America. This requires the strengthening of Latin American enterprise through vigorous financial and technical support. . . Foreign private enterprise will be able to fill an important function in assuring achievement of the objectives of integration within the pertinent policies of each of the countries of Latin America. . .[38]

The United States was also committed by Chapter III of the Action Programme to obtain access to world markets, a demand which had become prominent since the early sixties and had been brought out by the developing countries at the conferences of UNCTAD since 1964.[39]

There is reason to believe, however, that the Declaration of the Presidents was one of those international documents whose approval was obtained without a full commitment to its terms on behalf of many of the signatories. The United States appears to have offered additional financial aid to those countries which advanced toward integration and this factor evidently played some part in the acceptance of the final document by some of the Latin American Governments.[40]

Why the United States was anxious to secure the adherence of Latin American governments to the Declaration of the Presidents is not entirely clear. Some light may, however, be thrown on this phenomenon if we consider some of the criticisms which have been made in later years in Latin America on the US role in economic affairs of that region.

Let us consider the three major criticisms which have been made. The first relates to the quantum of aid under the Alliance for Progress; second, to the link between aid and US investment in Latin America, and third, to the question of terms of trade. There is also an additional criticism with regard to the question of bilateral versus multilateral aid which will be examined separately in the following section.

First of all, with regard to the quantum of aid, it is pointed out that although ALPRO called for a program of foreign investment of $20 billion in ten years, the impression which was created was that US aid would be of this order. This was not correct; actually $14.5 billion was to be private capital investment and commercial credits, not only from the US, but also from other parts of the world US aid was to be only of the order of about $4 billion in ten years, i.e., $400 million a year.[41] Besides, the content of the program did not compare favourably with that of the Marshall Plan, which along with other flows of aid from the US to Europe, provided for a massive transfer of some $24 billion from the end of the war to mid-1951. The aid to Europe, according to Felipe Herrera, was 90 per cent gifts and 10 per cent loans, while the aid to Latin America between 1957 and 1961 consisted of 30 per cent gifts and 70 per cent loans.[42]

Secondly, the aid given to Latin America is linked up in the minds of many Americans with support to private enterprise; and private enterprise in Latin America very often means US enterprise. The United States main interest in the region seemed to be to maintain stable conditions which would provide favourable conditions for investment, rather than to further social reform and economic change in the continent. The dilemma which faced the planners of economic development thus involved a choice between social reform and the furthering of private enterprise.[43] This conflict between the social objectives of ALPRO and the economic realities of US business in Latln America has been noted by the conservative Brazilian economist, Roberto de Oliveira Campos as follows:

> . . . the objective of accelerating institutional reforms in the receiving countries (such as the agrarian reform or the tax reform) may in the short run be incompatible with other desirable objectives, such as the creation of a favourable climate for private investment or the stabilisation of price levels.

He points out further that if "the decision. . . to press the case for fundamental reforms in Latin America" was a correct one, then:

> We ought not to hope sanguinely for a simultaneous improvement in the climate for private investment, or to take to the warpath if the tension and bitterness of reform movements destroy the passivity and predictability of conventional economic attitudes in relation to foreign investment. More often than not, irrational and emotional attitudes during periods of fast structural change give way to a more relaxed posture when a higher degree of social integration and a more equitable pattern of income distribution are finally attained.[44]

Not only was there serious resentment of the role of US capital in Latin America, even by conservative elements, but the situation was aggravated by the fact that US aid largely consisted of "tied public loans and of private suppliers' credits in lieu of untied public foreign aid." This strengthened bilateral rather than multilateral aid arrangements, and worked against regional economic integration as each country's industries were linked with a US manufacturer. Moreover, the US had given financial support to CACM from the start, even setting up a special regional office for Central America and Panama (ROCAP). On the other hand, LAFTA was not supported politically and financially. This distinction was ascribed to the fact that CACM members abstained from "any interference with free market forces and foreign investment.[45]

The third criticism made of US economic policies in Latin America raised a fundamental argument, viz. that the financial assistance which was being given was in reality not aid at all, since there had been no net transfer of resources from the US to Latin America and that the deteriorating terms of trade and the ever-mounting imbalance between the exports and imports of the developing countries of Latin America resulted in a net gain to the industrialised countries which far outweighed whatever transfer of resources might take place with the 'aid' given to the developing countries. The aid, according to this view, ought to be described in some other way, perhaps as 'partial compensatory financing.'[46]

The roots of this argument went back to the Prebisch thesis. The main thrust of Prebisch's argument was (1) to focus attention on the international trading system as the basic cause of Latin America's backwardness and (2) to urge that public policy be altered to correct the faults of the international trade system by protection and import controls.[47] While the first part of the thesis had received wide emphasis in the ECLA proposals for a Latin American Common Market, the problems created by the deteriorating terms of trade continued to take a heavy toll of the national economies. The preliminary meetings of the Latin American representatives at Brasilia and Alta Garcia, Argentina, prepared the ground for the first United Nations Conference on Trade and Development held at Geneva in 1964. The preparatory meetings also led to the creation of a Special Commission of Latin American Coordination (CECLA), "which has transformed itself, particularly after the Consensus of Vina del Mar of 1969, into a Latin American approach for the adoption of a common position in economic relations with the United States."[48]

In his report as Secretary-General to the Geneva meeting, Raul Prebisch took a stand in which he sought to reconcile his earlier advocacy of regional preferences for industry with his new advocacy of preferences for exports of developing countries in the markets of industrialised countries. He argued that this was a "logical extension of the infant-industry argument." The preference should be sought not only in other developing countries but also in the markets of developed countries.[49]

Although the two UNCTAD conferences held at Geneva in 1964 and New Delhi in 1968 did not achieve any spectacular results, the establishment of a new international organisation as a spokesman for the developing countries helped in widening the acceptance of the demands of these countries in the economic field, and furthered a better understanding of their problems in the industrialised countries. By October 1970 the developing countries seemed to be within grasp of achieving some of their long-held ambitions, when an accord on a system of generalised preferences was agreed upon. "Two hallowed rules on which world trade has long been built" were suspended in favour of the developing countries: the first, favoured-nation principle, and the second, the fact that the industrialised countries were not asking for any concessions in return for those they were making.[50]

These concessions were hedged in with conditions, some of which were difficult to fulfil, e.g. the US insistence on dismantling of preferential arrangements between some industrialised and some developing countries. Nevertheless the agreement, when implemented, was expected to constitute a major breakthrough in the relationships between the countries of the Third World and the developed countries.

President Nixon's New Economic Policy, announced on 15 August 1971, had an adverse effect on official thinking in Latin America. At a meeting of CECLA called to consider the matter, preliminary to the meeting of the Inter-American Economic and Social Council to be held in Panama in September 1971, it was decided to pursue a common strategy in regard to three major issues: (1) a role for the less developed countries (LDCs) in the reform of the international monetary system, (2) exemption of developing countries from the 10 per cent import surcharge imposed by the United States, and (3) the elimination of the 10 per cent reduction in "external development financing" for Latin America.[51]

The IA-ECOSOC meeting at Panama City, however, was

the scene of a confrontation between US and Latin American delegates on a number of economic issues which did not lead to any consensus.[52] It was only after the revaluation of the US dollar at a new rate of exchange that the US Government decided to lift the import surcharge for all countries, and ask Congress for commercial preferences for developing countries.[53] The demand of the developing countries for a say in the reform of the international monetary system was not conceded, and the President of Colombia pointed out that the economic situation of these countries would be adversely affected by the new monetary arrangements entered into by the ten rich countries.[54]

Keeping in mind these three criticisms of US economic policy in Latin America, it is possible to consider the change in US policy toward Latin America with greater clarity. There has always been a feeling in the United States that if Latin America could be "opened up" as the United States was during the nineteenth century, there would be a great future ahead for the southern continent. The idea of a hemisphere common market was originally brought up by the US Secretary of State, James G. Blaime, in 1889. It was revived in 1960 by the National Planning Association of the United States, although it was not seriously considered at that time. The US interests who made such a proposal were evidently inspired by the possibility of penetration of Latin America by US commerce, which they regarded as in the interests of Latin America as well as of the United States.[55]

Between 1964 and 1967 the earlier reluctance of American business to accept a Latin American Common Market began to give way to a new interest in the prospect of increasing benefits from the industrialisation of Latin America. The experience of US business with the European Economic Community and the CACM had shown that "integration could bring benefits to US as well as regional business groups. A number of large US companies with branches in several Latin American countries had discovered that LAFTA might afford them the opportunity to enlarge operations and reduce costs."[56]

Another reason given for the change is that the administration could by this means demonstrate to the US Congress, the interest of the former in establishing a link between self-help and the distribution of aid funds.[57]

The close link between some members of the US Congress and US business interests in Latin America was evident from the pressure applied by US business interests on Congress to obtain assurances from Latin American countries about a reduction in tariffs before agreeing to support economic integration,[58] as well as from the specific provisions made by Congress on US assistance to Latin America, such as the Hickenlooper Amendment which required the President to suspend assistance to any government which nationalised the property of a US investor, imposed a "discriminatory" tax, etc., unless the country took steps to discharge its international legal obligations to pay for the property.[59] Moreover, some US Congressmen became spokesmen for a particular view of the role of American business in Latin America.[60]

However, it would be too simplistic to assert that the US Congress reflects the views of US business in Latin America. The pressures operating on Congress included those of the US consumer, and of American public opinion generally. There was also an interplay between the views of the Congress and the administration which it was difficult for one outside the system to understand.

An assessment of the long-term prospects of US attitudes to Latin American integration and development is an extremely difficult task not only because of the lack of rapport which is often observed between the Administration and Congress in that country, but also due to the complexities of the US policy-making apparatus, and the complex position of the US in the world today. For instance, the stoppage by Congress of all aid to developing countries in November 1971 was evidently motivated by a desire to separate military from economic aid, and to prevent the US Administration from using economic aid to bolster military regimes, especially in Southeast Asia.

Taking these factors into account, a long-term projection of US role in Latin American integration would have to take account of a number of relevant factors. The factors listed earlier as having been put forward as explanations of the US acceptance of Latin American integration become clearer in the context of the overall strategic political and economic situation.

President Johnson's policy of "prevention" in relation to the spreading influence of Cuba in Latin America took two forms—first, the Dominican intervention in 1965 and aid to military forces for the suppression of internal revolts, and secondly, the support for liberal and constitutional political regimes such as those of Eduardo Frei in Chile. At the same time, the American business interests of the new, "progressive" type, represented by the Rockefellers and spokesmen like Senator Javits, began to see the advantages of Latin American integration to their prospects in Latin America. The role of the US economists, who played a prominent part in obtaining US support for integration, also became clear when seen in the context of the political and economic factors mentioned above. There was a change in US policy, but this change was intimately connected with the pressures of US interest groups and with the political and strategic factors operating on US policy-makers, rather than on a realisation of the desirability of Latin American integration for the countries themselves.

Multilateral Aid: The Inter-American Development Bank and Latin American Integration

There has been a tendency in recent years to urge that bilateral aid results in undue influence being exerted by the donor country on the recipient, and that multilateral aid should be preferred. Multilateral aid in this context refers to the agency through which aid is channelled, but may also refer to the receiving agency, as in the case of aid to a regional or sub-regional organisation like LAFTA, CACM, CABEI, etc. The assumption is that multinational organisations, or consortia of donors, which serve as media of aid, will be less subject to pressures of the donor countries, and will take a more objective view of the needs of the recipient countries.[61]

This assumption is unfortunately not always justified. Political pressures on international agencies concerned with the disbursement of aid are not unknown. Moreover, the set of economic ideas which have been accepted as official doctrine in most of the international agencies represent an established system of international finance and of international economic stability which have been increasingly challenged by the developing countries in recent years. The International Monetary Fund and the World Bank represent a certain position in world economic affairs, while UNCTAD represents the opposite view.[62]

The study of international organisations from the viewpoint of their internal structure and composition, the sources of their influence and authority and the role they play in world affairs is still not in a completed stage. It has to be noted, however, that international institutions do play a role, and that it is not simply a product of the collective interests of their members. Lagos has pointed out that regional economic organisations in the Americas have played a role in laying down the sphere of activity of a new sub-system within the inter-American system, and in asserting the autonomy which the Latin American countries would exercise as a result of the creation of the new sub-system.[63]

The role of multinational aid agencies has to be examined in the context of this situation. The assumption that international organisations are performing an "objective" role as representatives of some superior wisdom has to be rejected. On the other hand, it is not necessary to assume that they are acting exclusively as agents of the more developed countries. Rather, they have to be seen as the product of a political process, in which the interests of different donor and recipient nations are represented, and in which the institution has also acquired a certain strength, which enables it to operate on the basis of its own traditions, and the play of forces within the organisation itself.

The function of "mediation" between the "principal power" of the inter-American system and the "rest of the member nations" of that system[64] was seen both in the organisation of CIAP and of the Inter-American Development Bank. When CIAP was set up, there was much discussion as to "whether it should have the power to *decide* on the allocation of aid under the Alliance for Progress, or merely to advise on its allocation. In the end the United States threatened not to participate if Latin Americans insisted on the CIAP 'deciding'."[65] Its powers were therefore limited to the making of studies, reviews, and proposals and to promote the multilateralisation of aid. Its chairman was a Latin-American, and it sought to follow a middle course between the Latin American point of view and that of the US. Although it had no final say in the allocation of funds, it had on occasions questioned the traditional wisdom that "good performance" of a member country was to be judged by "high rates of growth, price stability, no structural change . . .," even though accompanied by high social tensions.[66]

The Inter-American Development Bank (IDB) also played an unusual role among international aid-giving agencies. Although located in Washington and enjoying a high credit rating in the New York money market, it seemed to represent the views of Latin America rather than of the United States in the dialogue between the two in economic matters. This situation was partly a product of its history and partly of the choices made by its early administrators, and the willingness of the US representatives to accept the position. A kind of equilibrium appeared to have been reached, as a result of which decisions were taken on the basis of an adjustment of the interests of the United States and the Latin American countries.

The establishment of a regional development bank for the Americas had been a long-standing demand of the Latin American countries, going back as far as 1889, when the first inter-American conference was held.[67] The US resolutely opposed the creation of such an institution, which would be in competition with private banks. The proposal was not entirely forgotten, however, and was revived several times after the Second World War, most recently at the Buenos Aires Conference in 1957, a year before the establishment of the Inter-American Development Bank. The Latin American proposals met with no greater success than in the nineteenth century.

The decision to support the establishment of such a bank, which was announced by the US government in August 1958, came as somewhat of a surprise, being evidently a reaction to the Latin American dissatisfaction with US policies which was evident after the Nixon visit.[68] The programme of work laid down in the Act of Bogota, approved on 11 October 1960, ten days after the Bank began its operations, was regarded as "a kind of political charter" of the Inter-American Development Bank.

Its stress on the close connection between social progress and economic development appeared to be "ahead of its time." However it provided IDB with a ready-made field on which to focus its activities.[69] The Social Progress Trust Fund, the main source of concessionary finance of IDB till 1965, originated with a fund of $500 million set up by the US Government under Eisenhower's administration.

The reasons for the establishment of the Inter-American Development Bank became clearer from the following statement of Dr. Milton Eisenhower, a brother of President Eisenhower who was his close adviser on Latin American affairs:

> First, decisions on loan application would be made cooperatively; thus there would be no justification for identifying the United States with project developments that might, while improving the economies, continue to strengthen the prevailing order. Second, if conditions were attached to loans in the hope of spreading more widely the benefits of economic growth, the intervention involved or implied would have been collectively determined. In other words an agency of the Americas might help to solve the dilemma; desirable social changes might be fostered through credit, while avoiding the malodorous charges that had arisen as the United States sought sincerely but unilaterally to promote economic development in Latin America.[70]

This was the American justification of IDB as a multilateral institution. Latin American motives in pressing for the establishment of a bank included "two more specific and directly relevant resentments, the Latin Americans' growing dislike of the policies of the World Bank, and their sense of grievance over their failure to secure even a modest share of American aid."[71]

We have now to consider the technical aspects of the Bank's work—its sources of funds, the method of its operation, the content of its programmes, and its position in the money market. All these factors were connected with its position as an intermediary between the United States and Latin American positions in economic matters.

The sources of funds of IDB may be classified as follows: (1) the ordinary capital resources, consisting of the subscribed amount of the authorised capital stock, funds raised by borrowings, repayments, and income from loans and guarantees; (2) the Fund for Special Operations (FSO); (3) the Social Progress Trust Fund (SPTF); and (4) resources mobilised from non-member developed countries.[72] The United States was the largest subscriber, having contributed 41 per cent of the authorised capital. The distribution of voting power was very close to the distribution of subscriptions, and the United States had a formal blocking vote in the Fund for Special Operations. However, according to White, "the bank and its Latin American members have come to terms with the reality of US financial power and have done so in a manner which ameliorates some of the worst effects to which the formal exercise of that power might give rise."[73]

The utilisation of the Bank's funds was not without controversy. Many in the US Congress for example, challenged the "somewhat flexible approach to project appraisal," its willingness to commit "resources to a project of doubtful economic utility" and its allegedly "insufficiently rigorous standards of project appraisal."[74]

This original focus of IDB was on social progress in relation to economic development. This gradually gave way to economic integration as a focus of the Bank's activities. Its first President, Felipe Herrera, made a series of speeches after 1964 bringing to attention this aspect of the Bank's work. The Bank in fact came to be known as the "bank for Latin American integration." Although the Charter of the Bank made no mention of integration as such, it required it "to cooperate with the member countries to orient their development policies toward a better utilisation of their resources, in a manner consistent with the objective of making their economies more complementary and of fostering the orderly growth of their foreign trade."[75]

The role likely to be played by the Bank in the integration of Latin America was the subject of speculation on the part of some writers. It was pointed out that the American chiefs of state at Punta del Este entrusted the Bank with specific functions in this field. It was hoped that the Bank would play a pioneering role in establishing "strong regional institutions to underpin the weaker national institutions."[76]

Writing in 1965, Haas and Schmitter expressed the possibility of Felipe Herrera performing the role of a statesman furthering the integration of Latin America, as Paun-Henri Spaak of Belgium did in Europe.[77]

The Bank, in actual fact, took a rather cautious approach to the commitment of funds for projects furthering integration. From an initial stress on urban water, housing, and agriculture in the commitment of funds the emphasis changed in later years to power, transport, and communications.[78] The activities which it had undertaken in support of integration could be classified into two main categories, viz. the provision of infrastructure and the furtherance of integration in industry, agriculture, and trade.

The first was a long-term function and was really laying the foundations for integration rather than furthering integration directly. The lack of adequate physical mobility and contacts within the region led to a stress on transportation, telecommunication, power and port development. In addition IDB was active as coordination agent in the preparation of preliminary technical studies for the development of the River Plate Basin at the request of five countries, viz. Argentina, Bolivia, Brazil, Paraguay, and Uruguay. An attempt was being made to coordinate the planning of the development of border areas. The Bank was also furthering the establishment of import-substituting industries at the Latin American level in accordance with the recommendations of ECLA and in coordination with LAFTA.[79]

The Bank pioneered in providing funds for the financing of exports of capital goods among the Latin American countries; thus enabling them to overcome partially the incentives offered by advanced countries in the form of suppliers credits.[80]

The Bank's "principal instrument of support" were the Institute for Latin American Integration (INTAL), a research and training institute at Buenos Aires set up in 1965, and the Pre-investment Fund for Latin American Integration set up in 1966. The latter undertook feasibility studies of projects affecting integration, ranging widely from multinational infrastructure works such as highway networks, communications, air, maritime, and river transportation to the development of economic regions and the establishment of basic industries on a regional scale.[81]

Apart from providing technical and financial support to measures involving the integration of Latin America, IDB made a "major commitment to integration" in the input of time and energy by its management. Thus IDB, "instead of seeking to isolate a special area of responsibility of its own, has consistently sought to identify itself with and merge itself into a broad political movement."[82]

Unlike the Asian Development Bank, IDB had not been obliged to "tailor its operations to fit the assumed expectations of prospective purchasers of its bond." This had been ascribed to the political support received from the United States and the high credit ratings it enjoyed in the New York and other financial markets as a result of the US guarantees, the strength of its Finance Department, and the close contact maintained with the world's capital markets.[83]

The Inter-American Development Bank was clearly playing an important role in the economic development of Latin America and in the assertion of the solidarity of the continent *vis-a-vis* the United States. Its position in relation to Latin American integration was, however, not a necessary one. Proposals for a separate development bank to serve the LAFTA Area were made. Such a bank would be an anomaly as not all Latin American countries were members of LAFTA (the Caribbean and the Central American countries being excluded) and the countries which are members "can by no stretch of the imagination be regarded as constituting an economic region." Moreover LAFTA did not constitute even a free-trade area, and there was little chance of its acquiring the other basic elements of regional integration, such as a customs union and the free movement of capital, labour, and business enterprise.[84]

The first truly regional financial institution in Latin America was the Central American Bank for Economic Integration. On purely economic grounds, a number of arguments could be adduced for and against external financing through regional institutions.[85] Most of the activities of IDB in the field of integration, including regional industrial integration, could be justified on economic grounds in terms of the return on the investment. But the justification for the priority given to these activities by IDB was a matter of some doubt. Regional institutions that owe their existence to external sponsorship or imposition were mushrooming; but economic, political, and administrative conditions essential for their operation were conspicuously lacking. Institutions should be created only when there is a genuine demand for such institutions and the necessary infrastructure as a base. "At its most meaningful, Latin American economic integration must begin with freedom of movement of commodities, capital, enterprise, labour and ideas. Seeking to mesh activities at the governmental level is highly impracticable, particularly in view of external disorganisation so often in evidence in the majority of governments of the region."[86]

In conclusion, we have to consider the question of the political role of the Bank and its position in the early seventies. It was pointed out by Teresa Hayter that

> the United States basic reason for promoting international institutions is to transfer some of the responsibility for making unpleasant decisions onto others; it has no desire for the decisions themselves to be different. . . The IADB probably demonstrates the limits of freedom of action likely to be achieved by an agency actually responsible for allocating a considerable proportion of 'aid'. It has nevertheless on the whole avoided controversial issues. . .[87]

Teresa Hayter also made it clear that IDB used its freedom by adopting a more flexible policy in relation to problems of economic development. It was generally reluctant to join the IMF, IBRD, and USAID in exercising "leverage." This was partly due to a reluctance to intervene in internal matters of member states, doubts about the policies of the World Bank, and the continuing links of some IDB officials with Latin American countries, whom they were reluctant to criticise. By refusing to apply leverage, IDB was giving up the opportunity of influencing the policies of member states as the only way she could do so would be by following the US "policy line" observed by other international agencies.[88]

In fact, the IDB was accused of making loans to dictatorial regimes in violation of the Social Progress Trust Fund Agreement.[89] In his address when handing over the Presidentship of the Bank, Felipe Herrera, admitted that the institution did not discriminate among the recipients of its loans on the basis of the economic and political position of the regime in power.[90]

On the other hand, the Bank sought to play a critical role in the integration of the Latin American area, both by providing technical and financial support to measures involving integration and also by commiting the time and energy of its management in this direction. It appears to have used leverage in this direction in preference to furthering progressive political regimes. The shift in focus from social progress towards economic integration was reflected in the speeches of Herrera and in the promotion of integration through such activities as the setting up of INTAL.

The role of the IDB in regard to integration was a catalytic one of providing technical support and incentive rather than of committing large funds for integration activities. This could conceivably become the major activity of the Bank. It was suggested that the Bank should concentrate exclusively on integration, leaving other financing agencies to assist non-integration activities.[91]

The physical integration of Latin America is an immense task, and the funds provided were completely inadequate for the provision of infrastructural facilities and the integration of the Latin American economics. The most appropriate solution would be to take the integration criterion into consideration along with the need to provide for integrated institutions of an infrastructural type at the sub-regional level, the sub-regions being defined on the basis of carefully collected data, which was already under compilation at the Bank.

There were indications that the political support which had hitherto been given to the IDB by the US government had been reduced. Although President Nixon declared his intention of shifting from bilateral to multilateral aid programmes administered by the IDB, "Congress is less than interested because of domestic problems and the pressures being exerted by US investors whose interests are increasingly imperiled by rising nationalism in Latin America."[92] The IDB was also subjected to criticism for its allegedly "political" loans. The tradition of giving loans irrespective of the political position of the government concerned was being eroded by the insistence of the United States that loans to countries like Chile and Peru, which were causing problems to US investors, be stopped. The traditional readiness of the US Congress to provide additional funds for the IDB was not likely to continue, in spite of the record business of the Bank during 1970.[93]

Although the appointment of the President of the Bank, Antonio Ortis Mena, former Finance Minister of Mexico, was made under circumstances which gave the impression that he was a US nominee, not widely acceptable to Latin Americans, the policies of the Bank did not appear to have undergone any substantial change as a result of his appointment.[94] In fact the Bank was attempting to counter some of the pressures of the United States on the lending policy by ensuring the member governments discriminated against access to sources of funds outside the IDB membership, mainly in Europe.[95]

The IDB's original ideological basis was that of a mediator between US and Latin American goals. Some kind of a synthesis was arrived at between the two approaches.

The Bank's role changed gradually from that of a supporter of social reform and political liberalism in the early sixties to that of an exponent and supporter of Latin American integration. Both the United States and Latin America seem to have acquiesced in this change. Unfortunately the concept of integration came to be gradually deprived of some of its original developmental and social content.

The concept of integration appears to require further definition. The furtherance of physical integration would be more appropriate at the sub-regional level in view of the limitations of funds and organisational resources, and to enable a contribution to be made to the development of the Latin American region within a reasonable time-span.

There is no doubt that the Bank has made a contribution to the development and integration of Latin America and has opened up some avenues for a multilateral financial institution, independent of the highly industrialised nations. However, Latin America will have to depend more on its own resources in future in view of the deteriorating economic relations between the United States and Latin America. The IDB's efforts to find external funding for development should help both to reduce Latin American dependency on the United States and to assist the balanced development of the southern continent.

REFERENCES

1 The argument here follows that of Norman A. Bailey, *Latin America in World Politics* (New York, 1967), pp. 4-5, 38-54.

2 Joseph Grunwald and Miguel S. Wionczek, *Latin American Economic Integration and the United States* (Washington, D.C., 1971), p. 111.

3 Iris Mabel Laredo, "Posicion de Los Estados Unidos frente a la Integracion de America Latina: Afirmaciones y Tendencias," *Revista de la Integracion* (November 1968), pp. 59-60.

4 See *supra*, Chapter I (b).

5 Robert Edwin Denham, "The Role of the US as an External Actor in the Integration of Latin America," *JCMS* (March 1969), p. 200.

6 See *supra*, Chapter II (a).

7 Laredo, n. 3, p. 63.

8 R. Harrison Wagner, *U.S. Policy Toward Latin America: A Study in Domestic and International Policies* (Stanford, Cal.), pp. 76-7.

9 Laredo, n. 3, pp. 64-6.

10 Wagner, n. 8, p. 78.

11 Ibid., pp. 123-4.

12 See *supra*, Chapter II (a) (i).

13 See *supra*, Chapter II (b) for a discussion of the views of critics of the Prebisch thesis. Younger Latin American social scientists have pointed out that industrialisation has increased rather than reduced the dependency of Latin America on the US economy. A recent formulation of the approach outlined above will be found in Helio Jaguaribe, "Dependencia y Autonomia en America Latina," in Helio Jaguaribe, et al, *La Dependencia Politico-Economica de America Latina* (Mexico, 1970), pp. 1-85 and a paper presented by Osvaldo Sunkel at the Conference on "The Economic and Financial Relations of Latin America with the Industrialised Countries," organised by the International Economic Association at Mexico City, 6 to 11 December 1971.

14 (New York, 1967). For a critique of Galbraith's approach from the viewpoint of Latin American economists, see Alonso Aguilar M., "El Capitalismo Opulente de John Kenneth Galbraith," in *Problemas del Desarrollo* (October-December 1969), pp. 113-40.

15 Celso Furtado, "La Reestructuracion de la Economia Internacional y las Relaciones entre Estados Unidos y America Latina," in Osvaldo Sunkel, ed., *Integration Politica y Economica: El Proceso Europeo y el Problema Latinoamericano* (Santiago de Chile, 1970), pp. 367-8.

16 Ibid., pp. 384-6. Celso Furtado was Minister of Economy in Brazil under Goulart, and is a leading exponent of the dependency thesis in Latin America.

17 In January 1963, three prominent members of the American business community, including David Rockefeller, and representing the Standard Oil Company, the First National City Bank of New York and the Chase Manhattan Bank, issued a statement urging a greater participation for American private enterprise in the Alliance for Progress. This statement

shocked many Latin Americans who regard private enterprise as a continuation of nineteenth century patterns of exploitation, and take a mixed, state-directed economy for granted.
Peter Nehemkis, *Latin America: Myth and Reality* (New York, 1964), pp. 190-1, 268-74.

18 Between 1960 and 1967, US investments in manufacturing increased from 20 to 32 per cent, while the share of extractive sectors fell from 53 to 40 per cent of all US direct investment in Latin America. Grunwald and Wionczek, n. 2, p. 114.

19 US investment per person employed is $7,900 in Latin America as against $3,800 in Europe. If petroleum and mining are excluded, the figure still comes to $4,500 in Latin America. Ibid., p. 119.

20 Laredo, n. 3, p. 98.

21 Ibid., p. 99.

22 Ibid., p. 13. A more cynical view of the demonstrations against Nixon was taken by the State Department, which explained them as a community plot. See the remarks of Deputy Under Secretary Murphy quoted by William D. Rogers, *The Twilight Struggle: The Alliance for Progress and the Politics of Development in Latin America* (New York, 1967), p. 16. For the views of the then US Ambassador in Argentina on the Nixon trip and the Cuban revolution see Willard L. Beaulac, *A Diplomat Looks at Aid to Latin America* (Carbondale, 1970), pp. 1-12.

23 Milton S. Eisenhower, *The Wine is Bitter: The United States and Latin America* (Garden City, N.Y., 1963), p. 230.

24 Rogers, n. 22, p. 19.

25 Ibid., pp. 19-25. See also Connell-Smith, *The Inter-American System* (London, 1966), pp. 167-72.

26 Denham, n. 5, pp. 199-200.

27 Ibid., pp. 200-1. For a well-argued critique of several criteria prescribed by the industrialised countries for the underdeveloped world's integration programmes, see Miguel S. Wionczek, ed., *Latin American Economic Integration: Experiences and Prospects* (New York, 1966), pp. 7-11.

28 Rogers, n. 22, p. 34. See also pp. 27-35 *passim*.

29 For the text of the Declaration to the Peoples of America, The Charter of Punta del Este and the appended resolutions, see *Alliance for Progress, Official Documents*.

30 Rogers, n. 22, pp. 41-5.

31 Resolution I-M/63, 7 January 1964, in OAS Document, OEA/Series H/XII, 6, quoted in Raul Saez S., "The Nine Wise Men and the Alliance for Progress," *International Organization* (Winter 1968), p. 266.

32 Ibid., p. 258.

33 Interview with Senor Manuel Trucco, Special Assistant to the Chairman, CIAP, Washington, D.C., 9 September 1971. For an account of the working of CIAP see *The Alliance for Progress and Multilateral Economic Cooperation*. Document presented by the Chairman of CIAP to the Second Meeting of UNCTAD, New Delhi, India, February 1968 (Washington, D.C., n. d.)

34 Denham, n. 5, pp. 202-4.

[35] Arnold Toynbee, *America and the World Revolution and Other Lectures* (London, 1962), p. 229, quoted in Saez, n. 31, pp. 257-8.

[36] For a general critique of the Alliance for Progress see Cesar Sepulveda, "Reflexiones Sobre la Alianza para el Progreso," in *Foro International* (July-September 1967), pp. 67-79. Denham, n. 5, pp. 206-8.

[37] See *supra*, Chapter IV (b) and (c).

[38] Inter-American Institute of International Legal Studies (IILS), *Instruments Relating to the Economic Integration of Latin America* (Dobbs Ferry, N.Y., 1968), p. 399.

[39] See ibid., pp. 405-6 for the text of Chapter III. For a discussion of these points, see Wionczek, "Latin American Integration and U.S. Economic Policies," pp. 149-56.

[40] Denham, n. 5, pp. 208-10.

[41] Hernan Echavarria (Colombian Ambassador to United States, 1967-68), "The Alliance for Progress," in Alberto Martinez Piedra, ed., *Socio-economic Change in Latin America* (Washington, D.C., 1970), pp. 3-4.

[42] Quoted in Roberto de Oliveira Campos, *Reflections on Latin American Development* (Austin, 1967), pp. 3-4.

[43] For a discussion of this point from the viewpoint of the Latin American Left, which looks upon the national bourgeoisie in Latin American countries as allies of the US capitalist system, see J.P. Morray, "The United States and Latin America," in James Petras and Maurice Zeitlin, eds., *Latin America: Reform or Revolution?* (New York, 1968) pp. 99-119. See also John Gerassi, *The Great Fear in Latin America* (New York, 1966), pp. 266-8. Gerassi points out that ALPRO Funds could be used only for restricted purposes and all purchases of goods and services had to be purchased in the US; thus the debtors were "hooked" to the banker but had good credit. Both Gerassi and Morray are Americans, but present the Latin American viewpoint in this matter.

[44] Campos, n. 42, p. 100. See also the remarks of K.H. Silvert, an American political scientist specialising in Latin America: "The ultimate measure of the worth of a Latin American Government should not be whether or not it is a paradise for foreign capital." Quoted in Gerassi, n. 43, p. 292. The former President of Colombia, Alberto Lleras Camargo strongly urged in 1963 that ALPRO "should not take on the character of a campaign for capitalism and free enterprise." See Sydney Dell, *A Latin American Common Market? (A LACM?)* (London, 1966), p. 175.

[45] Miguel S. Wionczek, "The Rise and the Decline of Latin American Economic Integration," *JCMS*, no. 1, 1970, p. 62. See also Grunwald and Wionczek, n. 2, p. 77.

[46] Campos, n. 42, p. 101. Some economists from the industrialised countries support this view. See Dell, *Trade Blocs and Common Markets* (New York, 1963), pp. 363-5.

[47] See *supra*, Chapter II (b).

[48] Felipe Herrera, "Nationalism and Economic Integration in Latin America," Lecture at Georgetown University, Washington, D.C., October 1969 (Washington: IDB, n.d., mimeographed), p. 9.

[49] United Nations Conference on Trade and Development, *Towards A New*

Trade Policy for Development: Report by the Secretary of UNCTAD (E/CONF. 46/3), 12 February 1964, Chapter II B, p. 80.

50 Victor Lusinchi, "Poor Nations Win Trade Advantage," *New York Times*, 13 October 1970, For accounts of the two UNCTAD conferences, see Branislav Gosovic, "UNCTAD: North-South Encounter," *International Conciliation*, No. 568 (New York) (May 1968) and A.S. Friendeberg, *United Nations Conference on Trade and Development of 1964: The Theory of the Peripheral Economy at the Centre of International Political Discussions* (Rotterdam, 1968).

51 Letter dated 6 September 1971 from Juan Alberto Quilici, Minister of Finance of Argentina and President of the XIth meeting of CECLA at Ministerial level, to Dr. Walter J. Sedwitz, Executive Secretary of IA-ECOSOC (Washington, D.C.: OAS, n.d., mimeographed).

52 Address by Dr. David Pollock, ECLA Representative in Washington, D.C., at a meeting of the Society for International Development, Washington Chapter, 22 September 1971.

53 "Pedira Nixon al Congreso Preferencias para Ibroamerica," *Excelsior* (Mexico City) 21 December 1971, p. 1.

54 "Los 10" Cearon mas Desequilibrio Para los Pobres: Pastrana: Ausentes, los "chicos," *Excelsior*, 22 December 1971, p. 1.

55 Grunwald and Wionczek, n. 2, pp. 67, 73.

56 Business International Corporation, *LAFTA, Key to Latin America's 200 Million Consumers* (New York, 1966), quoted in ibid., p. 78, footnote.

57 Grunwald and Wionczek, n. 2, p. 78.

58 Wionczek, n. 39, pp. 134-43.

59 Rogers, n. 22, pp. 241-2.

60 Senators Jacob Javits and Hubert Humphrey sponsored the Atlantic Community Development Group for Latin America (ADELA), made up of American, Japanese, and European companies set up to provide investments for joint ventures. Nehemkis, n. 17, p. 265.
For an exposition of Javits' views on Latin American integration, see Jacob J. Javits, "Last Chance for a Common Market," *Foreign Affairs* (April 1967), pp. 449-62.

61 For example, Grunwald and Wionczek, n. 2, pp. 93-4 quote the objections put forward by Hirschman and Bird in an article, "Foreign Aid: A Critique and a Proposal" to programme aid. Grunwald and Wionczek argue that these objections are applicable to all bilateral aid. See also p. 92 for a justification of multilateral aid for industries.

62 An account of the growth of UNCTAD and its connection with the Latin American integration movement will be found in part (d) of this chapter.

63 Gustavo Lagos, "The Political Role of Regional Economic Organisations in Latin America," *JCMS*.

64 Ibid.

65 Teresa Hayter, *Aid as Imperialism* (Harmondsworth, 1971), p. 103.

66 Ibid., pp. 103-6. The quotation is from p. 106.

67 The date 1889 is based on the view of Henry S. Bloch, "Regional

Development Financing," *International Organisation* (Winter 1968), p. 188. However the formal proposal seems to have been based on an earlier suggestion. See Julio Broide, *Banco Interamericano de Desarrollo, sus antecedentes y creacion* (Washington, D.C., 1961).

68 John White, *Regional Development Banks: A Study of Institutional Style* (London, 1970), pp. 146-7.

69 Ibid., p. 148. For a summary of the provisions of the Act of Bogota, see Saez, n. 31, pp. 251-2.

70 Milton S. Eisenhower, "The Alliance for Progress: Historic Roots," in John C. Dreier, ed., *The Alliance for Progress: Problems and Perspectives* (Baltimore, 1962), p. 12.

71 White, n. 68, p. 144.

72 See ibid., pp. 157-64, for a discussion of these sources of funds.

73 Ibid., pp. 152-4. The quotation is from p. 154.

74 Ibid., p. 168.

75 Article 1, 2 (a) (iv) of the *Agreement establishing the Inter-American Development Bank*.

76 Bloch, n. 67, pp. 189-90. See also the comments by Denham, n. 5, p. 213.

77 See Ernst B. Haas and Philippe C. Schmitter, *The Politics of Economics in Latin American Regionalism: The Latin American Free Trade Area after Four Years of Operation* (Denver, Colo., 1965), pp. 59 and 63.

78 White, n. 68, p. 172.

79 Inter-American Development Bank, *The Inter-American Development Bank and the Economic Integration of Latin America* (Washington, D.C., April 1969), pp. 15-28.

In actual financial terms the allotment by the end of 1968 for integration projects was about $275.3 million or less than 10 per cent of its total commitment at that time. White considers this a small proportion of its total allotment. In absolute terms, however, it constitutes a substantial figure.

80 White, n. 68, p. 178.

81 n. 79, pp. 29-32.

82 White, n. 68, p. 179.

83 Ibid., pp. 182-4.

84 Raymond F. Mikesell, "External Financing and Regional Integration," in Wionczek, n. 27, p. 206.

85 Ibid., pp. 211-2.

86 Ibid., p. 213. For a critical analysis of the concept of integration component in the IDB, see Maria del Rosario Green, "The Inter-American Development Bank and the Economic Integration of Latin America: The LAFTA Case," Masters' Thesis, Columbia University, Faculty of Political Science and Dept. of Latin American Studies, pp. 73-8, 130-1. For an explanation of the integration criterion by an official of the bank see R. Alberto Calvo, "El Banco Interamericano de Desarrollo y el Proceso de Integracion," in Gustavo Lagos, ed., *La Integracion Latinoamericana, Situacion y Perspectivas* (Buenos Aires, 1965), pp. 80-2.

87 Hayter, n. 65, p. 186.

88 Ibid., pp. 99-102. Somewhat similar views are expressed by John White.

89 Gerassi, n. 43, p. 277.

90 "One of the basic principles of the Bank's view of Latin America is to recognise the fact that the region is at the same time indivisible and divergent and that in its work of transferring financial or technical assistance resources there are no "ideal" conditions regarding economic and political systems in the recipient countries. We are not professional reformists or ideologists but public servants; our contribution to change can only be made through the channels indicated by the member governments, regardless of their ideologies. This pragmatic attitude. . . has enabled the Bank to successfully overcome difficulties or changes. . ." *Address by Felipe Herrera, President of the IDB, at the Special Meeting of the Board of Governors, Buenos Aires, March 1, 1971* (Washington, D.C., n.d.), p. 8.

91 Green, n. 86, p. 134.

92 H.J. Maindenberg, "Latin Bank and Critics: Meeting in Peru will chart Future of IDB," *New York Times*, 9 May 1971, section 3, (Business and Finance), pp. 1, 5.

93 Ibid.

94 For a report on the controversy regarding the selection of Ortiz Mena as the President of IDB, see "Hemisphere Bank Picks Mexican," *Washington Post*, November 1970, p. 2. See the statement by Antonio Ortiz Mena, President of the IDB, at the Special Meeting of the Board of Governors, Buenos Aires, 1 March 1971 (Washington, D.C., n.d.), *passim*. There is considerable stress on the need for physical infrastructure and on the pressing need for economic growth and population control in Latin America.

95 The speech made by the President of the Republic of Peru and the addresses of several of the Governors very strongly rejected possible forms of intervention in the internal affairs of borrower countries through conditions imposed by international financing. As a practical solution to the dilemma in which the Bank was placed in the administration of resources placed at its disposal under certain conditions which it could not evade, the Bank was seeking to "diversify the sources of soft funds so that the borrower country can choose the type of credit that suits it best." Thus the capital-exporting countries would be competing to provide soft credits. As a first step, the Spanish government had offered to establish a fund to be administered by the Bank amounting to $50 million at an interest of 6 per cent. Address by Antonio Ortiz Mena, President of the IDB, at the closing session, IDB, XII, Meeting of the Board of Governors, Lima, May 1971. Documents of the Meeting, No. AB 279, 14 May 1971 (Washington, D.C.: IDB, n.d., mimeographed), pp. 1-2.

CHAPTER VI

THE POLITICS OF LATIN AMERICAN INTEGRATION

INTRODUCTION

We have listed in Chapter One four factors which contributed to the success of the Western European integration movement. These were (1) the common fear of an outside power; (2) the expectation of massive US aid; (3) the urge for unity and the tradition of democratic government, and (4) the need to prevent a military threat from Germany.

The situation in Latin America during the formative period, 1948 to 1960, at first sight appears to bear some similarity to that in Western Europe.

There was an outside power which played a powerful role in the economic life of the region, and was therefore regarded with suspicion tinged with fear, owing to the memory of armed interventions in the Caribbean area. Secondly, there was the possibility of large-scale aid, which unexpectedly developed, mainly as a result of the threat of Castroism, during 1959 and the early 1960's. Thirdly, there was an affinity among the Latin American countries which enabled them to speak of a common tradition of unity, going back to the time of Simon Bolivar. While there was no internal "problem state" like Germany to be contained, there developed in the late 1950's an economic crisis which gave rise to serious difficulties and made economic integration a credible alternative to import substitution at the national level. Lastly, there were pressure groups operating both at the political level and among economists who were working for the idea of integration, whether political or economic.

However, the two situations were in fact only superficially

comparable. Apart from the major differences in the levels of development of the countries and the degrees of communication among them, the political situation in Latin America was not really parallel to that in Western Europe.

The major outside power which was looked upon with fear and suspicion could not be ejected from Latin America because of the "penetration" of the economic and political life of the country by its commercial and industrial firms.

The earlier attempt by the Latin American countries to work out a pattern of monetary integration led to protests from the IMF at the instance of the USA. Subsequently, the Latin American integration movement shifted its course to accept aid from the United States for integration, both in the Central American and LAFTA areas.

In fact, an examination of both CACM and LAFTA would indicate that the economic issues were in many cases superficial, and fundamental problems were political in nature. For example, the slow rate of progress of negotiations for reduction of tariff barriers in the LAFTA area could be ascribed to economic nationalism, or to a lack of acceptance of the bonafides of a regime which was in control of another country. Similar reasons could be found for the failure of the provisions regarding complementarity in LAFTA.

A comprehensive analysis of the political factors involved in the Latin American integration movement at the national level would be a worthwhile task. It would supplement the studies undertaken in regard to the internal situation in the Western European countries, especially the important study of Haas. However, it is possible at present only to indicate a few internal political factors which might help us to understand the international developments in regard to the LAFTA and CACM.

THE CENTRAL AMERICAN CASE: INTEGRATION, GROWTH AND DEPENDENCY

Towards the close of the Second World War, a sense of restlessness began to surface in Central American countries which was most marked in Guatemala. This country had been the seat of the Captaincy-General in colonial times and of the Federal Republic of Central America in the nineteenth century, and occupied a dominant position in the isthmus. The fall of the Ubico dictatorship in Guatemala in mid-1945 as a result of popular demonstrations was accompanied by a similar change in El Salvador and a revival of the spirit of Central American unity under the auspices of the Unionist Party. This party which had been founded by the University students in 1899 saw a close link between the unity of Central America, the ending of despotism, ignorance and exploitation, and the beginning of a "regeneration" of the region. During the thirties, the Unionist thinkers divided themselves into three lines of thought, the conservative idealism of Napoleon Viera Altamirano, the realistic idealism of Juan Jose Arevalo, and the development-oriented (*desarrollista*) views of Francisco Villagran Kramer.[1] The intellectuals in Central America retained in a certain measure the high social prestige which had been lost to their fellows in Europe and North America.[2]

There emerged during the late forties in Central America a revolutionary situation which was most markedly seen in the successful armed revolt of Jose Figueres Ferrer, founder of the Partido Social Democrata (PSD) which was later called the Partido Liberacion Nacional (PLN), of Costa Rica, against the larger forces of the leader of the ruling party, Dr. Calderon Guardia and Teodoro Picarlo. In his revolt Figueres received the support and participation of Central Americans of other countries, members of the "Legion del Caribe," and of the Guatemalan regime of Juan Jose Arevalo (1945-51). Figueres was attacked for allegedly aiding revolutionary forces of Nicaragua against the dictatorship of the Somoza family (which had either directly or indirectly controlled the state of Nicaragua since 1935), and for maintaining close ties with the Arevalo regime of Guatemala and its successor, the regime of Jacobo Arbenz (1951-53).[3] The latter regime was removed in 1954 by a military coup, aided by a counter-revolutionary force with US support, because of its alleged communist affiliations.[4]

During the 1950's it became clear that the promise of basic changes in the political systems of the Central American countries was not to be fulfilled. Even the three states which were the supposed vanguard of the movement, El Salvador, Honduras, and Guatemala, reverted to authoritarian regimes. The progressive movements stagnated in each Central American country for different reasons.[5] Figueres and his party, the PLN, became identified with the international social democratic movement, which took an increasingly anti-communist stance after the take-over of Cuba by Castro.[6]

During the 1950's there emerged a number of political leaders who were proponents of what has become known as "desarrollismo." They have been described as "descendants of Keynes, directly or through Franklin D. Roosevelt." They believed in the reform of captialism by socio-economic controls invented by Socialism; they wanted a reformed capitalism, and rejected the old US policy of protecting monopolies and the landed oligarchy. They looked to the US for assistance in their attempt to reform Latin America. The leaders of this group, Romulo Betancourt of Venezuela, Jose Figueres of Costa Rica, and Luis Munoz Marin of Puerto Rico, were identified with President Kennedy's Latin American policies, and the Alliance for Progress. The ideologues of "desarrollismo" constituted a nucleus of planners, sociologists, advocates, and especially economists and financiers who came to be known as 'tecnicos' or technocrats.

> From the ideological point of view this international and 'modern' team employs fluently Marxist terminology in its dealings with the left, and liberal terminology to win over the industrialists. Their academic training is pragmatic and, like their sources of information and techniques of work, basically Anglo-Saxon.[7]

From our examination of the Central American governments, it will be clear that the governments could not form a strong force for the integration of the Central American republics. This explains the crucial role played by the tecnicos in the integration process. Whereas the Organisation of Central American States (ODECA) was buffeted by strong political winds throughout the fifties, the meetings of Economic Ministers were marked by shirt-sleeve diplomacy. The technocrats were "marginal members of the elite" who were allowed to use their economic and technical training to futher certain economic activities which the political elite regarded as comparatively unimportant. Some of the Ministers of Economy during a crucial period in Central American integration belonged to this economic elite, and were able to isolate the economic integration process from the major political issues that disturbed the progress of the parent organisation, ODECA, which consisted of Foreign Ministers. Even the political tension between Guatemala and the rest in 1952-53, and the serious tension between Presidents Somoza of Nicaragua and Figueres of Costa Rica, did not prevent the meetings of Economic Ministers.[8]

The major actors in the integration process in the Central American countries may be classified into two groups, the internal and the external. The internal actors were the traditional landed oligarchy, the newly emerging bourgeois class, the trade unions, the political parties, and the intellectuals.

The landed interests were generally opposed to integration, but were rapidly losing ground. The interests of manufacturers and commercial interests varied according to the nature and size of their business, and their attitudes toward foreign competition. Many of them were willing to sell out to foreign investors at a profit, and this prevented the emergence of the autonomous internal development of the region by a national bourgeoisie. The political parties and trade unions tended to take a position on the basis of their political position at the right, centre or left of the political spectrum. Generally the Centre and socialist parties, many of which emerged during the ferment of 1945-48, as well as the Christian Democrats, supported integration. The parties of the Right and the extreme Left opposed integration, the former because it tended to modify the traditional power structure and the latter because it was identified with a newly emerging bourgeoisie and with US capital in the region.

Although the intellectuals played an important role in the early period, they tended to take Central American unity for granted as a desirable goal. However, they did not play a substantial role in the achievement of this goal.

The conflicts between the various interest groups could not be reconciled by the State, as was originally visualised by ECLA, because the governments in Central America were often so weak that either they were creatures of pressure groups or mortgaged to them. One of the most powerful of these pressure groups was the group of industrialists, which had the backing of the tecnicos and the Ministers of Economy.[9]

Two external actors on the Central American scene played a crucial role in giving an impetus to the process. The importance of ECLA's role in the region is clear from the early fifties.[10] Aaron Segal has stated that two external factors, US and ECLA, played an important part in ensuring the "viability" of CACM, and these factors distinguish the Central American from the East African Common Market.[11]

The combination of these two factors did not prove an unmixed blessing for Central America. ECLA's original plans for Central America provided for a "balanced development" of the region. The United States was indifferent to Central American integration in the early fifties. However, the financial aid offered by United States proved an important, perhaps the most important factor in actually bringing Central American decision makers to the conference table. US financial supports, particularly the setting up of a special Regional Office for Central America and Panama (ROCAP) also provided an important basis for the continued existence of Central American integration.[12]

The changed attitude of the United States toward Central American integration coincided with the decline in ECLA's influence. It is well known that the United States was opposed to ECLA's work in general and in particular to its "socialistic" ideas. It is significant therefore that the Tripartite Treaty between Guatemala, Honduras, and El Salvador, which gave a shock to the other two members and instigated the negotiation of the Treaty of Managua later in 1960's, was negotiated without ECLA's advice, and that the offer of US aid was a significant factor in this unexpected action of the three states. The treaty did not contain the important provision for integrated industries, which the US governments had openly opposed because it was supposed to limit competition.[13]

Although ECLA officials refrained from criticising the existence of the Tripartite Treaty, Victor Urquidi, then head of the Mexico City office of ECLA, has indicated disapproval of the absence of the provision for integrated industry.[14]

It has to be noted that the industrial integration scheme was an important part of the ECLA programme for balanced development, and given the very rudimentary nature of Central American industrialisation prior to the Managua Treaty of 1960, it should have played an important part in the development of local industry in Central America. The arguments put forth by the

US government against the scheme were refuted and the benefits of the scheme made clear. The argument that the scheme interferes with the "free play of market forces" indicated the real nature of the US opposition to the scheme. In all probability the pressures of US industrialists on Congress and on the administration, and the desire of the administration to obtain Congressional support for Central American integration, led to the insistence of the US on the abandoment of this scheme. Although the US did not take concrete action against the scheme, its statements of disapproval and the ban on lending to CABEI for this scheme proved completely adequate to render the scheme completely innocuous in the Central American context.[15]

Although the figures of exports and imports between the United States and Central American countries would seem to indicate a decline in both, thus indicating a lessening of the dependency of these countries on the United States in fact the dependency increased, owing to the vast increase in US investments in the region. Moreover the industrialisation of the region was of a capital intensive nature. The balance of payments position had worsened probably due to the import of machinery for finishing plants and import of semi-finished products and technology. The main beneficiaries of the increased industrialisation were Central American captalists and US investors. The existing power structure had not altered, and in fact the stability of the military supported regimes seems to have been strengthened. Labour intensive industry had not been fostered and the standard of living had not risen.[16]

Central American integration faced two principal difficulties in the early seventies. In the first place, the presumption of ECLA that the state would play a major role in the planning process was negatived by the fact that the governments were either too weak to resist the influence of powerful interest groups; or, were themselves identified with powerful conservative interests in the body politic.

> On the one hand the integrationist policy requires a type of dynamic activity for which the State ought to convert itself into an instrument of planning, and become the initiator and executor of many basic tasks. On the other hand it rejects planning and state intervention.[17]

The second major defect of the Central American integration process was the failure of the programme of social change which provided the original impulse for the unification movement in the 1940's, and which was based on the idea of reviving the Central American unity of the 1840's on the one hand, and the provision of greater autonomy and the reduction of dependency on the other.[18]

The tendency for integration to become an end in itself, divorced from the original goal of development, was a product of this situation. It was necessary that the basic socio-economic changes were tackled so that integration could restore its original link with the developmental process.[19]

The LAFTA Experience: From Autonomy through Imitation to Dependency

(*i*) *The Ideal of Latin American Unity*

The experience of Central America in regard to economic integration provides a fitting introduction to a study of the same question for the LAFTA area. It should be noted in the first place that LAFTA as it was constituted then included not only most of the countries in the continent of South America, but also Mexico, which was separated from the rest of the members by the Caribean and Central American countries some of which were members of CACM, while others belonged to neither group. We have seen in earlier parts of this study, LAFTA faced serious difficulties in the economic sphere. It is very difficult to justify this grouping on the basis of a high degree of political community. It is true that most of these countries constituted a part of the Spanish American Empire, but this Empire was ruled through two major Viceroyalties located in Mexico and Peru, while Brazil was under Portuguese rule. The Viceroyalty of New Granada, with jurisdiction over the northern part of South America was created in 1717. The Latin American territory thus consisted of a mumber of disparate regions which soon developed their own personality based on local variations, as Spain consisted of a number of kingdoms incorporated into the realm on the basis of equality.[20]

The liberator of the northern republics of South America, Simon Bolivar, had a grandiose scheme for combining Venezuela, Colombia and Ecuador in a state to be called Gran Colombia. But this amibition came to nought, as did his later attempt to set up a permanent organisation of the Latin American Countries at the Congress of Panama in 1826.[21]

Inspite of the failure of Bolivar's first attempt to create a sense of unity among the Latin American countries, some of which were his own creation, the idea of Latin American unity has continued to haunt the minds of thinkers and writers to the present day. Among those who kept the idea alive were Andres Bello, an educator and man of letters who was Bolivar's tutor; D.F. Sarmiento, a liberal reformer who was President of Argentina for several years from 1868; Jose Marti, a Cuban revolutionary and national hero killed by the Spanish shortly before the Spanish American War of 1898 which liberated Cuba from Spanish rule; Jose Enrique Rodo an Uruguayan essayist whose *Ariel* was probably the most influential book written by a Latin American author; and Ruben Dorio, the Nicaraguan poet. In 1862 a Society for American Union was formed, with members from many countries.[22]

During the 1920's the idea of Latin American unity received a considerable impetus with the rise in anti-imperialist sentiment. The Peruvian political movement known as APRA (Alianza Popular Reuolucionaria Americana) provided a set of ideas in justification of the political and economic unification of Latin America to counter the US dominance. The Mexican revolution, with its stress on the "indigenista" traditions of the pre-Hisponic past, provided a further sense of distinction from the United States and a bond among the countries of Latin America (or Indo America, as APRA called it).[23]

Inspite of the fact that there was a long tradition of Latin American unity which provided a background in which the movement for economic integration has operated, it cannot be said in regard to the LAFTA area that there was a strong political urge which provided the base for economic integration. In this respect, the situation has to be contrasted with that in Central America where, at the end of the Second World War the collapse of authoritarian regimes gave a new impetus to the idea of Central American unity under the anspices of the liberal reformers of the Unionist Party.

In order to understand this difference, two significant factors should be noticed. First of all, the Central American countries had constituted a single unit in the early nineteenth century although it subsequently broke up into a number of small states. Secondly, even if Central America had been reunited politically, it would have been one of the smaller Latin American states with a population approximately comparable to Colombia. Even a superficial comparison between the political situation in Central America and in the LAFTA area will immediately indicate the great differences in regard to the political urge for unity. Latin American countries inspite of their literary movements and similar background were not characterised by any strong urge for political unity. Considering the size of many of the countries, the lack of communications and the many divisive factors which operated on the Latin American scene, this is hardly surprising. What is surprising is that an atmosphere could be built up which enabled some observers to think that there was a strong urge for unity which could be used to further the economic integration of the area as a whole.

(ii) The Political Situation in the LAFTA Countries

In order to understand the circumstances in which the concept of political unity was converted into that of economic integration we will have to look deeper into the political situation in the LAFTA area. The analysis of these factors will also throw much light on the politics of the economic integration movement and enable us to examine some of its strong and weak points.

It is possible to quote statements of the various governments in the favour of integration,[24] but it is necessary to consider these in the light of the internal political situation of each country. This is in keeping with the general proposition that the foreign policy of most Latin American countries is an extension of their domestic policies, serves the interests of internal elites, and is directed more toward preserving the social order than toward serving the national well-being in the abstract.[25]

In this connection we are faced with the dilemma which has troubled many students of Latin American affairs: to what extent is it justified to consider developments in the various countries as a pattern? Some Latin Americans deny that such comparisons are meaningful, pointing to the separate development of each of their countries and arguing that the countries are developing in different ways. There is some truth in this view. It is unwise to assume that institutions in different countries have the same significance, even though the terminology used may be similar. Nevertheless it cannot be denied that there have been common influences working on the countries of the region from outside, such as the impact of the Positivist ideas from France in the nineteenth century and the American and Soviet influences in the twentieth century. Moreover, as we have noted already, a common set of ideas had arisen in relation to the concept of Latin American unity. Many Latin American intellectuals have lived in countries of the region other than their own during political exile; and consciously or unconsciously, there seems to be a tendency to imitate institutions, customs and habits in other countries of the area. Thus some basic similarities in the economic pattern and social structure are supported by contacts among the elites which enable us to speak of a common Latin American pattern, although considerable allowance has to be made for local variations in different countries and within each country.

The traditional political parties in many Latin American countries were the liberals and the conservatives, which originated out of the anti-clerical and clerical sections of the old ruling classes. The influence of European political movements is seen in the existence of Radical and Social Democratic parties, modelled on those in France or elsewhere in Europe. The Christian Democratic parties, which gained importance during the 1950's, especially in Venezuela and Chile, continue this tradition of European influence.

Most Latin American political systems are a product of local conditions and of the impact on these local conditions of ideas imported from abroad. The traditional police state of Latin America owed much to the tradition of Caudillismo, a kind of authoritarian dictatorship headed by a strong man with a strong rural or military base.

The twentieth century has given rise to two or three new types of political parties. The first is the Partido Revolucionario Institutional (PRI) of Mexico, which has been for all practical purposes a one party state since about 1930. Although it has a monopoly of power, PRI is not dominated by a single individual for any prolonged period of time. The President cannot succeed himself and the party provides for representation to various sectors of society.

A number of parties appear to be modelled on the APRA party of Peru, founded originally as an international party working for Latin American unity, APRA was later forced to confine itself to Peru. It was, however, imitated by other parties, such as the Accion Democratica of Venezuela, the Movimiento Nacionalista Revolutioniaro (MNR) of Bolivia, and other parties in Costa Rica and Puerto Rico. These parties, although generally anti-American during the 1930's and 1940's, tended to accept American influence during the 1950's and early 1960's, as has been mentioned in the previous section of this chapter when discussing developments in Central America.

Another type of political party which emerged during the 1940's and 1950's is based on what may be called Populism. The two most important leaders of this trend were Peron of Argentina (1946-52) and Vargas of Brazil (1930-45 and 1951-54). Both Vargas and Peron are said to have been influenced by Mussolini's Corporate State, but both were pragmatic and innovative with roots in the native soil. Both gave importance to the working class and tried to reduce the power of foreign enterprise in their respective countries. They had an influence on the thinking of political leaders in other parts of Latin America.

Lastly, we may mention the parties of the extreme Left. The traditional Communist parties of Latin America were, ironically enough, not revolutionary forces, and had little success in capturing popular support, although the party in Chile was a partial exception. The influence of Fidel Castro on the Latin American countries was revolutionary precisely because he broke away from the rigid party discipline of the Communist parties, and injected an element of dynamism which had hitherto been absent.

As we have seen, political developments in Latin America during the 1950's were moving away from the traditional military dictatorship toward a pattern of liberal regimes which were interested in using American aid for the economic development of their countries.[26] Let us observe this trend with reference to the member countries of LAFTA.

In Brazil, Vargas was deposed by a military coup in 1945

which tried to establish a constitutional regime. However, Vargas was elected President in 1950 with strong labour support. Vargas shot himself in August 1954. After a short interregnum, Juscelinio Kubitschek, a liberal who enjoyed the support of Vargas' followers became President in January 1956. During his Presidency, which lasted till 1961, Kubitschek gave an impetus to economic planning and development, and started the construction of the new capital in the interior, Brasilia. He was followed by two radical Presidents, Janio Goulart, who raised the hopes of the people for reform, but these hopes ended in frustration. Quadros resigned a few months after taking office in August 1961, and Goulart was removed by a military coup in 1964, which replaced him by Marshal Castelo Branco.[27] In March 1967 Marshal Artur de Costa e Silva took over as President, but in August 1969 he resigned. Under the new Constitution promulgated in October 1969, the first election since 1966 was held in November 1970. The government's National Renewal Alliance (ARENA) defeated the Brazilian Democratic Movement (MDB), the official Opposition. Though ARENA won overwhelmingly, the legitimacy of the government was doubtful if one took into consideration the invalid votes which amounted to 30-50 per cent of the total votes cast. Also the government's action against the opponents came under severe strictures by International Heads. Thus Pope Paul VI in October 1970 denounced the strong arm tactics of Brazilian government.

Argentina had been governed during the 1930's by a series of undistinguished Presidents who enabled British and American capital to strengthen their position in the country. Public opinion tended to favour the Germans in World War II because Argentina had experienced the exploitation of the British and the Americans, but not of the Germans. When the military coup of 1943 deposed the civilian President Castillo, Colonel Juan Peron began to prepare the way for a takeover with the help of the labour unions and his future wife, Eva Duarte. By his strong support of labour and his policy of economic nationalism, he built up Argentina as a bulwark against the foreign interests who had dominated it. But his policies led to financial chaos and he did not move against the powerful industrialists and the landowning class of Argentina. His regime began to cave in from lack of internal support and he was deposed by a military coup in 1955. However, even in exile he continued to exercise considerable influence through the trade unions which he continued to control from his exile in Madrid.[28]

The provisional governments of Generals Lonardi and Aramburu succeeded Peron in 1955. General Aramburu continued in office till 1958, when elections were held, which gave power to a Radical politician, Arturo Frondizi. During the four years he held office, Frondizi was unable to implement his economic programme of making Argentina self-sufficient in steel; he succeeded only in adding to the inflation and thus hitting the masses. His poltical machinations were no more successful. Abandoning his own Radical party, Frondizi clamped down on civil rights and tried to play off the Peronist labour unions against the military. After twenty-three minor uprisings against him had failed, he was deposed in 1962.[29]

Frondizi was succeeded by Dr. Jose Guido as provisional President. In the elections of 1963, Dr. Arturo Illia, a mild-mannered medical doctor was elected President. Within a month of taking office, he fulfilled his election pledge by nationalising the foreign oil interests. But after that his government had become too slow and inefficient to survive, and was ultimately overthrown by the army late in June 1966. The immediate cause of his overthrow seems to have been a fear that he was negotiating with the Peronists. He was succeeded by General Ongania, who promptly dissolved Congress, the provincial legislatures, the Supreme Court, and the political parties.[30]

General Ongania, however, did not last long. He was deposed in June 1970 and was followed by Brigadier General Robert Marcelo Levingston, who was also ousted in a bloodless coup in March 1971. General Alegandre Augustin Lenusse then came to power. He tried for a national reconciliation with Peron who was living in exile in Spain. However, the breakdown of law and order continued and the civilian President, Dr. Hector Campora, who took office in May 1973, invited Peron to return and the latter became President once more in October that year with his wife Isabel as Vice-President.

Only one of the three major countries to enjoy a stable political life was Mexico. The Mexican Revolution received a considerable impetus during the Presidency of General Cardenas from 1934 to 1940. He laid stress on rural schools and stepped up the pace of land reforms considerably. In 1938 he took over the petroleum industry from the foreign corporations. However from the time of his successor, Manuel Avila Camacho (1940-46), the governments shifted the emphasis from land reform to agricultural productivity and industrialisation. A new industrial bourgeoisie, largely dependent on US investment, began to grow up. During the period 1958 to 1964 President Adolfo Lopez Mateos attempted to move towards the Left within the Constitution but this effort was frustrated, and his successor, Gustavo Diaz Ordaz (1964-70), moved back to the Centrist policies of the past.[31] The 1968 Olympic games were held in Mexico City in October and were accompanied by violent workers and student demonstrations against the Government. Luis Echeverria Alvarez won the presidential elections of 1970. He established diplomatic links with Third World countries, and was keen to considerably reduce economic dependence on the United States.

Among the middle countries of Latin America, Chile enjoyed fair stability. President Ibanez was replaced in November 1958 by Jorge Alessandri, who continued in office till November 1964 when he was replaced by Eduardo Frei, the Christian Democratic leader. Neither Allssandri nor Frei was able to tackle effectively the need for drastic land reform and the rising inflation in the country.[32] In the election of September 1970, Dr. Salvador Allende Gossens, the Marxist candidate of Unidad Popular, a coalition of five Left-wing parties, including the Communist Party, was elected President. Nationalisation, agrarian reforms, and more government control over foreign trade characterised Dr. Allende's rule. The country suffered acute shortages of many basic foodstuffs and consumer goods. Thus in 1972 the Government faced a deteriorating economic situation adding fuel to a turbulent political uneasiness. On 11 September 1973 President Allende was deposed by the military and Carabineros (para-military forces).

Colombia had emerged from ten years of *violencia* (a period of large-scale guerilla and bandit activity of a semi-political type), only in the end of 1957. According to a political formula approved by national plebiscite, the Conservative and Liberal parties were to alternate in high political offices for twelve years. Alberto Lleras Camargo became President in 1958. He was succeeded by the Conservative Guillermo Leon Valencia in 1962 and another Liberal, Carlos Lleras Restrepo, followed in 1966. Political divisions, inflationary pressures, an economic crisis due to the weak price of coffee in the world market, and guerrilla activity marked the period 1962-66.[33] In August 1970 Lleras Restrepo completed his four year term. Dr. Misael Pastrana Borrero of the Conservative Party was elected President by a very small majority over General Rojas. Dr. Pastrana was forced not only to face the formidable opposition of Generals Rojas and his supporters, but also the warring faction of his own partymen. However in 1972 the two main factions within the Liberal Party agreed to unite their forces.

Venezuela emerged from the military dictatorship of Perez Jimenez in January 1958. Romulo Betancourt of the Accion Democratica Party was President of a coalition government from 1959 to 1964 when he was succeeded by Raul Leoni of the same party.[34] In 1966, supporters of ex-President Perez staged an abortive military uprising. After Dr. Leoni completed his five-year term in 1960, Dr Rajael Caldera Rodriguez got elected as Venezuela's first Christian Democratic President. Though Dr. Rodriguez was in control of the economy, to some extent, the political assassinations and abductions went unabated. In the election of December 1973, Carlos Andres Perez Rodriguez, candidate of Accion Democratica, the main Opposition party, was chosen President.

Peru was ruled by the dictatorship of General Manuel Odria from 1948 to 1956. Dr. Manuel Prado was President from 1956 to 1962 when he was deposed. The elections of 1962 were annulled and an architect, Fernando Belaunde Terry, became President in 1962.[35] He was removed by a military coup in 1968. General Velasco Aluarado became President of the revolutionary government and he aimed at a complete structural transformation of the country.

Bolivia was ruled by a revolutionary regime between 1952 and 1964; but the President, Victor Paz Estenssoro, moved gradually to the Right and lost the support of his own followers. He was replaced by a military revolt in October 1964 by General Barrientos, and Bolivia has undergone several changes of regime since then.[36] In fact, General Barrientos had to share power with General Ovando Canida as Joint President for a while before the latter replaced him for an interim period of around eight months in 1966. General Barrientos became the Constitutional President in August 1966. But he got killed in an air accident in 1969, when, therefore, the then Vice-President Dr. Siles Salinas succeeded to the presidency. In September Gen. Ovando Candia assumed power by coup d'etat and established a Left wing military government. He antagonised the United States and the Right wing very much. In 1970 Gen. Torres Gonzales emerged as President after a military coup. Gen. Torres allowed a People's Assembly inclined to socialism to meet. The disquietened Right wing nationalists and the military ousted Gen. Torres in favour of Gen. Banzer in August 1971 as the 58th President in 146 years. During 1972 cracks developed within the Right wing ruling coalition and many members of the MNR (Movimiento Nacionalista, Revolucionario) were arrested. In 1973 President Bauzer "promised" an imminent return to constitutional government. The Church meanwhile joined hands with the Left and the labourers to give a difficult time to Gen. Banzer.

Ecuador has been dominated by Jose Maria Velasco Ibarra who was President five times, most recently in 1952-56, 1960-61 (withdrew) and 1968-72 (deposed). Galo Plaza was President from 1948-52 and Camilo Ponce Enriquez from 1956-60. Ecuador went through a period of chaos between 1965-66.[37] In February 1972 Velasco Ibarra was deposed by the armed forces, and this event ushered in the era of Brigadier General Guillermo Rodriguez Lara.

Uruguay, called the first welfare state in Latin America enjoyed a fair degree of stability under a constitutional regime but there has been considerable disaffection with the regime in recent years, as is clear from success of the armed urban guerrillas known as the Tupamaros, in their disruptive activities.[38] In order to supress the Tupamaros, in April 1972, under the then civilian President Juan Maria Bordaberra Arocena of Colorados (Liberals), promulgated a law declaring a "state of internal war" under the full control of the Army. In the process, the President became a puppet in the hands of the Army. In June 1973 Congress got dissolved. In December 1973, a 25-member Council of State, a new legislature, was appointed.

The Army was thus well entrenched.

Paraguay has enjoyed the doubtful benefits of a military dictatorship of one man, General Stroessner, since 1954.[39] He was re-elected as Colorado candidate in 1958, 1966, and 1973 too.

Before proceeding to an analysis of the forces working for and against integration in the LAFTA area, it has to be noted that the Latin American political systems were subject, in varying degrees, to "penetration" in the economic, military, political, and cultural spheres, by US and to a lesser extent, by European interests. The result of this penetration was that local pressure groups aligned with foreign interests or foreign powers, tend to prevent the development of independent foreign policies, not withstanding the power of the state embodied in the Presidency. During the early sixties, two major Latin American countries, Argentina and Brazil, attempted to coordinate their foreign policies in the direction of greater independence of the United States. This culminated in the famous episode at the OAS meeting of Foreign Ministers at Punta del Este, Uruguay, in January 1962, when six Latin American countries opposed the proposal to exclude Cuba from the OAS. These six countries were Argentina, Bolivia, Brazil, Chile, Ecuador, and Mexico. Between them they represented two-thirds of the population of Latin America. The fall of Frondizi in Argentina in 1962 and of Goulart in Brazil in 1964 have been traced partially to the loss of internal support caused by their shift in foreign policy as symbolised by their vote at Punta del Este. Mexico, on the other hand, followed a more cautious policy of adjusting its views to those of the United States.[40]

The leaders of the Centrist political parties were faced with the dilemma of either moving to the Left and implementing radical measures like land reform, or of accepting American aid for their administration, which would enable them to retain the support of important interest groups in the country. Most leaders chose the latter path; some of those who chose the former paid for it by losing power, and were replaced by military or Right wing regimes which were more amenable to the powerful interest groups and to US influence.[41]

(iii) Actors in the Integration Process

During the 1930's and 1940's, a number of political parties with ideas of some kind of "continental nationalism" and with a stress on socialistic and anti-imperialist policies emerged, including the Aprista Party of Peru, the Accion Democratica of Venezuela, the Febreristas of Paraguay, the MNR of Bolivia, and the revolutionary parties of Guatemala and the Dominican Republic.[42] In the 1950's these parties were further strengthened by the rise of Christian Democratic parties.

The Christian Democratic Movement which owes its inspiration to the inspiration of a similar movement in Europe, bases its philosophy on the papal encyclicals and the liberal Catholicism of writers like Jacques Maritain. Their devotion to the cause of Latin American integration seems to be based first of all on their belief in the value of the individual human being, as against the devotion to the State and their consequent stress on constitutionalism and internationalism; secondly, on the European example, where Christian Democrats like Konrad Adenauer of Germany, Alcide de Gasperi of Italy, and Robert Schuman of France, and Christian Democrat parties in Holland and Belgium played an important role; and thirdly on the personal contact with integrationist sentiments of ECLA economists. Eduardo Frei, who became President of Chile in 1964, embodied in himself all these influences and was able to provide a focus for the integrationist sentiment at the political level at a crucial period.[43]

The activities of social democratic social parties of the APRA type and Christian Democratic parties on a continental level led to the creation of a Latin American Parliament, which was decided to be set up at Lima in December 1964, when delegates from thirteen countries met, representing not the governments but the national parliament of Argentina, Brazil, Colombia, Costa Rica, Chile, El Salvador, Guatemala, Nicaragua, Panama, Paraguay, Peru, Uruguay, and Venezuela. The creation of the Parliament followed a proposal by the VI Congress of the Christian Democratic Organisation (ODCA) at Caracas in May 1964 to set up a parliament, Councils of Ministers of Economy and Education, and a Latin American Court of Justice.[44]

The idea of a Latin American Parliament was evidently

modelled on the Council of Europe at Strasbourg which also represents a federal rather than a confederal approach to European unity. However, the frequent changes of regimes in Latin American countries has led to anomalous situations whereby the Parliament sometimes seats representatives of legislative bodies which have been dismissed by military coups d'etat.

The location of the Parliament at Lima was evidently a tribute to the background of APRA'S interest in Latin American unity. However, there seems little possibility of it becoming a nucleus of future growth of a federal type in Latin America.

The main actors in the integration process at the national level were politicians, industrialists, and tecnicos. A Mexican Commercial Mission which visited eight countries in South America between July and September 1964, found that while all three groups were excited at the prospect of building LAFTA, there were differences of opinion as to the way in which this should be done.

The mechanisms established were insufficient and reforms were necessary. While the tecnicos held politicians responsible for lack of support, politicians blamed industrialists for putting a brake on more effective measures. The industrialists blamed the tecnicos for suggesting radical solutions. This vicious circle created a gulf between the "generally" favorable attitude to economic integration, and the actual attitudes in the face of urgent problems to be solved.[45] At the international level, as we have seen in part (a) of this chapter, the major forces working in the integration process were the three groups of countries, i.e. (1) the three major countries, (2) the middle countries like Chile, Peru and Colombia, and (3) the least developed countries, like Ecuador and Paraguay.

The international economic organisations also functioned at the international level, directed mainly by international economists and tecnicos.

(*iv*) *Motives of the Actors*

Thus the main actors in the Latin American integration movement were member-governments and international organisations at the international level, and tecnicos, politicians, and industrialists at the national level. It is necessary to consider the motives of the principal actors in the Latin American integration process.

First of all, as we have noted earlier, Latin American unity was not put forward seriously by anyone as a goal of the integration movement. In fact, during the 1920's and 1930's there was a shift from a political to an economic approach to Latin American integration. However, during the 1960's, according to Lagos, the different schools of thought began to converge, and there was a kind of synthesis of the economic, political and intellectual aspects of integration.[46] One cannot avoid feeling that the economists who prepared the Report of the Four were thinking in terms of some kind of long-term political goal, whether federal or confederal methods were to be applied to this goal. The speeches of Felipe Herrera during this period convey the same impression, and it is clear that the European example of achieving political goals through economic means had influenced them greatly. This is not to say, however, that politicians were influenced by such concepts. Most of them used integration to serve their personal or national goals.

The second possible object of the integrationists would be the pursuit of prestige, power, and influence. This is an important factor which evidently influenced not only the economists but the politicians and probably the elites of Latin America as well. The assertion of Latin America's autonomy against the United States has been a long standing demand of Latin American statesmen.

However, the solidarity of Latin America was weakened by the fact that Latin American countries often competed with one another for US favours, and secondly, that the ruling elites were the ones who benefited most from links with the United States. Closely connected with the pursuit of prestige, power, and influence is the desire for an improved position in world trade, and increased trade within Latin America. This was something on which almost all power groups could agree.

Another motivating factor was the desire for economic growth and development, a goal which went back to the Prebisch thesis with its stress on industrialisation as a basic need of the peripheral countries.

A fourth reason for taking up integration was the importance of social change and economic distribution. Although the Prebisch thesis included the concept in its argument, it was not stressed till much later, and there were powerful groups who rejected it or sought to underplay it.[47]

(v) *The Demand for Acceleration: From the Treaty of Montevideo to the Summit of Punta del Este*

We have already noted the crucial role played by the economists and international organisations in the creation of the Latin American Free Trade Area. It has also been noted that Prebisch had published a study in 1964 in which he had expressed dissatisfaction with the achievements of LAFTA, which he wanted strengthened.[48] In fact the ECLA economists had been unhappy with the Montevideo Treaty from the beginning. They regarded it as a poor substitute for the Latin American Common Market which was their goal.

The concern of the new President of Chile and the leading technocrats of Latin America coincided in 1964 when President Frei asked four economists, all of them already associated closely with the integration movements, to report on the state of Latin American integration movement. Their report, as we have seen, called for an acceleration of the integration process and a four-fold institutional system, consisting of a Bank for Latin American Integration, a Latin American Parliament with the Lima Parliament as a nucleus, a Council of Ministers with a permanent executive board, and a Latin American Court of Justice. The significance of the Report of the Four lies in the fact that the economists, who had till then remained in the background, came out publicly and stated not only that Latin American integration could not succeed without political decisions, but even recommended institutions which could be seen as steps toward the creation of federal institutions for Latin America. In other words, they gave up the functionalist strategy for a frontal attack on the question of sovereignty, i.e. for a federal approach.

It is not surprising that the proposals for stronger political, legal, and parliamentary institutions were not accepted. But the key to the question of an accelerated approach to a common market was the setting up of an institutional basis which would have provided day-to-day guidance for the whole scheme. The collapse of this proposal at the preliminary stages of negotiations for the Punta del Este meetings meant in practice that the decisions at the meetings were doomed to oblivion—because the

Declaration of the Presidents, for all its high-sounding declarations, had no legal and binding force.

The executive board proposal in the Report of the Four was evidently modelled on that of the High Commission of the European Economic Community at Brussels. It should be noted that about this time the EEC went through one of the worst crises of its history. General de Gaulle rejected both the functionalist and federal approaches to European unity and asserted the confederal approach, based on the continuance of a "Europe des parties."[49]

Thus the lesson of the European experience for Latin American integration is that the original idea that one action in the economic field would give rise to another, and there would be a spill-over also from the economic to the political field, has to be given up. The functionalist strategy has to take account of what Haas has later called the "dramatic-political" aims of statesmen as against the functionalist strategy of incremental economic goals.[50]

The rupture between the political and technical elites in Europe was clear in July 1965. The assumption that an economic strategy would lead to political decision-making turned out to be incorrect in the case of Europe. How much more incorrect was this view in Latin America, where the EEC had been taken as the model? One of the principal protagonists of Latin American integration, Gustavo Lagos, has drawn two conclusions from the European experience: (1) that it shows the risks of an integration process which does not incorporate in its project common policies in the industrial, financial, foreign investment, scientific, and technological fields; (2) that it has to be recognised that Latin America is in an initial stage of a regional common market.

It is unfortunate that this realisation did not dawn on the protagonists of Latin American integration between 1964 and 1967, when there was still time to alter the basic pattern of Latin American integration. The high hopes which were raised by the Report of the Four, the speeches of Felipe Herrera and other protagonists of Latin American integration, and finally the summit meeting of Punta del Este were instrumental to some extent in devaluing the concept of integration in the public mind.

The internal situation in each country was different, but the political leaders who went to Punta del Este were not in a position to make any positive commitments for integration either due to lack of sympathy or due to internal weaknesses of the regime. Probably each had a good reason for going to Punta del Este—to strengthen his internal postiion, to obtain US aid, or simply to avoid being left out.

When President Belaunde of Peru commented after the Declaration of Presidents was approved, "The score is a good one; now everything depends on how we play the music,"[51] he did not realise how soon the personnel of the orchestra would be changed. Moreover there are difficulties involved in an orchestra playing a piece of music without a conductor. When the Presidents failed to set up an adequate machinery to implement their decisions, there was little chance of effective results.

Techniques in the Integration Process: The Mexican Case

We have now to consider some of the methods used to further integration and the results of the policies adopted. As we have seen in the Central American case, the attitudes of traders and industrialists to the changing situation varies according to their type of business. Moreover they tend to be conservative in their attitudes to change.

Schmitter and Hass pointed out that "the Mexican government had to expend considerable effort to sell a skeptical and reluctant business community on the idea of regional integration." This was done effectively by the tecnicos who "launched a series of conferences and round table discussions in the Fall of 1959, designed to convince private businessmen that they had everything to gain and nothing to lose by participating in LAFTA . . ." They concluded that "Mexico's decision to join LAFTA was a future-oriented decision by a restricted political and technical elite."[52] However the results of the first three years of LAFTA showed "the tendency for Mexican intrazonal trade to develop in a *non-reciprocal* manner."[53] Mexico became one of the most conservative members of LAFTA because she was able to achieve her immediate objectives of expanding trade even without the full scale achievement of a common market.[54]

The role of the tecnicos in convincing the industrialists of the necessity of economic integration therefore tended to defeat its own purpose, while the object was to expedite the creation of a common market, the very success of Mexican export-drive in Latin America, and the surplus enjoyed by the country led to a sense of complacency. Moreover, some sectors of the Mexican economy strongly opposed a lowering of tariff barriers. The presence of foreign capital in Mexico which had a tendency to take the main benefit from regional integration, and the fact that import substitution at a national level had not adequately exhausted itself, contrary to ECLA's claims, were other factors which discouraged Mexico from taking a strong stand in support of regional integration.

The favourable balance of trade which Mexico enjoyed both with ALALC and Central America had been expanding since 1960. Konig argued that Mexico was experiencing a conflict between two positions, one "commercialists-exportadora" and the other "desarrollista-integracionista." The former was identified with groups linked to the traditional agricultural and export-oriented economy, while the latter focused on economic development, favored state intervention and looked to the long term benefits of economic integration. While the benefits of the second view had yet to be proved, he suspected that the main objection to regional integration was the fear of opening up the economy to foreign competition. Those who held this view forgot the contribution which regional integration can make to the improvement of distribution of the national income and the economic and social benefits which would ensue."[55]

The techniques adopted by the proponents of integration in ECLA during the period before the signature of the Montevideo Treaty have been described as follows:[56] (1) the maintenance of a close link between industrialisation and integration; (2) the recruitment of allies at the national level; this activity was jokingly described as an infiltration of state governments by an "Integration Mafia"; (3) stressing those aspects of the program which were more acceptable, e.g. the stress on the "non-political" and "technical" nature of the project and de-emphasis on plan harmonization, which was earlier regarded by ECLA as an important part of its programme; (4) capturing all the options. Prebisch and ECLA were supposed to have two alternative plans, one for the Southern cone countries, and the second for Latin America as a whole. The first was said to have been used as a weapon to win support for the latter.

Judging by the Mexican case, the tecnicos at the national level also adopted techniques comparable to those of the ECLA economists. In order to obtain the support of Mexican industrialists for the Montevideo Treaty, they appear to have explained it in terms of the interests of the industrialists for expanding exports, and soft-pedalled its wider implications. This was probably an important factor in the subsequent reluctance of the Mexican industrialists to reduce tariff barriers and take other steps to convert the treaty into a genuine free trade area. The tecnicos at the state level tried to serve two masters, their national interests and integration. In this they had to seek allies, and this was not always an easy task. While they received important support from heavy industry and raw materials producers, especially in the Southern cone countries. there was a large "silent group" consisting of trade unions and some politicians in high places. There was also an element that was opposed to integration, like investors in light and medium industries, and large agricultural interests. This opposition would not always be stated openly. They would often agree "in principle" and then qualify their agreement.[57]

The Crisis is Integration and the Demand for Sub-Regionalism

Although the limited results of the efforts of the international tecninos were seen in the weakness of the Montevideo Treaty, there emerged, as a by-product of LAFTA, a number af international interest groups, in the form of associations of manufacturers and international workers' organisations, which could be expected to play an increasingly important role in the creation of a regional consciousness and the gradual building up of the integration process.[58]

As has been noted,[59] there was a shift in the centre of international integration activity from ECLA to LAFTA, but LAFTA in this respect faced competition from the other organisations in the field, including the IDB, and OAS, and in some respects UNCTAD.

Inspite of the provisions in the Montevideo Treaty for the

equalisation of benefits, there was a marked trend towards the concentration of benefits in the three major countries, which gave rise in turn to the demand for special treatment not only by the most backward countries like Ecuador and Paraguay, but even by the middle-sized members, Chile, Colombia, Peru, and Venezuela.

The crisis which was evident in LAFTA in 1964 gave rise to two sets of actions—the first, which we have already discussed, was the demand for a rapid acceleration of the integration process which culminated in the Declaration of Punta del Este. The second effect was a sharpening of the dissatisfaction by middle countries and their initiative for the setting up of a separate sub-regional agreement to deal with the problems of the Andean countries.

It will be recalled that there was an attempt to set up sub-regional groupings in Latin America during the 1950's, but this attempt was given up due to the feeling that Latin American solidarity would be broken up by smaller groupings, i.e. primarily for political rather than economic reasons. When the failure of the Common List preparations became obvious, five Andean countries, Colombia, Chile, Ecuador, Peru, and Bolivia, took the initiative and proposed the establishment of separate sub-regional arrangements for themselves. The basis for a sub-regional agreement and norms for sub-regional agreements in general were approved somewhat grudgingly as a "transitory" measure by the Foreign Ministers of LAFTA in September 1967.[60]

The Andean group was set up as a result of the Treaty of Cartogena in 1969. The demand for sub-regionalism in general was strengthened by the failure of the three large countries to take the necessary steps to carry on the integration process. They saw LAFTA as a means of improving their foreign trade and their balance of payments position rather than of furthering economic integration. We have seen this clearly in the Mexican case. This position was "recognised and consecrated" by the Caracas Protocol in December 1969, which postponed the implementation of the common list of products, and reduced the obligations of member-countries for tariff cuts.

In view of the fact that President Frei of Chile was the initiator of the actions which gave rise to Punta del Este summit of 1967, it is interesting to note that Chile was also one of the chief sponsors of the Andean agreement. This was because of its disillusionment with the role of the higher countries, which it regarded as interested in preserving the status quo, while Chile and other countries were anxious to achieve a common market which would enable them to industrialise rapidly. Since the first position was imposed on LAFTA, the smaller countries were forced to enter into a separate agreement for the solution of their common problems.[61]

The objects of the Andean Pact were as much political as they were economic. The disappointments with the results of LAFTA were parallelled by a suspicion of the motives of the larger countries in the political sphere, although these fears were not openly expressed. For example, Chile has always feared Argentina's position as a greater power of the Southern cone, and the Northern Andean group countries tend to fear the possible move of Brazil toward the Pacific. The possibility of building up the Andean bloc as a practical-cum-economic force cannot be excluded. However, there are many difficulties in the way of such a development. The per capita income of Venezuela is much higher than that of the other Andean countries and she joined the Pact only in February 1973 as she was reluctant for a long time to accept the controversial Decision 24, according to which foreign owned enterprises have to be converted into mixed companies by 1986. Venezuela was granted exemption from tariff cuts for a long list of 450 products which would have to be free of all duty only by 1985 and not be subjected to annual 10 per cent tariff reductions.

There were old rivalries among the countries of the group, such as those between Ecuador and Peru, and Peru and Chile. The regimes of the countries were following widely different political and economic systems. Chile (till 1973) and Peru took a negative attitude to foreign investment, while Colombia, Bolivia, and to some extent, Ecuador took a positive view. The coordination of policies became a difficult task in these circumstances.

If in spite of these differences the Andean countries were able to hold together as a group, in spite of the many obstacles that faced them, they could show the way to sub-regional groups in other parts of Latin America and elsewhere in the Third World. They would also be able eventually to negotiate a fuller Latin American integration agreement with the three major countries of Latin America from a position of strength.[62]

Political developments during the 1950's and early 1960's were moving away from traditional military dictatorship towards a path of liberal regimes. These regimes were generally favourably disposed to economic integration which they considered as a desirable goal partly for economic reasons and partly because of their interest in furthering political cooperation in Latin America and solidarity against outside forces.

In the yearly sixties the regimes of Frondizi in Argentina and Goulart in Brazil fell. During the period from 1965 till 1975 there was a reversion to the earlier trend of military dictatorship.

In 1973, Brazil was under a military President Emilio Garrastazu Medici, since October 1969. Argentina had gone through a period of military rule since 1966, and Peron was recalled from Spain by the civilian President, Dr. Campora. In Chile the Marxist regime of Dr. Salvador Allende was overthrown by a military coup. Bolivia had been ruled by a Right wing military government under Colonel Hugo Banzer Suarez since August 1971. The civilian government of Ecuador had been overthrown by General Rodriguez Lara in February 1972. Paraguay had been controlled by General Stroessner since 1954. Peru was under Left wing military rule since the overthrow of Belaunde in 1968, with General Alvarado as President. Even traditionally democratic Uruguay had a military-supported civilian regime under Bordaberry since June 1973.

Of the major countries of Latin America, only Mexico, Argentina, Colombia, and Venezuela were functioning under constitutionally established civilian regimes.

We have seen that the politics of the Latin America favoured the Integration Movement in the late 1950's and early 1960's because of the nature of the regimes which ruled a large number of Latin American countries at that time. The reformist ideas, which characterised the liberal regimes of Argentina, Brazil, and Chile were also reflected in the regimes of Colombia, Venezuela, Peru, Mexico, and Costa Rica. The Christian Democratic Movement of Europe influenced Chile, and the concept of Latin American unity nurtured by APRA, part of Peru found expression in the setting up of a Latin American Parliament in Lima in 1964.

The economic compulsions of the situation, however, were such that Latin American countries were unable to maintain the same commitment to integration as they had done earlier. The attempt by President Frei of Chile to revitalise the movement by an injunction of urgency through the Report of the Four (which recommended not only a Latin American Bank, but also political institutions like a Parliament, an executive and a court) was unsuccessful. The summit of Punta del Este passed high sounding resolutions but did not lead to concrete results. Our examination of the Mexican case showed that the internal factors in a country are decisive in determining its attitude to integration.

Towards the end of the sixties, the crises in integration led to a revival of the demand for sub-regional economic cooperation. Of the two important attempts in this direction, CARIFTA and the Andean Pact, we have examined the latter and found that although it had a clear focus and limited goals it faced difficulties in the early years because of the unequal benefits expected by its members, and the reluctance of Venezuela to join without special concessions, which were finally made in 1973. The outlook for Latin American integration was therefore largely negative in 1973. LAFTA had ceased to be a major force and the sub-regional alternative had not made a substantial impact. The failure of political will was seen everywhere including to some extent in the Andean countries.

REFERENCES

1 Mario Monteforte Toledo, "Los intelectuales y la integracicn centroamericana," *Revista Mexicana de Sociologia* (October-December 1967), pp. 844-5.

2 Ibid., p. 846.

3 Ulrich Fanger, "Costa Rica," in Claudio Veliz, ed., *Latin America and the Caribbean: A Handbook of Documents* (New York, 1968), p. 180. Suzanne Bodenheimer, "La crisis del movimien to social democrata an America Latina," *Estudices Internationals* (January-March 1970) pp. 551-53.

4 See *supra*, pp. 35-6. See also Alberto Fuentes Mohr, "Guatemala", in Veliz, n. 3, p. 201, where it is made clear that "the programme under which Arbenz was elected, and which he began to put into force, was

not a communist one. . ."

[5] Toledo, n. 1, p. 839. Honduras had constitutional regimes from 1949-54 (Juan Manuel Calvez) 1954-56 (Lozano), and 1958-63 (Morales). The second and third were removed by military intervention. See Franklin D. Parker, "Honduras," in Veliz, n. 3, p. 210. El Salvador had constitutional regimes from 1950 to 1960, headed by Major Oscar Osorio, his successor, Jose Maria Lemus. The latter was overthrown by a coup. A constitutional regime was restored in 1962, but there was considerable instability thereafter. See Alejandro D. Marro-quin, "El Salvador," in ibid., pp. 189-90. Guatemala's history has been equally unstable. Arbenz was replaced by Colonel Castillo Armas who was assassinated in 1957. The next constitutional president was General Ydigoras Fuentes (1958-63) who was removed by the military. The army kept power for three years when it allowed the election of the Partido Revolucionario's candidate, Julio Cesar Mendez Montenegro, a former dean of the National University's law faculty. A. Fuentez Mohr, "Guatemala," in ibid. pp. 201-2.

[6] Bodenheimer, n. 3, pp. 553-63, especially pp. 562-63.

[7] Toledo, n. 1, p. 842. This writer's translation.

[8] Joseph S. Nye, "Central American Regional Integration," *International Conciliation* (New York) (March 1967), pp. 17-9, 26-31.

[9] The above analysis is based on the comprehensive account by Mario Monteforte Toledo, "La Integracion Centroamericana," *Problemas del Desarrollo* (October-December 1970), pp. 40-60.

[10] See *supra*, pp. 56-63.

[11] See *supra*, pp. 82-4.

[12] Nye, n. 8, pp. 51-4.

[13] James D. Cochrane, *The Politics of Regional Integration: The Central American Case* (Tulane Studies in Political Science, v. XII) (New Orleans, 1969), pp. 65-6, 82.

[14] Victor L. Urquidi, *Free Trade and Economic Integration in Latin America: The Evolution of a Common Market Policy* (Berkeley, 1964), p. 98.

[15] See James D. Cochrane, "US Attitudes Toward Central American Integration," *Inter American Economic Affairs* (Autumm 1964), pp. 33-50; James D. Cochrane, "Central American Economic Integration: The Integrated Industries Scheme."

Cochrane, n. 13, pp. 209-18, for detailed discussions of this question. US hostility to ECLA is mentioned as a possible factor on pp. 211-2, in Gustavo Lagos, *La Integracion Latinoamericana: Situacion y Perspectivas* (Buenos Aires, 1965).

[16] See Toledo, n. 9, pp. 51-3 and Jack J. Rosenblum, "The United States' Interest in Central American Economic Integration," *Foro Internacional.*

[17] Edelberto Torres-Nivas, "Desarrollo, integration y dependencia an Centroamerica," *Estudios Internacionales* (January-March 1970), p 511 This writer's translation.

18 Ibid., pp. 491.

19 For a discussion of this point see Isaac Cohen Orantes, "Funcionalismo integracion centroamericana," *Foro International* (October-December 1968), pp. 179-81. He favours a reconstruction of the Central American federation with a revival of its original goals.

20 Salvador de Madariaga, *The Rise of the Spanish American Empire* (London, 1947), p. 9. George Pendle, *A History of Latin America* (Harmondsworth, 1965), pp. 52-3.

21 Pendle, n. 20, pp. 101, 114-5.

22 Gustavo Lagos, "The Movement toward Integration," in Samuel Shapiro, ed., *Integration of Man and Society in Latin America* (Notre Dame, 1967), pp. 244-46. See also Pendle, n. 20, pp. 136-7, 173, 180-1.

23 Arthus P. Whitaker, *The Western Hemisphere Idea* (Ithaca, 1954), pp. 128-9.
For a study of the ideas of the APRA movement, see Harry Kantor, *The Ideology and Programme of the Peruvian Aprista Movement* (Berkeley, Calif., 1953).

24 See Heracio Godoy, "Actitudes frente ala Integration," in Gustavo Lagos, *La Integracion Latinoamericana: Situacion y Perspectivas* (Buenos Aires, 1965), pp. 144-47 for quotations from Heads of State committing themselves to integration.

25 See Carlos Alberts Astiz, "The Latin American Countries in the International System," in Astiz, ed., *Latin American International Politics: Ambitions, Capabilities and the National Interest of Mexico, Brazil and Argentina* (Notre Dame, 1969), pp. 5-6 for a discussion of this point.

26 See *supra*, pp. 35-6.

27 Emaneuel de Kadt, "Brazil," in Veliz, n. 1, pp. 49-51.

28 John Gerassi, *The Great Fear: The Reconquest of Latin America by Latin Americans* (New York, 1963), pp. 46-50.

29 Ibid., pp. 50-60.

30 John Gunther, *Inside South America* (New York, 1966), pp. 187-98.

31 Rafael Segovia, "Mexico," in Veliz, n. 1, p. 159.

32 Frederic B. Pike, "Chile," in ibid., pp. 64-6.

33 Kevin J. Lyonette, "Colombia," in ibid., pp. 79-81.

34 Guillermo Moron, "Venezuela," in ibid., p. 141.

35 Frederic B. Pike, "Peru," in ibid., pp. 117-21.

36 Alistair Hennessy, "Bolivia," in ibid., pp. 29-32.

37 David Preston, "Ecuador," in ibid., pp. 91-3.

38 See Gerassi, n. 28, pp. 193-200, and Gunther, n. 30, pp. 220-37.

39 George Pendle, "Paraguay," in Veliz, n. 1, pp. 105-6.

40 Dardo Gunco, in an article on Argentine's foreign policy in Astiz, n. 25, p. 315, says flatly that "Frondizi fell because of Punta del Este." For an analysis of Quadros and Hoularta's foreign policy, see Vladimir Reisky de Dubnic, "Brazil's New Foreign Policy from Nonalignment to Solidarity with the West," in ibid., pp. 274-86. See especially p. 281. See also the Introduction to Section II "The Foreign Policy of Mexico," in ibid., pp. 83-4.

41 See J.P. Morray "The United States and Latin America," pp. 104-14 and Bodenheimer, n. 3, pp. 544-50 for discussions of the links set up between the US and Latin American "desarrollista" governments during the late fifties and early sixties.

42 Andres Townsend Ezcurra, "Political Integration in Latin America," in Hilton, ed., *The Movement toward Latin American Unity*, pp. 311-2.

43 For detailed accounts of the role of Christian Democratic parties in Latin American integration, see Thomas W. Walker, "El papel de la democracia cristiana en la integracion de America Latina", *Foro International* (July-September 1970) pp. 77-91 and Edward J. Williams, *Latin American Christian Democratic Parties* (Knoxvill, Tenn., 1967), pp.1 33-44, 262-3.

44 Godoy, n. 24, pp. 149-50, 153-4.

45 Ibid., p. 155.

46 Lagos, n. 22, pp. 249-53.

47 See Per Olav Reinton, "The Legitimacy of Latin American Integration," in *America Latina* (October-November 1969), pp. 3-23, for a discussion of the goals of the integracionistas. See also Per Olav Reinton, "Elementos Cognoscitivos y Valorativos en los programas Latino americanos de Integracion," *Revista de la Integracion* (November 1970), pp.'154-64.

48 See *supra*, pp. 84-8.

49 Gilbert Ziebura, "La Estrategia Politica de la Integracion Europea," in Sunkel, ed., *Integracion Politica y Economica*, pp. 392-4.

50 Haas, "The Uniting of Europe and the Uniting of Latin America," p. 329.

51 *Vision*, 28 April 1967, quoted in Mitchell, "Punta del Este and After," *IAEA* (Winter 1967), p. 87.

52 Schmitter and Haas, *Mexico and Latin American Economic Integration* (Berkeley, Calif., 1964), pp. 13-4, 17.

53 Ibid., p. 26.

54 Ibid., p. 31. These findings are confirmed by Wolfgang Konig in a manuscript study entitled "Posicion de Mexico frente al proceso de intogracion economico de America Latina," prepared for a course on "Mexico and Latin American Integration" at the Golegio de Mexico in September-October 1970. See p. 12 of the Introduction. The study is to be published by INTAL in Buenos Aires.

55 Konig, "Posicion. . .", pp. 12-22.

56 Christopher Mitchell, "The Role of the Technocrats in Latin American Integration," *Inter-American Economic Affairs* (Summer 1967), pp. 13-5.

57 Ibid., pp. 10-3.

58 Godoy, n. 24, pp. 150-52.

59 See *supra*, pp. 56-63.

60 See *supra*, pp. 63-6.

61 Alberto Baltra Cortes, "El Pacto Andino y el Capital Extranjero," *Problems del Desarrollo* (October-December 1970), pp. 69-71.

62 For discussions of the Andean Pact, including its background see Quarterly Economic Reviews: QER Special No. 1, *The Crisis in Latin*

American Integration (London, 1968), pp. 7-10; "The Andean Subregional Integration Movement," *Peruvian Foreign Trade News* (Lima, September 1969); Carlos Diaz-Alejandro, "The Andean Common Market: Gestation and Outlook" (New Haven, Economic Growth Centre, Yale University, Centre Discussion Paper no. 85, May 1970, mimeo.); William P. Avery and James D. Cochrane, "Sub-Regional Integration in Latin America: The Andean Common Market," *Journal of Common Market Studies* (*JCMS*), no. 2 (1972-73), pp. 85-102 and William P. Avery and James Cochrane, "Innovation in Latin American Regionalism: The Andean Common Market," *International Organization* (Spring 1973). Reports on the Andean Pact appear in *Commercio Exterior*, a monthly periodical issued in Spanish and English by the Banco Nacional de Comercio Exterior, S.A., Mexico City in the section "Monthly Report on Latin American Integration."

CHAPTER VII

ASSESSMENT OF LATIN AMERICAN INTEGRATION MOVEMENT

Isolated from world politics for a long time, Latin American countries began to play a role in the United Nations. A sense of dissatisfaction with the US rule in Latin America in the economic sphere was translated by the example of the Cuban Revolution into a feeling that something could conceivably be done about it. The Cuban revolution, unlike the earlier Latin American revolutions (the Mexican and Bolivian) had not come to a *modus vivendi* with the United States, nor like the Guatemalan regime of Arbenz had it succumbed to US pressure. Cuba continued to influence the thinking of Latin Americans, who regarded it as a symbol of independence from US dominance, even when they continued to vote for US resolutions in international conferences.

In this atmosphere, the Prebisch thesis, with its militant attack on the economic policies of the industrialised countries towards the periphery, became a focal point of attention.

Although it was realized in the beginning that the integration of trade should proceed side by side with industrialsation, and industrialisation was a cardinal principle of the Prebisch Thesis, this aspect received inadequate emphasis in the actual implementation of LAFTA's programme of work. Moreover, its achievements were not impressive even in the reduction of trade barriers. The term "LAFTA" is really a misnomer, as it never became a free trade area, but was on the way to becoming one, provided the bilateral and multilateral negotiations made adequate progress. In fact, the negotiations were proceeding very slowly, there was a decline in intra-regional trade after 1967 and the provisions for complementarity agreements were not utilised, so that industrialisation did not proceed in a coordinated fashion. There was some increase in intra-regional trade in the early years, although it is not certain as to the extent to which it was caused by the Treaty. There were also contacts among manufacturers across national borders which enabled them to utilise the issued capacity in their manufactures by dividing the market among themselves, and to learn about the latest developments in their fields.[1]

At the end of the sixties, ECLA analysed at length the difficulties facing LAFTA and several factors were identified as causes of the general lack of achievement. Some of these, like the lack of marketing networks, promotion machinery, and inadequate statistics could have been remedied with a certain amount of effort and with the provision of adequate expertise. There was a second group of factors whose solution requires decisions at the national policy-making levels. This presupposes an effective political machinery with a willingness to tackle the problems even if it involves unpopular measures. This group includes differences in economic, financial, labour, and social measures in different countries, balance of payment problems, and resources for financing intra-regional trade. A third category of problems may itself disappear in course of time, although it would be aided by government policies. This group would include, for instance, resistance to change among enterpreneurs who are said to lack competitive spirit.

There is, however, a fourth and fundamental level of problems which can only be described as "structural," the solution of which would involve a basic change in the institutions of integration themselves. These are such questions as (1) "differences in levels of development and economic potential, which mean that the countries' relative chances of benefiting by the process (especially by the broadening of market) are very unequal so long as no well-defined policy is adopted to prevent acute disequilibria"; (2) "marked contrasts in the internal development of each of the LAFTA countries," which raise difficulties at the national level; and (3) "deficiencies of transport and communications, which hinder the expansion or even preclude the development of intra-area economic relations."[2]

This analysis reinforces our main thesis, viz. that the major obstacle to the growth of LAFTA is the great economic disparity between the different member countries. The point is made by many of the writers on this subject. However, the assumption is too often made that the adverse consequences of having in a single integration unit a number of countries with wide variations in size and stage of economic development can be overcome by the provisions of economic complementarity agreements, escape clauses, and other devices. Sub-regional integration has also been put forth, but only as an interim measure to enable lesser-developed countries to develop economically always keeping in view the ultimate goal of continental integration as an ideal.[3]

It is time for Latin American integrationists to recognize that the escape clauses and other devices are brakes which can only mitigate the defects of market with countries at widely different levels of development and cannot create favourable market conditions. On the other hand, the array of concessions given to the lesser developed countries may discourage the manufacturer in the more developed country from benefiting, without necessarily providing the reassurance for the manufacturer from the less developed country, who may continue to be apprehensive about the possibilities of integrated industries putting him out of business. Moreover, the existence of complicated rules and regulations would necessarily restrict the possibility of expansion of trade and industry simply because of the fear of red tapism and harassment of minor officials. If regional economic integration is to be a reality, it must take the sub-regoinal unit as the main field of activity and give up the stress on the Latin American region, except in the very distant future.

It should not be assumed, however, that sub-regional integration will provide an adequate answer to all the problems of unequal development. The experience of CACM has shown that even sub-regional integration carefully planned and implemented by countries with a long history of attempts at political union, each having little economic viability on their own, can run into serious difficulties because of the lack of economic benefits accruing to the people and the problems generated by economic development concentrated in certain sectors and certain countries of the sub-region. Our examination of the working of CACM led us to the conclusion that although it had enjoyed a aspectcular success in the field of trade, Central American integration had made little contribution either to industrialisalion or to the develo; mental process in the five countries.

This was because the acceptance of US aid in the CACM led to the shifting of attention from the integrated industries scheme to the attraction of foreign investors—a shift from the model laid down by ECLA, which could have led to self-reliance, to a pattern based on dependence on foreign investment, which could not make a major impact on the problems of the area. The CACM was a statistical success in terms of foreign trade figures, but did not answer the needs of economic development. This situation was further exacerbated by the political weakness of the regimes during the 1960's when the intial impact of the liberal movement for unification had given way due to the emergence of authoritarian regimes, which were often dominated by vested interests linked to foreign capital.

The situation in the LAFTA areas, while different in some ways, was basically similar to that in CACM. As has been indicated in Chapter Five, the US attitude to Latin American integration was originally wholly negative, and it was only around 1964 that US policy became favourable to the idea. This trend culminated in the Declaration of the Presidents at Punta del Este in 1967. This change of attitude could be ascribed to an influence of Latin American thinking on US policy. In reality, however, there was a more fundamental reason for the change. This was the realization by US industrialists and business leaders that the integration of Latin America need not necessarily work against their interests. This was primarily a consequence of the experience of US business in Western Europe and in Central America. The natural consequence of this change was that US support for integration was not unconditional, but was closely linked with the presence of certain guarantees for foreign investors, or at least with the existence of circumstances favourable to American business in Latin America. The consequence was that a kind of *modus vivendi* was arrived at which enabled integration to take a certain shape between 1964 and 1967.[4]

There was a strong urge for unity in Western Europe which was strengthened by the sense of weariness engendered by two world wars in a quarter-century and a desire for Europe to emerge as a kind of third force between the United States and the Soviet Union. The Latin American integration movement did not enjoy such advantages. Conceived and planned largely by Raul Prebisch and his band of ECLA economists, the movement took advantage of the atmosphere of resentment towards US economic policies which pervaded Latin American countries and mobilized support at various levels, political and economic, in as many countries as possible. Economists exiled from their countries for political reasons were given employment in economic organizations. They went back years later as convinced advocates of integration.

All this, however, did not make a fundamental difference to the acceptability of the integration movement. The integration-minded tecnicos in international organisations had still to convince the politicians of their own countries. In a few cases the decision-makers had themselves been exposed to the integration philosophy or accepted it on its merits (Presidents Frei of Chile, Lleras Restrepo of Colombia, and Betancourt of Venezuela, for example). In other cases, Presidents were willing to use the integration ideas to build up their internal strength (Presidents Frondizi and Illia of Argentina), and in still others, the top executives had to be convinced of the necessity of integration, which was a delicate task requring an intermediary between the technicos and the President (e.g. President Velaso Ibra of Ecuador).

The Mexican case makes it clear that in order for integration to be accepted as an internal policy it has to have a high degree of acceptability to the important interest groups concerned with trade and industry.[5] If in a country like Mexico with its comparatively high political and economic stability it was possible to "sell" the integration programme only in terms of the promotion of exports, the situation could hardly have been different in the other two major countries of the region—Argentina and Brazil. The continuity that is provided by the Mexican political system is absent in Argentina and Brazil and a political chief, whether constitutionally elected or not, has to seek support for his policies among powerful interest groups in order to retain his authority. In fact, the integration programme in an unstable political situation has to take second place to the day-to-day needs of preserving authority within that system.

What of the politics of the Latin American integration

movement? Many of the political regimes which dealt with the problem of integration were politically weak and were concerned primarily with maintaining control of their own states. This was particularly true of the constitutional regimes in Argentina and Brazil. They were replaced by military regimes whose interest in integration was less evident. In Mexico the Government did not appear to be as concerned about integration as the tecnicos, who, in order to obtain the support of politicians and industrialists, had to soft-pedal some aspects of integration which were unpalatable to interest groups.

It should be remembered that there were industrialists and others who had something to lose from economic integration. Generally it could be stated that, as in Central America, the traditional agricultural interests and the extreme Left opposed economic integration; the former because it threatened their position, and the latter because it was regarded as a capitalist device to ensure US imperialist dominance. The socialist and internationalist parties supported integration, but the business and industrial interests regarded it with some caution and supported or opposed it to the extent it served their interests. Thus in all the three major countries integration was viewed as a minimal process concerning mainly the expansion of their external trade within the region, preferably on a non-reciprocal basis. In this respect the three major countries benefited from the introduction of the new trade arrangements. But the medium and small countries who could gain little or nothing from trade expansion within the region were concerned about the industrial development of their countries.

The response to this crisis on the part of the international tecnicos was the demand for the speeding up of the goal of a Latin American Common Market. This effort, which culminated in the Declaration of Punta del Este, did not lead to any fruitful result. On the other hand, the response of the smaller countries was to set up new sub-regional arrangements for which a limited sphere of operation was demarcated at Punta del Este.

The sincere efforts of the tecnicos to counter the defects of the integration movement led them into two errors. The first was a continued dependence on the European model, to which we have already referred. The fact that European integration was itself going through a severe crisis in 1965 did not have the necessary cautionary effect, and they pressed for a strong institutional base, which was not accepted by the member governments. The fact that the conflict between tecnicos and the politicians had now spread from Europe to Latin America was concealed from the general public for sometime because the rhetoric of the summit conference tended to induce a feeling of euphoria.

The second major error of the tecnicos was to accept the dominant position of the US at the summit conferences. President Johnson's presence was perhaps thought necessary on the assumption that integration could succeed only with American aid.[6] The changed attitude of the United States as a promoter of Latin American integration was explicable only on the basis of the realization among the industrialists of that country that they could take advantage of the Latin American common market as they had done in Western Europe and Central America. In fact, an attempt was made by Senator Javits to set up Action Committees consisting of the United States and Latin Americans from the "political, business and labour sectors to promote the acceleration of Latin American integration."[7] The strategy of the Action Committees might have had a significant impact if it had the backing of powerful Latin American political figures, men of the calibre of Monnet of France and Spaak of Belgium. Unfortunately the attempt to instigate an autonomous Latin American integration movement was sought to be taken over by US backers, who would have liked to use it for their own ends. This probably roused resistance in Latin American political circles and defeated the purposes of the technicos.[8]

This trend was in conflict with another development of the previous three years, commencing prior to the Geneva conference of UNCTAD in 1964. A series of international conferences purely of Latin American states had been held to enable these countries to take a joint stand against US policies in the economic sphere. This organisation, known as the Special Committee for Latin American Coordination (CECLA), had no permanent secretariat and met in various capitals whenever necessary. While its recommendations, such as the Consensus of Vina del Mar, suffered from having to adjust the views of countries with different sizes and interests, it did a great deal to provide for the emergence of a common approach by Latin America to the United States and to prepare the ground for the meetings of UNCTAD.

The Latin American integration movement has tended to regard integration as a goal in itself instead of as a means to the end of development because of its attachment to the European model and its willingness to accept US support. The concept of integration is of value only in so far as it serves this wider goal. In the context of the contemporary world, development includes not only the increase of GNP and per capita income, but a balanced development of different sectors of the economy and different regions of the country as well as a better distribution of the gains of development.

Our findings for the period to the end of the First Development Decade (1960-70) are as follows:

1) The movement for Latin American solidarity which was based on an assertion of the Latin American personality and a struggle for recognition by the United States and the world at large played a positive role in the building up of a regional consciousness in Latin America against the industrial countries. This was a political rather than an economic function.

2) There was inadequate geographic, economic, and political basis for integration at the Latin American level. The possibility of sub-regional groupings was not pursued due to political factors, such as the desire to maintain Latin American solidarity.

3) Latin American integration did not adequately stress the special criscumstances of Latin America. There was an imitation of the Western European model and integration tended to become an end in itself instead of being closely linked to the developmental goals of the regions.

4) The main factors in the integration process were the economists and other tecnicos operating both at the iniernational and national levels. There was inadequate support for their goals among other leading elite groups, such as politicians, industrialists, and intellectuals. They also lacked mass support.

5) The Governments which were favourably disposed towards inegration were oriented to "desarrollismo" ("developmentalism") but lacked adequate internal strength. The weaknesses of the regimes in power and the lack of support led the *integracionistas* to accept US support for integration. The changed United States attitude was attributable mainly to a realisation by US investors that they could adapt themselves to a Latin American Common Market and would benefit by it. Thus the integration movement moved from autonomy through imitation to dependency.

6) The main policy implication of these findings is that integration is likely to be more successful if it focuses on a subregion rather than on a continent and if it depends on internal resources and ideologies rather than on an imitation of foreign concepts and institutions and on an acceptance of foreign assistance.

The experience of Latin American integration till the begining of 1970s has thus tended to move from autonomy as a goal, through imitation as a means, towards dependency as an end product.

REFERENCES

[1] The argument is based on information collected during interviews with Dr. Raul Ray Alvarez and several other officials of the Inter-American Development Bank and Dr. Elba Kybal, Integration Adviser of the Organisation of American States, in Washington, D.C. These trends are confirmed by regular reading of reports on Latin American integration in *Comercio Exterior*, a well-known Mexican journal in the field of economic development and international trade.

[2] These items have been taken, through not in the same order and not exhaustively, from a note by ECLA reproduced in *Economic Bulletin for Latin America* (second half of 1969), p. 114.

[3] See the Action Programme, Part II of the Declaration of the Presidents of America and the norms drawn up by the LAFTA Foreign Ministers in September 1967, which declared subregional agreements to be transitory and as such required them to "fix the date of entry into effect and duration." Christopher Mitchell, "Common Market: The Future of a Commitment: Punta del Este and After," *IAEA* (Winter 1967), pp. 83-4. The documents will be found in Miguel S. Wionczek, ed., *Economic Cooperation in Latin America, Africa and Asia: A Handbook of Documents* (Cambridge, Mass., 1969), pp. 88-95.

[4] See *supra* Chapter V.

[5] See *supra* Chapter VI.

[6] In the course of discussions at the inter-American conferences it is fre-

quently stated that the United States offered or the Latin Americans expected economic aid as a reward or in order to ensure support for specific resolutions. See the accounts of the Caracas, Rio, and Punta del Este conferences in Connell-Smith, *The Inter-American System* (London, 1966), pp. 163, 177-8.

7 See Vodarsik, "Building the Latin American Community: The Meaning and Value of Latin American Integration" (unpublished Ph. D. dissertation, Department of Government, Georgetown University, 1970), p. 441; see also Lagos, "The Movement toward Integration," pp. 267-8.

8 See the discussions regarding Javits and Rockefeller's views in Chapter V.

CHAPTER VIII

ASIAN ECONOMIC COOPERATION AND THE RELEVANCE OF LATIN AMERICAN EXPERIENCE TO ASIA

Asia and Latin America: Similarities and Differences

The area covered by the Economic Commission for Asia and the Far East (ECAFE), which extends from Iran to Japan, is culturally heterogenous and can scarcely be described as a region in economic terms. The links of Asian countries with different metropolitan powers make it difficult for them to "speak the same language," either literally or figuratively, as the Latin Americans do. Asia has no Bolivarian tradition of continentalism to look back upon. Moreover, the countries of Asia are divided by mountain and sea barriers which often prevent or discourage communication among them.

At first sight, therefore, there seems little similarity between the two regions. But on closer examination, one finds that the homogeneity of Latin America is not as great as one might expect. The Andean mountains constitute a massive barrier obstructing communication and trade between the Atlantic and Pacific countries of South America. The Caribbean almost constitutes a region by itself. Moreover, many countries of Latin America and particularly the Andean countries are far from united. Argentina, with its strong regional pulls, often lays greater stress on national unification than on regional economic integration. Brazil is a country of continental proportions, and Mexico is as the saying goes, "so far from God and so near the United States."

When one looks at the trading and industrial pattern, other similarities emerge. As former colonial or semi-colonial areas, both the ECLA and ECAFE regions are primarily producers of of raw materials dependent on their exports. In recent years, both regions have undergone a considerable increase in population, which has pointed to the need for raising the rate of growth and reducing inequalities, as well as the urgency of controlling the growth of population. The main problem in both areas is not integration, but development, not coordinating existing institutions, but building new ones. Both regions have a variety of types of economies, ranging from those which welcome private enterprise to those which follow a strictly planned economy. The elites in Asia and Latin America are generally regarded as enjoying an influence disproportionate to their numbers. This may paradoxically be an advantage in planning integration as it makes it easier for countries to work together once the elites understand and accept one another.

Lastly, in both ECAFE and ECLA regions there are big countries with a large potential for growth, existing side by side with smaller countries which may benefit only marginally from economic integration. The fear of the major countries like Japan, China, and India dominating the economies of smaller ones has been a factor in discouraging economic integration in Asia. Although in Latin America the fear of the large countries was at first kept in abeyance by the common suspicion of the "colossus of the North." Unequal gains from economic integration and restrictive policies of the bigger countries have been a major complaint against LAFTA and one of the factors which encouraged the growth of sub-regional integration in the Andean region,

Asian Regionalism in the Early Postwar Period

The concept of a regional international organisation for Asia under the auspices of the United Nations was put forward soon after the Second World War, but did not lead to any concrete results. Asia is the home of at least three major civilisations, and Asian consciousness has only gradually emerged during the past hundred years or so, arising mainly out of a common opposition to the European presence in Asia. The cultural and linguistic diversity of Asia is well known, but it is not the diversity that has obstructed the development of a regional consciousness so much as it is the clash of political and economic interests. The Asian Relations Conference, held at New Delhi in March

1947 at the initiative of Jawahrlal Nehru, did not result in the establishment of a permanent organisation because of the rivalry between India and the Kuomintang regime in China and the suspicions entertained by the smaller countries of domination by these big powers.[1]

A proposal for an Asian regional organisation had been drawn up about this time by a study group of the Indian Council of World Affairs. The organisation was to be based on a "vast and prosperous economic unity based on planned development" and on the guidance and assistance of the United Nations. It was not to be "left to the make-shift expedients of the Western powers." A large capital inflow through the World Bank was executed and tariffs were visualised as a basis for the industrialisation of backward countries. The organisation was to be sponsored by India and China, who were to have a weightage in voting as against the smaller countries of South-east Asia. Japan and Australia were to be considered as members later on.[2]

The fact that the regional organisation was proposed to be created under United Nations auspices is indicative of the importance given to the new world organisation in the guaranteeing of the regional state pattern in Asia, and the expectation that it would play an impartial role in protecting the interests of developing countries in economic and political matters. Although the proposal does not appear to have been moved at the New Delhi conference, it evidently had some effect on the thinking of ECAFE because the Chairman of the study group, Dr. P.S. Lokanathan, became the first executive secretary of ECAFE.[3]

The ECAFE had 31 members and 6 associates in 1973. ECAFE was founded in 1947 as one of the four regional commissions of United Nations Economic and Social Council (ECOSOC). Its first session was held in Shanghai. The 31 members were Afghanistan, Australia, Bhutan, Burma, China, France, India, Indonesia, Iran, Japan, Khmer Republic of Korea, Laos, Malaysia, Mongolia, Nauru, Nepal, Netherlands, New Zealand, Pakistan, the Philippines, Singapore, Sri Lanka (Ceylon), Thailand, Tonga, USSR, UK, USA, Republic of Vietnam, Western Samoa, and Bangladesh. The six associates were British Solomon Islands, Brunei, Cook Islands, Fiji, Hong Kong, and

Papua New Guinea.

PROPOSALS FOR ECONOMIC COOPERATION IN ASIA

Unlike the Latin American region which had been till recent years somewhat insulated from the problems of the Cold War, the ECAFE region has been from the early post-war period one of the main foci of Cold War conflicts. Due to the presence in ECAFE of both the United States and the Soviet Union and due to the restrictions sought to be placed on the regional body by the representatives of Western powers as to the role it should perform in regard to the promotion of industrialisation and the administration of aid programs, ECAFE was unable during the early years to play an independent role as a spokesman for the countries of the area [4] It was further hamstrung by conflicts among some of the Asian countries themselves, and by the fear of big power dominance among the smaller countries, as well as by the exclusion of China, which lent an air of unreality to the proceedings. Moreover, the secretariat was unable to provide the sort of intellectual leadership which was provided in Latin America by the ECLA secretariat under the leadership of Raul Prebisch. The secretariat was less innovative and followed a tradition of caution; it did not actively seek to play a role in the national planning and development process by inculcating officials of the member countries with a common set of beliefs and ideals, as ECLA did.[5]

This difference in the approach of ECLA and ECAFE would appear to have been partly due to the differences in the personalities of the executive secretaries of the two organisations. Both Raul Prebisch and P.S. Lokanathan had intellectual stature and toughness of fibre; relations with the UN secretariat were not good in either case. However, there appeared to be in the ECAFE secretariat "an aura of apparent complacency" which contrasted with the tradition of "critical self-analysis" established in the ECE under Gunnar Myrdal.[6]

In spite of these difficulties, a number of attempts at regional cooperation in the economic sphere have been made in the ECAFE region. In 1955 the then Executive Secretary, Lokanathan, submitted an aide-memoire proposing: (1) the establishment of an economic development section to study conditions in

ECAFE countries, formulate programming techniques and study questions of economic growth and policy; (2) that ECAFE assist governments in examining their plans in a regional context with a view to their coordination later on by representatives of the governments, and thus counter the emerging surpluses in rice, textiles, and some minerals, as well as enable the countries to benefit from economies of scale; their own markets being too small; and (3) a strengthening of ECAFE's advisory services in the field of economic planning.[7]

Action on these and subsequent recommendations was disappointingly slow. Most of the member countries were opposed to the idea of regional economic integration, although they were not prepared to say so openly. A Working Party on Economic Development and Planning was set up in 1955 and the launching of the European Common Market in June 1958 gave some impetus to its activities in spite of the general preoccupation with national economic planning. As a result of the Bangkok resolution on Asian economic cooperation in 1960, Asian governments agreed for the first time to explore pragmatically all avenues of regional economic integration, a subject that till then could not even be discussed.[8]

A conference of Asian economic planners was held in New Delhi in late 1961, which could not come to any agreement on the coordination of regional planning because the smaller countries felt that such a step would benefit only India and Japan, both of which wanted to expand their markets in the region. An exchange of information was agreed upon and the coordination of planning was evaded. Although an expert committee consisting of K.B. Lall (India), L T. Sethanphanichakan (Thailand), and Saburo Okita (Japan) recommended the establishment of an executive agency for taking concrete measures in regard to regional economic cooperation, their proposal for an Organisation of Asian Economic Cooperation was openly supported at the 1962 annual meeting of ECAFE in Tokyo only by India. Both India and Japan seem to have been afraid of spoiling the chances of some kind of regional arrangement by showing undue enthusiasm for the proposal.[9]

The proposals of the expert committee for economic integration were considerably watered down by a Ministerial conference held at Manila in December 1963, leaving a set of high sounding resolutions, involving no commitment on the part of the member states. The most important result of the exercise so far has been the establishment of the Asian Development Bank which was set up under a decision taken at the second Ministerial conference on Asian Economic Cooperation held at Manila from 30 November to 2 December 1965.[10]

While events since the Manila meeting proved something of an anti-climax, the basic obstacles to regional integration could be discerned from a careful examination of the discussions at that meeting itself. The resolution on Asian economic cooperation passed at the meeting repeatedly referred to the need to protect the sovereignty of members and the interests of land-locked countries. The basic factor behind these provisions was the economic and political weakness of the smaller countries, which could hardly hope to stand up to giants like India and Japan. The difference became all the more glaring with countries like Nepal, Afghanistan, and Laos, which performed the role of buffer states between two or major powers of the region, and are denied access to the sea, thus accentuating their weakness. Thus the economic nationalism of the middle and smaller countries of the ECAFE region was a major objection to any kind of economic integration in Asia.[11]

Another major factor that stood in the way of Asian economic cooperation was finance. The advantages of regional economic groupings were necessarily limited if they were confined to their own financial resources.[12] It was not surprising, therefore, that the discussions on regional cooperation at the Manila conference of 1963 were partly overshadowed by the preparatory discussions for the meetings of UNCTAD (United Nations Conference on Trade and Development),[13] which had been planned to be held in Geneva the following year, and were expected to provide a dramatic breakthrough in the economic problems of developing countries.[14]

A number of studies undertaken by the ECAFE secretariat, reports of committees appointed by the organisation, and studies by economists pointed out that although intra-regional trade in Asia was comparatively high, the region's share in the world trade tended to decline, and the terms of trade became steadily less favourable to the countries of the region. These studies urged therefore the necessity of expanding intra-regional trade on the one hand and import substitution at the regional level on the other.[15]

Developments in the field of trade cooperation since the Manila meeting of 1963 indicated that there was considerable interest in the working out of concepts and undertaking of studies. At the same time there was a reluctance to commit the members to any concrete course of action.[16] In its *Economic Survey of Asia and the Far East* for 1969, ECAFE separated three main issues for consideration by the member countries during 1970, which marked the beginning of the second Development Decade. These were: (1) The issue of unequal development and the provision of "reciprocity" and escape provisions to compensate the weaker countries. This had not been successful in Latin America. (2) The issue of grouping countries, whether on the basis of sub-regional groups or on the basis of 'regional sub-groups.' The distinction was based on the assumption that contiguity was not the only factor in forming a viable group of countries. Affinity on the basis of size, stage of economic development and ideology (as with Pakistan-Iran-Turkey, Australia-New Zealand, and India-UAR-Yugoslavia) might prove to be more effective than proximity as in ASEAN (Association of South-East Asian Nations). To protect the interests of countries outside the sub-region, a free trade area was to be preferred to a customs union (3) The issue of plan harmonization as a precondition for trade liberalization. This would be desirable in the case of infrastructure facilities like transport and communications as it would enable the most economic sites to be selected and permit specialization and enable plants of optimum size to be set up.

On the basis of these general principles, a phased programme of agreements was laid down. A gradual liberalization of regional trade was to be accomplished by the freeing of trade within the region for some commodities by stages rather than by a major breakthrough in the liberalisation of regional trade. Concessions were to be provided for the weaker countries of the region and the first step was to be the setting up of a clearing house and a payments union.[17]

The cautious and pragmatic approach of ECAFE to integration was based on a realization that the difficulties in the way of economic integration in Asia were great and included not only a suspicion of the larger countries, but also a general unwillingness to surrender control over one's economic life. Nevertheless there was some progress, in the words of an ECAFE report, from "the early projects of sound information-building, surveys and studies to cooperation in physical resources (Mekong), infrastructure (Asian Highway), institutions (Asian Institute for Economic Development and Planning), commodities (coconut) to more complex areas such as finance (Asian Development Bank), payments and shipping."[18]

In 1970, the ECAFE secretariat, after years of effort and elaborate preparation, was unable to obtain their signatures from the member countries present at the fourth ministerial meeting at Kabul, Afghanistan, for a modest proposal that an Asian Clearing Union be established, and that the setting up of an Asian Reserve Bank be approved in principle. True to its past traditions of postponement of decisions the Ministerial conference appointed committees to look into these matters further, thereby delaying these steps.

The concept of an Asian Clearing Union (ACU) designed to promote the use of regional currencies for current transactions, conserve foreign exchange and help expand trade called for the use of an "Asian Monetary Unit" (AMU). AMU was to be the common accounting unit of ACU. The ACU was actually set up, it appears, only in 1973. Though modest in scale it was the first time that a monetary agreement appeared in the ECAFE region. The proposal contained in the "Kabul Declaration" of 1970 to establish an Asian Reserve Bank (ARB) with the object of pooling reserves under joint management for regional trade expansion and development was a non-starter even after four years of prolonged visualisation, as of 1973. Cambodia, Sri Lanka, the Philippines, and Thailand initialled on March 1973 a draft agreement setting up a 50 million Asian Rice Fund that would ultimately become self-financing[19] This gave a new dimension to the rice trade on a system of deferred payments to finance and refinance rice sales. Thus the concept of cooperation in the field of commodity trade began to take concrete shape.

Aid and Asian Integration

One of the most important institutions for the coordination of economic assistance of the developing countries of Asia was the Colombo Plan for Cooperative Economic Development in South and Southeast Asia. As the name implies, the intention was to dovetail technical assistance and cooperation with the needs of the countries in the sphere of economic development. It was a product of the initiative of Australia and originally consisted only of members of the British Commonwealth. It was subsequently joined by the other Southeast Asian countries and some from outside the region.

All the members of the Colombo Plan, an association of donors and recipients of aid, operate on the basis of equality; in fact, many of the recipients are also donors. There was an annual review of the activities and gains of the member-countries in the economic and social fields. A Bureau was maintained in Colombo to serve as a clearing-house of information and provide secretariat facilities for meetings. Although the membership of the Plan included almost all the non-Communist countries of South and Southeast Asia, as well as the Republic of Korea, Australia, Canada, Japan, New Zealand, United Kingdom, and the United States, there seemed little possibility of it becoming a centre of integration activities in the area or an effective instrument of plan harmonisation. The aid and technical assistance which it coordinated were actually bilateral rather than multilateral aid.[20] Its comparative lack of effectiveness was particularly unfortunate in view of its accumulated experience, since its establishment in 1951, of dealing with matters of aid in relation to economic development.

It is interesting to note that the first attempt at the multilateralization of foreign aid in Asia was made in 1956 at a conference held in Simla, India, at the instance of the United States. The conference was marked by strong reluctance on the part of the smallest countries, particularly Ceylon, to the idea of coordinated aid from the United States, probably because they felt that bilateral aid would be more generous and that the major countries like India and Pakistan would tend to take the lion's share of any aid which might be given on a coordinated basis. The failure of the Simla Conference was, however, at least partially ascribable to the lack of advance preparation of the invitees, and to the lack of high-level commitment to the idea of multilateral aid in the United States itself.[21]

The Asian Development Bank was established in 1966 with its headquarters in Manila. It originated from a proposal from ECAFE, but acquired its own ties with international agencies, including the World Bank, other regional banks, the United Nations, and its specialised agencies. The main source of funds consisted of subscriptions of $217.14 million each from the US and Japan, $100.97 million from India, and $92.29 million from Australia. It is worthwhile to note here that 14 non-regional members including the United States had subscribed an amount up to $412.57 million. In the early stages it suffered from a lack of adequate "soft funds" or concessional lending. The impact of its activities appeared to be more promising in the *quality* of the contribution it made, rather than its volume.[22]

In this respect the Bank was criticised for being too conservative in contrast to the Inter-American Development Bank and for over-stressing in its lending policies the "sound banking principles" which were supposed to enable it to raise more money in the world money markets. White believed that the Bank should play a more active role in promoting development activities, and specifically in the field of economic integration, as the ILB had done. The dominant role played by the United States and Japan in the Bank seemed to him a major factor in preventing the Bank from playing a more developmental role. Whereas Japan wanted the loans to be tied to Japanese goods and services, the US government faced difficulties with Congress, which refused to authorise additional funds for Asia in June 1968.[23]

To look at ADB through its annual report of 1973, the Bank commenced lending in 1968 and by the end of 1973, it had lent $1,376 million. This was about one third of the total amount lent by multilateral agencies to the Bank's borrowing countries during the period. In the second half of that period, the Bank provided nearly 40 per cent of multilateral lending. An important "milestone" was reached in 1973 with the approval in principle of the establishment of an Asian Development Fund with initial resources of $525 million for the period 1974-76. By the end of 1973, the Bank had approved loans to meet the direct and indirect exchange costs of 150 selected development projects in 21 developing member countries.

The outstanding external public debt in the Bank's borrowing countries was about $20.8 billion at the end of 1972 on which the annual debt service payments were estimated to have been $1.6 billion in 1973 (about 300 per cent over the figure for 1968). The Bank was thus caught in the growing problem of debt servicing.

The Bank placed its initial emphasis on the identification and evaluation of the possibilities for economic cooperation among countries. This led to the completion of seven studies on various features of the regional economy. The Bank visualised its role as a "catalyst of productive investment" in developing member countries.

The average amount lent for each project financed by the Bank continued to increase—$5.9 million in 1968, $10.5 million in 1972, and $10.8 million in 1973. In 1973 the Bank lent $421.48 million compared with $316.09 million in 1972. Thus there was a 33 per cent increase over 1972, against an increase of about 24 per cent in 1972 over 1971. During 1973, 39 projects were financed with 54 loans.[24]

The Bank's authorised capital stock was about $3300 billion on 31 December 1973. The subscribed capital was then about $2,720 billion having increased by $275 million during the year. The total repayments received upto 1973 were $10.0 million out of which $6.8 million was during 1973.

Attempts at Subregional Integration in Asia

The most important subregional groupings in the ECAFE region in the economic sphere were the Association of South-East Asian Nations (ASEAN) and Regional Cooperation for Development (RCD). In spite of their orientation, they inherited the anti-Communist image which had been a feature of the South-East Asia Treaty Organisation (SEATO) and the Baghdad Pact (CENTO). There were indications that Japan, a major trading partner of almost all the countries in Southeast and East Asia, would welcome an opportunity to play a hegemonial role in relation to a subregional organisation in Southeast Asia.[25] There was also a proposal for a Pacific Free Trade Area consisting of the advanced countries of the Pacific Ocean, i.e. the

United States, Canada, Japan, Australia, and New Zealand.[26] The developing countries of Southeast Asia would presumably acquire a sort of associate status comparable to that of the Francophone African countries in relation to the EBC.

The members of ASEAN were Malaysia, the Philippines, Thailand, Indonesia, and Singapore. The trade of the members among themselves was small and the stress on partial plan harmonization rather than on immediate trade liberalisation. A number of committees were set up to go into various fields of possible collaboration, including food production and supply, air transportation, communications, and shipping.[27] Although the reestablishment of diplomatic relations between Malaysia and the Philippines (broken due to the dispute over Sabah) gave some impetus to the discussions of proposals for regional economic cooperation in ASEAN, it generally took a cautious approach to cooperative projects and instead stressed mass media, cultural cooperation, and the furthering of tourism within the region. The association did not take any overt political position.[28]

Regional Cooperation for Development had a comparatively uneventful, though cautious, period of growth since 1964. It focused on plan harmonisation on a project-by-project basis, mainly with a view to establishing joint industrial ventures in the three member countries, viz. Pakistan, Iran, and Turkey. In comparing it with ASEAN, the ECAFE secretariat observed that projects in RCD were capable of being fully integrated into national development plans, while in ASEAN projects were considered more or less independently, as there was no permanent coordinating body like the RCD Regional Planning Council, which links the regional and the national projects and the regional projects themselves.[29]

The 29th session of ECAFE held in Tokyo in 1973, was an important one. Faced with the problems of aggravation of the stagnant agricultural production, the population problem, mass poverty, large scale unemployment, and coordination of the development of each country to that of the entire region, there was much rhetoric.

The Executive Secretary, U Nyun, relinquished his office. China's vociferous maiden speech on its debut was a scathing attack on the Soviet proposal for an Asian Collective Security

System. China criticized the proposal as a disguise of Soviet hegemonic ambition to "control and divide Asian countries and incorporate them gradually into its sphere of influence." The United States was also denounced by China.

The general mood was to evolve a new strategy for economic development wherein industrialisation and development of natural resources were to be more closely coordinated with agricultural development. "Concerted international efforts" were called for towards the achievement of these goals.

The ASEAN group vigorously supported a Philippine proposal for "reassessment" of the ECAFE conference structure, so as to implement ECAFE projects more effectively on a "sub-regional approach" at the initiative of countries concerned rather than on a "general" approach under the ECAFE secretariat—largely staffed by nationals of certain countries like India.

Another notable feature of the meeting was that developing countries in the region assumed an attitude of "Let's get started by ourselves first" instead of merely pleading for aid from developed industrial countries.

In his farewell speech, U Nyun struck an optimistic note, arguing that Asian regionalism would not be reversed or become merely nominal. He added: "We are now at the threshold of a whole new era of regionalism," after witnessing progressive regional and sub-regional cooperation in a very wide range of fields, including institution building, infrastructure, natural resources, trade, commodities, joint industries, and monetary schemes of cooperation inspite of disturbed conditions in Asia. "An Asia that is one" was the concurrent expression of solidarity throughout the occasion.

The Policy Issue: What Kind of Integration for Asia?

It will be noticed that unlike the situation in Europe and Latin America political motivations came into the field only at a comparatively late stage. The efforts of ECAFE were directed towards the achievement of trade and payments arrangements covering the entire ECAFE region, and to a lesser extent, to the furtherance of sub-regional arrangements with an emphasis on plan harmonisation. However, there has been little stress on the definition of regions, and on the determination of the most feasible economic units for integration. Although plan harmonisation of a limited kind was attempted in RCD and ASEAN, it was not effective because the governments gave it a low priority and continued to plan for economic development without consulting the other member-governments. There was no general consciousness of a need to integrate in order to fight for a better international position, and the distribution of foreign aid on a bilateral basis was preferred to multilateralization.

However, this is not to say that regional integration has no economic basis in Asia. The historian of ECAFE pointed out in his concluding remarks that "Asia cannot afford to contract out of the movement toward closer regional economic groupings in the world community." International organisations, he said, could serve to "mobilise and maximise the collective strength" of the weak and institutionalise their will "to alter the distribution of economic power and guarantee the interests of the weak against the policies of the strong."[30]

The Latin American integration movement was not as successful as was expected in the achievement of the goals of regional development. Therefore, it is necessary for Asian planners to avoid an unduly optimistic view of integration on the one hand, and counter the kind of pessimism which tends to inhibit any action on the other.

Relevance of Latin American Integration for Asia

Some questions which remain to be answered are: Is integration a viable goal for Asia in the light of the Latin American experience? What could the Asian countries gain from regional or sub-regional groupings? What are the lessons for Asia of the Latin American integration movement?

Apart from the problem of attempting to extend the Latin American findings to an Asian setting there is a further problem that the benefits from integration are technically non-qualifiable and therefore not subject to rigorous analysis. Quantitative studies are limited mainly to intra-regional trade—itself an insufficient indicator of the success of integration.

Policy recommendations for Asia from the Latin American experience must be cautious. The mere fact of being a less developed area is an insufficient leveller. There are far too many crucial variables which differ from country to country and which must not be lost sight of in planning for regional integration. These include the stage of development, the political regime, the composition of the country's exports and imports in world trade, foreign policy, both in relation to the region and the rest of the world.

Since increased bargaining power with the rest of the world is viable through regional cooperation, a strong case has been put forward for regional cooperation as a forerunner to integration in Asia.

In some respects, the countries of the region stand in a powerful bargaining position. The Asian countries are major exporters of timber and timber products. The ECAFE region produces more than 90 per cent of the world's combined output of jute and allied fibres. India and Sri Lanka together dominate the world's export supply of tea. Favourable bargaining position is also possible in rice, crude rubber, and sugar. The bargaining strength provided by oil and petroleum has come to the fore only since 1973.

Though the several factors or combination of factors which led to the formation of the EEC and the LAFTA are not present in the Asian situation, there is a possibility that regional cooperation may go a long way in solving the region's economic problems. In other words, there is no strong case against regional cooperation in Asia on theoretical grounds. The problem as such merits closer investigation.

We have, thus to re-examine the concept of integration in the light of the Latin American experience and consider the extent to which integration has taken place in Latin America. Economic cooperation was taken to refer to the process of collaboration between independent sovereign states, each retaining its right to participate in any particular project. There is certainly considerable evidence of economic cooperation in Latin America, but the process of integration has made very slow progress. The achievement of interdependent economies in the LAFTA area is an extremely remote prospect. In Central America the social and political obstacles have proved a major stumbling block to the success of integration.

We had expressed doubts about the proposition that economic integration leads to political unification. Our study of Latin America does not lend much support to the view that there is likely to be a shift of attitudes and interests from the nation-state to a supranational focus. The members of ECAFE, and particularly the smaller Asian countries, have regarded with suspicion any attempt at regional economic integration as they feared any surrender of their sovereignty; it is for this reason that words like "cooperation" and "collaboration" are preferred to "integration" in Asia. An examination of the Latin American experience would indicate that there is nothing to fear in the word "integration" itself. The surrender of sovereignty is a political concept which may alarm the representative of a small state unduly; in fact, the interdependence of all countries in the modern world is increasing rather than diminishing and membership of any international organisation with some regulatory power (the International Civil Aviation Organisation, for example) can be construed as a surrender of some decision-making power. The crucial question is not whether some power is being surrendered to a body outside the state, but whether the benefits being derived therefrom and the role which that state itself plays in the decisions taken by the body counter-balance the loss of "sovereignty" which may be involved. It is not necessary to start out with the conception of a supranational body which will dominate the decisions of a nation-state and make a mockery of its independence. The Latin American experience shows that the smaller states can exercise some influence in the regional organisations at least to the extent of preventing their effective functioning. Although this is a negative role, it should serve to reassure the smaller states in Asia about the possibility of retaining control over their own affairs. Both in Latin America and in Asia, the existence of economic integration would appear to have no necessary connection with the conception of political unification.

In order to avoid the mistakes of Latin American experience in the field of trade integration, several important lessons can be drawn by planners in Asia.

In the first place, large countries with the possibility of diversified development on the basis of a substantial internal market (like India and China, which can themselves be described as regions), should not be grouped together with countries with a small area, population, and small market potential. There may be some exceptions to this rule, e.g. where a small country neighbours a large one, has close relations with it, and desires to benefit from the larger economic market of the neighbouring giant. On the other hand, it is conceivable that some small countries, like Afghanistan and Nepal, may prefer to establish direct ties with non-contiguous countries rather than accept a position of dependence to major economies like those of the Soviet Union, Pakistan, or India. Trade groupings, which may be for limited purposes, should be based on factual studies undertaken by competent researchers, although political considerations affecting governments would have to be given due weight. The total actual determination of sub-regions would come at a comparatively late stage, after the compilation of data on the geographic and economic factors operating in the area.

Secondly, reasons for the lack of success of the industrialisation programme has been the lack of plan harmonisation, which would seem to be an essential feature of integration in the developing areas. The goal of industrialisation of the developing areas would appear to be a chimera unless there is a perceived equality of benefits derived from the integration process and a willingness to share the benefits received. In order to be really effective, such an experiment would require not only careful planning and the dovetailing of national plans, at least in limited sectors, but also the support of an outside agency in the form of technical assistance, and perhaps financial assistance as well.

Our proposal for the acceptance of sub-regional integration of countries at approximately the same level of development would imply a partial acceptance of the view that countries at different levels of economic development should seek to specialise in the production of those commodities for the manufacture of which they are best qualified. The acceptance of this principle would, however, have to be hedged in with several restrictions because of the inherent complexity of intra-state relations and the many social and economic pressures operating on the government of each country.

A third aspect of the Latin American integration movement which we have to consider is the need for infrastructure and for the planning of regional development. This factor has received inadequate attention from the promoters of the Latin American integration process till recently, and there has not been a full realisation of its social importance for the further development of the region. There are two aspects of the question which demand urgent attention: (a) the first is the need for comprehensive planning in the context of what has been described as the "special pattern" of industrial development as opposed to the "sectoral pattern" of development. If this is not done, there is a danger of having pockets of development scattered over the continent having contacts with one another but isolated from the rural areas of the national territories in which they are located; (b) the second is the desirability of infrastructural arrangements to focus on a smaller area than the continent as a whole. Thus, communications among the Andean countries should rate a higher priority than communications between Peru and Brazil where the border areas do not constitute an important area for development and where the possibility of building up trade relations would seem to be small.

The stress we have laid on the need for comprehensive planning in Latin America is even more applicable to the ECAFE region. The major obstacle to communication in Latin America are mountains and impenetrable jungles; in Asia, the sea is an important factor. However, the Asian Highway has similar goals to the Pan American Highway and the project for the development of the Mekong Delta is comparable to that of the River Plate Basin in South America. What kind of institutions are most suitable for the purpose of such long-term planning and for the implementation of the plan? The Latin American scene is characterised by a certain amount of duplication of functions. In Asia, ECAFE seems to have chosen the opposite path of attaching to itself directly the administration of projects like those of Asian Highway and the Mekong Delta project. This would seem to lead to a diversion of attention of the organisation from its main function of chalking out new lines of thought and action. The duplication of functions by different organisations like ECAFE, the Asian Development Bank, and the Colombo Plan is not necessarily undersirable provided it leads to a rethinking of basic issues in development. Recent studies of social and economic development indicate that there are no final answers in these fields, and there is always scope for different approaches to the problems of a region. One area which requires urgent attention is the application of geographic and socio-economic data to the problem of regional planning cutting across national boundaries. This kind of study would provide a basis for a determination of sub-regions in the ECAFE area, drawn up on the basis of objective criteria.

The most important criteria to be considered for determining a grouping may be mentioned here. These include proximity, area, and population. The size of the market, based on a combination of the level of productivity, population, income level, and other factors, would be a major, but not the sole deciding, factor in forming a grouping. Not only should markets be of approximately equal size, but countries should also be grouped with others at approximately the same level of development. In order to do so it may be necessary to begin with the smaller groupings of two or three countries (e.g. Laos, Cambodia or Phlippines-Malaysia) rather than a grouping of countries of widely disparate levels of development. If these sub-groups work effectively, they can be expected to lead to further attempts at integration with a larger group of countries (as Benelux prepared the way for further integration of the three member countries with EEC). The main basis of integration should be plan harmonisation rather than the increase of trade. In order to achieve this it is necessary to begin the process of integration before vested interests in industries get established as these tend to oppose changes in the industrial pattern of the area and demand protection. There would seem to be greater scope for integrated industries in new lines of production or in countries yet to be industrialised rather than in fields where there is already industrial activity.

A fourth aspect of the Latin American integration process which we have to examine is the financing of integration. As we have seen, the earlier idea of an autonomous movement, seeking to build integration without US financial participation had to be given up because the IMF and the United States would not permit a regional payments union. The establishment of the Alliance for Progress and the IDB led to a tendency to depend on US funds rather than to mobilize internal resources and to take hard decisions at a regional level. It is well known that there was a flight of capital from Latin America during this period.

The Latin American experience suggests that the hegemonial role played on the economic and political life of the region by a single outside power is not conducive either to the building up of a healthy relationship or to the balanced economic development of the countries concerned. An attempt by Japan to play a similar role in Southeast Asia may succeed in the short run due to the financial assistance which it may provide. It should be remembered, however, that the role of a major investor or donor is not a happy one. Instead of building up the kind of relationship that the United States had with Latin America, Japan would be well advised to multilateralise her aid programmes and channelise them through institutions on which other Asian countries are represented, such as the Asian Development Bank and the Colombo Plan. This would avoid the kind of confrontation that has frequently occurred between the United States and the Latin American countries in regard to economic matters. The hegemonial-type relationship which existed in the OAS was maintained only at the cost of considerable resentment and long-term friction. If the kind of multilateral machinery that has been built up by CIAP is set up in Asia, it would go a long way to reduce the tensions and fears brought about by the aid programme and make for a wider acceptance of coordinated economic development both in the developed and the developing countries.

Thus, the tasks which need the immediate attention of these organizations are: (1) defining the role of and strengthening the region-wide financial institutions like the Asian Clearing Union and the Asian Development Bank; (2) the provision of essential infrastructural facilities like the Asian Highway and strengthening shipping and telecommunications in Asia which further economic and cultural contacts; (3) the promotion of region-wide commodity agreements, like those in the fields of coconut, and taking up new commodity areas for joint action; (4) the determination of viable sub-regions on the basis of geo-economic criteria; and (5) the furthering of financing investment within the sub-regions by the oil rich countries of West and Southeast Asia, especially in countries which can provide the essential skills required for their own development.

REFERENCES

1 For accounts of the Asian Relations Conference, see Sisir Gupta, *India and Regional Integration in Asia* (Bombay, 1964), pp. 33-8 and G.R. Jansen, *Non-Alignment and the Afro-Asian States* (New York, 1966), pp. 51-75.

2 Indian Council of World Affairs, "India and Security in Southeast Asia," Report by a study group of the ICWA, New Delhi (New York, n.d.) (1947), mimeographed.

3 A much less ambitious scheme for an Asian Relations Organisation was mooted by Jawaharlal Nehru at the Asian Relations Conference, but even this had to be considerably watered down to allow for the strong opposition to the proposal from China and the Philippines. The non-official body which was set up maintained a shadowy, halting existence till 1955, when it was wound up. Jansen, n. 1, pp. 67-73. The quotation is on p. 71.

4 The first Executive Secretary of ECAFE, reviewing the history of ECAFE by Wightman, agreed with the latter that British and American policy in Asia worked against the interests and development of the Asian countries. P.S. Lokanathan, "Verdict on ECAFE," *Far Eastern Economic Review* (*FEER*), 21 November 1963, pp. 393-5. See also Wightman, *Toward Economic Cooperation in Asia: The United Nations Economic Commission for Asia and the Far East* (New Haven, 1963), pp. 344-51.

5 Gregg, "The UN Regional Economic Commissions and Integration in the Underdeveloped Regions," *International Organization* (Spring 1966), p. 224.

6 Wightman, n. 4, pp. 324-26, 340.

7 Ibid., pp. 104-5.

8 Lalita Prasad Singh, *The Politics of Economic Cooperation in Asia: A Study of Asian International Organization* (Columbia, 1966), pp. 149-54.

9 Ibid., pp. 160-1.

10 United Nations, ECAFE, *Regional Economic Cooperation in Asia and the Far East: Report of the Second Ministerial Conference on Asian Economic Cooperation* (E/CN. 11/716), Rev. 1, pp. 4-5.

11 The issue according to the Indian journalist Jansen, arose as early as January 1947 when General Aung San of Burma spelled out in a broadcast from Delhi his idea of an Asian commonwealth: "While India should be one entity and China another, South-East Asia should form an entity of its own; and then finally we should come together in a bigger union," and "there was still a long way to go before that stage." Jansen, n. 1, p. 73.

12 See Miguel S. Wionczek, *Economic Cooperation in Latin America, Africa and Asia: A Handbook of Documents* (Cambridge, Mass., 1969) p. 18 for a discussion of this point.

13 See *FEER Yearbook, 1964*, p. 45.

14 These expectations were not fulfilled even at the second UNCTAD conference held in New Delhi in 1968. See Branislav Gosovic, "UNCTAD:

North-South Encounter," *International Conciliation* (May 1968), pp. 76-89.

15 United Nations, *Economic Survey of Asia and the Far East 1969* (E/CN. 11/935), pp. 53-5. Some economists have also accepted the arguments for expanding inter-regional trade in Asia. See for example P.E. Stoneham, "Intra-regional Trade Cooperation in Developing Asia," *JCMS* (December 1967), pp. 197-210 and D.T. Lakdawala, "Trends in Regional Cooperation in Asia," in Margaret Grant, ed., *South Asia Pacific Crisis* (New York, 1964), pp. 77-100.

16 See Chapter IV, "Evolution of Ideas," in United Nations, *Economic Survey of Asia and the Far East, 1969* (E/CN. 11/935), pp. 67-72.

17 See Chapter VI, "Some Beginnings," and Chapter VII, "The Next Steps," in ibid., pp. 81-9.

18 United Nations, ECAFE, *The United Nations Economic Cammission for Asia and the Far East. One Times One Hundred, Selections from the Work of ECAFE* (Bangkok, 24 October 1970), p. v. The Asian Coconut Community is an association of Asian producers organised on a commodity basis in order to further a cooperative regional effort toward better production, processing, marketing, and research. The formation of other communities of producers of commodities like pepper, rice, and tin is being encouraged by the ECAFE secretariat. Ibid., pp. 19-20. For accounts of the Mekong Basin Project, see Wightman, n. 4, pp. 183-202 and W.R. Derrick Sewell and Gilbert F. White, "The Lower Mekong: An Experiment in International River Development," *International Conciliation* (May 1966). An account of the Asian highway will be found in United Nations, *Economic Bulletin for Asia and the Far East* (June 1968), pp. 45-8.

19 Kabul Declaration on Asian Economic Development, Appendix II to ECAFE Report of the Meeting of the Council of Ministers for Asian Economic Cooperation (E/CN. 11/961), 25 January 1971 (mimeographed), pp. 37-9.

20 Singh, n. 8, pp. 169 211. *The Europa Yearbook 1971. A World Survey*, Volume I, part I, *International Organisations* (London, 1971), pp. 145-7. For comparisons between the Colombo Plan and the aid programmes of the Inter-American system, see Lagos, *International Statification and Underdeveloped Countries* (Chapel Hill, 1963), pp. 70-7, 215.

21 Singh, n. 8, pp. 9-11.

22 Interview with Dr. Thelma Vettel, Economist at the United States, Department of State, Washington, D.C., 7 September 1971.

23 White, *Regional Development Banks*, pp. 71-4, 78, 80, 85

24 Asian Development Bank, *Annual Report for 1973* (Manila, 1974), pp. 2-31. (Amounts expressed are in US dollars at its current value of 0.73662 gm. of fine gold).

25 See Bernard K. Gordon, *Toward Disengagement in Asia: A Strategy for American Foreign Policy* (Englewood Cliffs, N. J., 1969), pp. 92-130, for an exposition of the role of regionalism in Southeast Asia. He advocates a regional pact built around ASEAN, with Japan and Australia playing an important role in the security field.

[26] See Kiyoshi Kojima, ed., *Pacific Trade and Development* (Tokyo, 1968), especially Chapter 12, ''Japan's Role in Asian Econ omic Development,'' pp. 359-89.

[27] See Intra-Regional Trade as a Growth Strategy, Chapter VI, "Some Beginnings," in United Nations, *Economic Survey of Asia and the Far East, 1969* (E/CN. 11/935), p. 81.

[28] *FEER Yearbook, 1971*, pp. 56-9.

[29] Chapter VI, "Some Beginnings," *Economic Survey of Asia and the Far East, 1969*, p. 83. For descriptions and analyses of RCD, see Nurul Islam, "RCD: Pakistan, Iran and Turkey," in *JCMS* (March 1967), pp. 283-301 and Parvez Hasan, "Regional Plan Harmonization: A Case Study of RCD," (Karachi, January 1968), mimeographed. However, RCD has not been able to provide effective consulation between the countries, according to a World Bank economist who has worked in Pakistan. Interview with Jack M. Baranson, Industrial Economist, World Bank, Washington, D.C., 17 September 1971.

[30] Wightman, n. 4, pp. 363-4.

CHAPTER IX

RECENT TRENDS IN INTEGRATION

LATIN AMERICA

We have seen in Chapters Four and Seven that the Latin American integration movement in the early 1970's was facing a crisis. The institution on which the greatest stress had been laid, namely LAFTA, was considered as a step towards a Latin American Common Market. The feasibility of this ultimate goal which had gained importance due to the example of the European Economic Community (EEC) was, however, a matter of doubt. The Central American Common Market (CACM), on the other hand, did achieve some early successes, but faced an equally serious crisis on account of internecine political disputes among the member countries. Our findings for the first decade of LAFTA and CACM were therefore largely negative and some suggestions were made at the end of Chapter Seven as to how the movement could be sustained by giving it a new direction. We have now to see the extent to which the movement took a new turn during the 1970's and the measure of its success.

(*i*) *LAFTA and the Andean Group*

Throughout its early history the doubts entertained by many as to the workability of LAFTA were held in abeyance. Once, however, LAFTA had been established and it was conclusively known that trade would not expand under its auspices to any satisfying degree, a number of Latin American nations which still felt integration of some sort was necessary to the solution of the economic impasse in which they found themselves began to consider the formation of subregional groups within LAFTA to be treated as a unit. The hope was that within such groups, integration could proceed more rapidly and that ultimately these subgroups could be integrated themselves at the old LAFTA level.

Agreements for the Andean, Rio de la Plata, and Caribbean subregions were signed and financial institutions set up for each area. Meanwhile the Central American Common Market declined in effectiveness for the same reasons as LAFTA.

The first stage of effecting structural changes in LAFTA was due in 1972. However, in 1969 the Caracas Protocol offered postponement of this until 1980, as we know. As of today in the early 1980's, "diagnostic" seminars and studies have conclusively and vociferously demanded a thorough-going and decisive restructuring of LAFTA. With the rise of new instruments and means of integration, there is genuine doubt as to the practicability of continuing to breathe artificial life into this moribund organisation. All the same, the pioneering work of LAFTA, inspite of its original schema being over-ambitious, has been sustained to this day although in attenuated form. Perhaps a new treaty, different from that which was signed in 1960, would salvage LAFTA as a broad scheme of regional integration.

The manifest stagnation of LAFTA has ushered in the era of sub-regionalism in integration. In this direction the resurrection of the original Cono del Sur (Southern cone) group did not prove possible, but the two subregional agglomerations, Andean and Rio de la Plata, which developed in the late 1960's were of the same order of magnitude. The most unified group to emerge was the Andean Pact of six Pacific Coast nations: Peru, Chile, Ecuador, Colombia, Bolivia and as a later member, Venezuela. The market was only 75 million and the states, by and large with the exception of Chile and to a slight degree Colombia, were neither industrially developed nor adequately linked by transport and communications. The pact, established in 1969, was not a classic free trade area, but represented a Latin American approach which involved the coordination of foreign economic policy, harmonization of development planning, and integration of industries, which it was hoped to develop in the area by means of explicit complementarity agreements. One of the most important areas of cooperation was to be the integration of the transport network which was discontinuous and thus prohibitively expensive for normal intrazonal trade. The emphasis was on state development projects and only secondarily to reduce tariffs with the goal of achieving a free trade zone.

While the Andean group has been able to achieve some of its aims, and in particular, until the departure of Chile in 1976, a coordination of policy towards foreign direct investment, and overtly on the issues in the North-South dialogue, the economic results have not been impressive. Only 5 per cent of the member countries exports are reported to go to other countries in the subregion after the Chilean departure and there has been no significant growth of this figure since the trade liberalization programme began in 1970. Such trade as exists, while diversifying, consists mainly of agricultural products.[1] There has been no obvious stimulus to growth and industrialization beyond what would have probably occurred in any case. Thus economically, while not yet devoid of momentum, the Andean group is less successful than the CACM, measured in terms of the growth of intrazonal trade as a proportion of total number trade (though this particular measure was not matched by equal development gains in the CACM). The refusal of Venezuela, and secondarily of Bolivia and Ecuador, to distribute benefits accruing from the rise in oil prices or to agree to guarantee the group's oil supply in return for trade rather than hard currency has demonstrated once again that the probability of major cooperation at considerable national expense is minimal and that even a fairly strong agreement such as binds the Andean Group is incapable of overcoming this in the absence of strong countervailing interests and clear economic pay-off.

In 1976 the Andean Pact faced a crisis owing to a dispute over trade diversion policy, which Chile and Colombia wished to minimise, while the other states demanded an extremely high common external tariff, averaging about 70 per cent. This would have protected assigned industry in the least developed member countries, but at considerable cost in economic welfare to consumers. Moreover, there had been a shift in Chilean growth strategy after the coup which deposed Allende towards encouraging foreign investment in the export sector. This brought Chile into sharp conflict with the foreign investment guidelines enunciated in the Group's "Decision 24". The divergence on these issues, between a Rightist, free enterprise growth theory consistent with the desires of the industrialized nations, and a somewhat statist development strategy with discouragement of foreign direct investment, led to Chile's acrimonious withdrawal from the Pact in 1976. The remaining five countries "vowed to continue the integration process." They concentrated on politically non-controversial programmes, nonetheless essential to trade growth, in the area of infrastructure development.

The withdrawal of Chile from the Andean Pact appears to have been the result of a dispute which was inward and economic in nature and not the result of external struggles for influence by the United States, Brazil, Mexico, and Argentina. The bigger Latin American powers perhaps felt that the Andean agreement potentially threatened their own development by closing off markets and there was certainly an attraction for an authoritarian style of government on the part of Chile, which had adopted their growth model. The declining economy of Chile before it left the pact (leading to the loss of its former leading position in the group in favour of the newly oil-rich Venezuela) also played a part as Chile was politically sensitive to the loss of prestige and influence, and its inability to counter strident attacks from the Left.

The original plan for the Andean Group was probably over-ambitious. The foreign investment control regulations were too inflexible, being consistent only with a single growth model. The sectoral production-sharing agreements probably could not have been carried out in an economically gratifying manner because delays, lack of adequate transport networks, and inexperience in manufacture and quality control would have led to severe cost overruns. Multilateral coordination of industrial production without a strong central authority is an extremely difficult planning task. The Andean states appear to have been too inexperienced to realize that the attempt was likely to encounter serious difficulties.

In 1978 the Andean Pact faced an uncertain future. LAFTA also remained a fairly stagnant holding operation. The transition period fixed by the Treaty of Montevideo and the Caracas Protocol is to end in 1980, and by the end of this year, member countries will have to decide whether to continue the Association with new measures aimed at increased regional integration or whether the proposal for a common market in Latin America should be dropped altogether.[2]

An abandonment of the treaty would, however, open the LAFTA countries to the danger of having to apply the most-favoured-nation principles of the General Agreement on Tariff and Trade (GATT) (which exempts customs unions and free trade areas from the principle).[3]

On 26 May 1979, exactly a decade after the "little summit" of five nations (Bolivia, Chile, Colombia, Ecuador, and Peru) wherein the Cartagena Agreement set in motion the process of Andean subregional integration, the heads of state of member countries of the Andean group met again in Cartagena to take stock and to consolidate their cooperation.

The Andean group was not formed as a breakaway splinter group of LAFTA. Rather, with the benefits of LAFTA at the beginning cornered by Brazil, Mexico, and Argentina, the smaller states wanted to ensure their rapid economic progress so that they could in time participate in LAFTA on an equal footing within the three major countries. The Cartagena Agreement represented only the economic sphere. There are also agreements in the cultural and social spheres. Thus the Andean group took strides towards total integration by taking an interest in other fields. An International Integration Institute, Andean Enterpreneurs' School, Commission of Higher Education, and an Andean Association of Universities are testimomials to the progress in non-economic areas.

On the economic front, we have seen that the Andean group desired a community model of economic development This was termed the "rationalisation of capitalism" as the play of the free market was to go hand in hand with intervention by the state as chief agent in the assignment of resources. This fundamentally reflects the approach of ECLA strongly influenced by Raul Prebisch. The leading basic mechanisms involved in this model are:

1) the regional trade liberalisation programme (as per the schedules set by the Constitutive Treaty);
2) the adoption of a common external tariff (but postponed for several years by the Lima Protocol of 1976);
3) joint industrial programming of two major types:
   a) industrial rationalization programmes of existing industries;

b) sectoral programming dealing with future industrial specialisation on equal participation.

4) preferential treatment to relatively less developed countries and special programme of support;

5) harmonisation of economic and social policies (e.g. adoption of a regional code for investment and transfer of technology).

The positive outlook, keenness, and togetherness of the technocrats coupled with the fairly strong similarity between the political intentions of the governments of Bolivia (until 1972), Chile, and Peru explains the successful start the Andean group had in its first four years. But the integration process came to an almost standstill from 1974 to 1976 due to the serious deterioration of the international economy precipitated by the oil crisis and nationalism superseding the need for regional cooperation.

Ultimately Chile withdrew in 1976. Then there was a diluting and reworking of several provisions of the Cartagena Agreement to facilitate the entry of Venezuela.

It should be said to the credit of the Andean group that in spite of the lack of homogeneity on the countries themselves, the age-old animosity that still persists in the region as a result of the scars of border conflicts and the experiments they had to pioneer like the industrial programming, preferential treatment, etc., considerable progress has been made in taking up new and complex projects.[4]

The Andean Pact is, however, now a far second to SELA, as the leading organization of the Latin American integration movement, notwithstanding the high hopes raised by the Cartagena mandate.

(ii) The Building up of Infrastructure

We have observed in Chapter Six that economic growth tends to concentrate in certain parts of a country and to sharpen the differences between different regions. We have noted also that the IDB has devoted much attention to the preparation of technical studies and feasibility reports geared to the building up of infrastructure, the development of natural resources, the exploitation of river valleys, etc.

The preliminary work undertaken by the IDB helped in the establishment of Rio de la Plata or River Plate Group by a treaty signed in 1969, and other projects which seek to develop the infrastructure of the areas in their jurisdiction.

The Rio de la Plata Group

The contracting parties consist of those states with territories in the Rio de la Plata basin, viz. Argentina, Bolivia, Brazil, Paraguay, and Uruguay. As originally conceived, the group was a multilateral river basin development arrangement, which aspired to conjointly plan navigational and hydroelectric development and water utilization with the cooperation and aid of various international development agencies led by the Inter-American Development Bank.

Clearly the Plate Agreement was never an ambitiously conceived scheme of full and rapid economic integration such as the Andean Pact. It is not a trade liberalization scheme, nor are there any common rules for treatment of transnational investors. As originally envisaged, there was to be some coordination of industrial development plans around joint infrastructure development, especially certain major hydroelectric power dams. The pact involves only part of the territories of the contracting parties and does not exclude participation in other integration schemes.

Politically the Plate Agreement includes the border regions of Argentina with Brazil and the buffer states between them, which were the arena for an intense Brazil-Argentinean struggle for influence in large part because of their rich natural resources. The main projects undertaken by the organization, which has become more active of late, are massive hydroelectric power scheme on the Parana River which have been given an impetus by the 1973 oil price hike.

There has occurred considerable bickering over these power schemes, especially Argentinian objections to the $8 billion dollar, eleven million kilowatt Itaipu Dam being jointly built by Brazil and Paraguay in the latter country to supply power to the Brazilian south. Argentina claimed that it would interfere with the efficiency of the joint Argentina-Paraguay dams being built downstream at Corpus and Yacireta Apipe. As late as July 1977 Brazil and Argentina were accusing one another of hegemonial geopolitical schemes in the subregion and there was a dispute over highway transport which the press called "the war of the trucks". However, at the ninth conference of Plate River Basin Foreign Affairs Ministers in December 1977 there was a mysterious reconciliation on the part of Brazil and Argentina. At the same time, relations between Brazil and Paraguay deteriorated.[5]

The establishment of the Financial Fund for the Development of the Plate River Basin in March 1977 with a capital of $100 million is perhaps evidence of increasing commitment of the member countries to the scheme mainly because of the energy resources (of which both Brazil and Argentina are short) to be found abundantly in Paraguay and Bolivia. It remains unclear whether there will be sufficient political support for the Fund to live up to its objectives of promoting subregional industrial complementarity especially in border zones, developing infrastructure, and possibly aiding in improvement of environmental, health, and educational conditions.

Though the Plate Agreement was only a limited infrastructure development oriented scheme, it is to be noted that it includes the three most affluent and developed Latin American nations (as well as the two least developed, viz. Paraguay and Bolivia), and it may soon have a fourth in Chile in some sort of *de facto* associate status. In contrast to the Andean pact, there seems to be a trend toward upgrading of cooperation in the Plate Group. Should this process, still extremely fragile and subject to severe stress, continue, the Plate Grouping, roughly the original Cona del Sur scheme area, is potentially the strongest economic bloc and most active trade region in Latin America. Perhaps two thirds of intra-Latin American trade already takes place within the area. This reflects not only the population and affluence of contiguous developed regions of Argentina and Brazil, but also the sophisticated level of industrial production occurring there. Despite the existence of other integration schemes, the trade links of many Latin American countries are stronger to the Plate Group than to the integration schemes to which they belong.

The Amazon Pact

The Amazon Pact, created by the Amazon Cooperation Treaty signed on 3 July 1978, is an agreement aiming to promote integration of the contiguous Amazon basin territories of the eight signatory countries. The contracting parties are Bolivia, Brazil, Colombia, Ecuador, Guyana, Peru, Surinam, and Venezuela. The contents of the treaty were not immediately made fully public, but it appears (because of widespread suspicion of Brazilian intentions) to be a weak scheme for technical cooperation, and scientific research into the biological and social problems of the region. However, because of the vast area and multitude of important countries involved, should cooperation and integration with this group be upgraded in years to come, it could emerge as highly significant. Should Brazil-Argentinean rivalry lead to stagnation of the integration of the Plate group of countries, the future economic pattern of Latin America could be a stabilized Amazon Pact group centring on Brazil.

Resistance to the scheme was at one time strong from the non-Brazilan parties which feared that Brazil might develop hegemony over their Amazon regions once infrastructure was developed, particularly if the schemes linked the resource-rich, but largely uninhabited, Amazon territories of the peripheral nations more strongly with Brazil than with the central zones of these countries themselves. No doubt residual fears remain despite Brazil's attempts to counter them.[6]

In a speech in Brazil Admiral Emilio Massera, member of the Military Junta of Argentina, proposed that the two countries "join their destinies in a confederate union as the only proper way of responding to history's challenge to exploit all their natural resources, not only for the benefit of Argentina and Brazil, but for all the countries of Latin America." This appeared to be an attempt to counter US hegemony in the area. Although the proposal for a South Atlantic Pact advanced insistently by Argentina, especially by its Admirals, did not find an echo in Brazil, there is still a possibility that it may bear fruit at some time.[7] The alternative to such a joint hegemony would be a series of regional groupings in Latin America which might eventually link up in some informal way to an integrated Latin American movement.

One of the main obstacles to trade in Latin America is the high transport cost between the regional states in contract to the relatively cheaper sea transportation between the continent and the metropolitan centres of Europe and the United States.

It was only fairly recently, and with strategic as well as

economic motivation, that serious efforts were made, usually by the public sector, to improve the infrastructure by joining the various national settled areas along the coast, building roads between the Atlantic and Pacific, across the Amazon and Andes, and introducing modern telecommunications. Attempt are also being made to establish Latin American multinationals to compete with established and foreign transport services within the zone, especially in the Caribbean.

The realisation of the need for a transport network in South America devloped only after easy import substitution had been done, when it was necessary to regionalise the development of a capital goods industry and heavy consumer durables, and when income and population had risen. Had transport facilities been provided before World War I (as was done, for example, in the Indian subcontinent) the continent of South America would have been more diversified and prosperours. The efforts now being made are expected to provide the basis for substantial changes in the economic scene in the years to come. There is a danger, however, that the benefits of these changes may go largely to the multinationals or to exploitative state systems in the region.

(*iii*) *Aid, Trade, and Investment and the Role of SELA*

We have seen in Chapter Five that the original plans drawn up by ECLA for regional economic cooperation were based on the assumption that foreign assistance would not be available. In fact, one of the objects of the Latin American economic integration movement was to make Latin America less dependent on the United States. However, the effect of the policies adopted by the integrationist movement did not conspicuously further this goal. In fact, one of the valid criticisms against the movement has been that it tended to increase the hold of American business interests in Latin America.

The criticism of US aid being linked with private investment in Latin America has been less applicable to the Inter-American Development Bank. The IDB has worked with other organs of the inter-American system and with ECLA in furthering the cause of Latin American integration, although its creation in 1959 antedated both the Treaty of Montevideo and the Charter of Puntedel Este, which set up the Alliance for Progress (AFP).

Along with LAFTA and the AFP, it was a product of a period of optimism in the early 1960's when there was great hope that reforms could be accomplished by regional institutions in Latin America.

The decision by the United States Government to give in to the long-standing demand by the Latin Americans for a regional development bank diffused the responsibility for decisions in regard to loan applications. The bank seems to have been permitted by the United States to play a role as spokesman for the Latin American nations rather than as an instrument of US policy. The bank had ordinary capital resources of $850 million when it commenced operations in 1961. Ordinary and concessionary funds amounted to $9.75 billion in 1978. A Fund for Special Operations, which was created with small initial resources of $150 million, had increased to $1.75 billion by 1978.

The IDB enjoys a good credit rating in the New York money market and in other financial centres. This is ascribed to the strong political support it receives from the US Government, the strength of its own financial department, and its location in Washington. By the end of 1978, outstanding loans came to about $14 billion, and the projects on which the bank was involved came to $57 billion.

The policy followed from 1971 to 1978 was to give the bulk of the funds to the less developed countries ($657 million) and to those with insufficient markets ($135 million). Stress was also laid on physical regional integration projects ($305 million).

Funds were allocated in the following manner from its inception in 1961 to 1978: energy 25 per cent; agriculture 22 per cent; industry and mining 16 per cent; transport and communications 14 per cent; health 10 per cent; export financing, pre-investment, and tourism 5 per cent; and urban development and education 4 per cent each.

For the period 1979-82, the IDB has proposed a programme reserving 50 per cent of the funds for the projects benefiting the lowest income groups, especially those which encourage the creation of productive employment.

At the 20th annual meeting of the IDB, its President, Antonio Ortiz Mena, stated that stress would also be laid on (1) the reduction of imbalances within societies and between the countries of Latin America; (2) strategies aimed at the integral development of national resources, including energy; (3) stepping up the efficiency of productive systems and opening up economies to the outside world. A multinational fund for fomenting industry in Latin America was being set up. He also stressed the need for greater efforts to integrate and cooperate.[8]

Notwithstanding the constructive role of the Inter-American Development Bank in aiding the development of Latin America there has been an increasing feeling during the seventies that unless drastic steps are taken Latin America's share of the world market will continue to decline and growth rates will not increase commensurate with expectations of the countries themselves. The stress which had been laid in the sixties on financial assistance from outside and the wresting of trade concessions began to give way to new mechanisms based on the building up of solidarity of the Latin American nations and the mobilistation of other Third World countries against the industrialised countries. This time the stress was on a variety of measures to mobilise resources for the rapid industrialisation of the Latin American region. These resources are to come both from within and outside the region.

Earlier during the sixties, the Special Coordinating Committee for Latin America (CECLA) was set up to work out a common regional position for Latin America at the first UNCTAD meeting of 1964. It was a highly flexible grouping without any permanent organisation. Apart from preparing common positions for UNCTAD, CECLA tried to establish itself as an agent of bloc bargaining between Latin America on the one hand, and the United States as well as the European Economic Community on the other. However, it was unsuccessful in its attempts to reverse the EEC's Common Agricultural Policy, which had placed the bulk of agricultural commodities under heavy protection duties. This had a serious effect on beef imports from Latin America. The Lome Agreement of February 1975, under which the EEC gave forty-six African, Asian, and Caribbean countries special access to the EEC in direct competition with Latin American producers, was a major setback for CECLA. Under the Treaty of Madrid of December 1974, Belgium, Denmark, the Federal Republic of Germany,

Spain, Switzerland, the United Kingdom, and Yugoslavia become non-regional members of the IDB, joining Israel and Japan. (This was, however, an achievement not of CECLA, but of the IDB). CECLA was wound up in early 1973 perhaps due to the energy crisis. The first meeting of SELA took place only three years later in January 1976.[9]

In the meantime the Latin American countries were searching for new instruments to forge their solidarity and to accomplish their common economic goals. When President Echeverria of Mexico addressed the third United Nations Conference on Trade and Development in Santiago in April-May 1972 he put forth the idea of a Charter of Economic Rights and Duties of States. The late President Allende of Chile took up the same theme when he addressed the United Nations General Assembly at New York in December 1972, and pleaded for the right of developing countries to protect their economic and political systems against transnational corporations. A charter was finally adopted by the United Nations General Assembly on 12 December 1974. The Charter enunciates the sovereign and inalienable right of every state to choose its own economic system without outside interference, coercion or threat. In the exercise of its full permanent sovereignty over "all its wealth, natural resources and economic activities," a state has the right to regulate and exercise authority over foreign investments and supervise the activities of transnational corporations within its jurisdiction. "No State shall be compelled to grant preferential treatment to foreign investment." It also forbids transnational corporations from intervening in the internal affairs of host countries.

States also have the right to nationalise, expropriate, and transfer the ownership of foreign property, with "appropriate compensation" to be paid by the States according to "its relevant laws and regulations and all circumstances that the State considers pertinent." In cases where the question of compensation is controversial, "it shall be settled under the domestic law of the nationalising State and by its tribunals," unless it is freely and mutually agreed that other peaceful means be sought.

The Tlatelolco conference of American foreign ministers in January 1976 was held outside the scope of the Organisation of American States. It set up a Committee to study the Inter-American system and to propose measures for its restructuring (CEESI). This Committee worked out a formula, later accepted by the OAS, under which each American country was free to have relations with Cuba or not, as it thought fit. The realisation that they could influence US policy towards Latin America seems to have reminded the Latin American countries of the benefits of block bargaining. A new pan-Latin American organisation (Sistena Economica Latino Americana—SELA) was therefore mooted at the initiative of Venezuela and Mexico in October 1975 in Panama. The new organisation was justified in the context of (1) the growing deterioration of the global economic system, which made Latin American self-help a necessity; (2) the success of Oil Petroleum Exporting Countries (OPEC) in collective bargaining with industrial nations; and (3) the role the new organisation could play in clarifying the dialogue with the United States although it would not displace the OAS.[10]

SELA was described by the President of Mexico as "a permanent regional agency for consultation, coordination, co-operation and joint economic and social promotion, with legal international personality, constituted by sovereign Latin American States." Its supreme organ is a Latin American Council with representatives from each member state. The council sets general policies, approves by-laws and regulations for SELA's other permanent bodies, sets up a working programme, and examines, guides, and approves the activities of SELA agencies.

An important feature of SELA is the Action Committees, made up of member states, which carry out study programmes and specific projects and adopt joint negotiating positions of interest to two or more member states. The Committees are financed by the participating countries. SELA also has a permanent secretariat at Caracas, the capital of Venezuela, the leading oil producer in Latin America.[11]

It is difficult to mention briefly the major steps taken to further the integration process in Latin America by SELA. The fifth ordinary meeting of the SELA Council held at Caracas from 30 July to 2 August 1979, achieved agreement on a wide range of issues, including proposals for the reconstruction of Nicargua, cooperation with Panama for the development of resources in the Canal Zone, solidarity with OLADE (the Latin American Energy Organisation) whose San Jose declaration was endorsed, and support for Bolivia's tin industry in the context of a US threat to place part of its strategic reserves on the market. The meeting adopted joint positions towards the US and the EEC. It also took steps to formulate the Latin American attitude to the forthcoming UN meetings and set up the first Multinational Company for Marketing of Fertilizers (Multifert), resulting from the report of the Fertilizer Action Committee. Reports of the existing Action Committees were received and new ones set up in areas like technological information and pharmaceutical products. A new Permanent Secretary was appointed and a cooperation agreement was signed with Spain.[12]

(*iv*) *Findings*

The Latin American movement for integration is thus getting away from its earlier preoccupation with a European-style common market. It is laying more and more stress on the forging of common policies towards multinational corporations, which are now generally recognised to exercise enormous economic power. These new policies are being promoted not by the traditional great powers of Latin America—Argentina and Brazil—but by the newly emerging oil-rich countries like Mexico, Venezuela, and Peru. The oil wealth of these countries seems to have given them the internal strength to enforce policies of economic independence, to take over foreign investments in crucial fields, and to offer moral and financial support to other Latin American countries so as to enable the latter to assert their own independence from multinational corporations and the major world powers. The fact that Cuba is associating itself with SELA is an indication that United States influence (at least in the economic sphere) may be on the decline. The unit of operation in future is likely to be the nation-state, with a stress on the positive policies to be followed to ensure its survival as a decision-making unit rather than on ideological factors of a revolutionay type or the pursuit of traditional European models of customs unions and common markets.

ASIA

In Chapter Eight we have examined the relevance of the Latin American experience to Asia and tried to draw certain lessons in order to avoid the mistakes of Latin American integration. Developments in Asia since 1973 indicate that the process of economic cooperation has made considerable progress and that some effort has been made to rectify the mistakes of the earlier years. While saying this, it must be considered, however, that Asia has always been a less favourable ground for the application of economic integration principles than Latin America because of the greater incidence of political conflict and war and uncertainties of various kinds. It is proposed now to consider the developments which have taken place in regard to integration in the ESCAP region since 1973.

(*i*) *ESCAP and Asian Economic Cooperation*

The trade conference sponsored by the ESCAP in New Delhi in August 1978 ended on a successful note with the adoption of a wide ranging programme of trade expansion and cooperation on a regional basis. In order to a promote a greater awareness of the import and export prospects within the region a trade information network was decided to be set up using the facilities of the ESCAP trade promotion centre and national trade promotion agencies. Long-term trade contacts were decided to be encouraged and promoted. Financial assistance was suggested to commodity associations and communities to help them enlarge the scope of their activities, especially to benefit the least developed, land-locked, and island developing nations.

An improvement in monetary and credit cooperation between member countries, the harmonising of trade statistics, tariff nomenclatures, and the facilitating of shipping, road, rail, and air transport were other decisions taken at the conference. In regard to the reduction of tariff barriers, however, the conference did not take positive decisions. Some member countries were unwilling to make tariff cuts, which they said would have to wait till the GATT decisions on the subject were finalised. A trade cooperation group was set up with sub-groups for countries interested in particular measures. The United Nations Development Programme (UNDP) was urged to cooperate with ESCAP and it was declared that regional trade expansion was proposed to promote the objective of the new international economic order and be consistent with the international and regional obligations of the member countries.[13]

At the 35th session of ESCAP held at Manila in 1979 it was reported that a regional development strategy was being drawn up for the 1980's taking into consideration the region's vulnerability to external factors. It was noted that some of the member countries had achieved growth rates exceeding 10 per cent. However, the economic picture was generally gloomy. It was proposed that technical and economic cooperation among developing countries should be promoted as an instrument for developing collective self-reliance. The major problem to be tackled in the 1980's were identified as food scarcity and the need for reasonable self-sufficiency in the area in order to tackle the widespread poverty and massive unemployment. Among the areas which required the establishment of viable policies were (1) transnational corporations and their role in the area; (2) the spectre of protectionism on the part of the developed countries; (3) plight of the land-locked least developed and developing island countries; (4) lack of firm commitment for international aid; (5) problems of the enviroment and the organisation of human settlements on the regional level; and (6) problems of social development, population growth, and the need for an integrated programme of rural development. To these could be added the need for a rational energy policy keeping in view the likelihood of a long-term rise in energy prices.

ESCAP has formulated a transfer scheme under which large amounts of concessional aid would be transferred to the developing countries. A Global Development Fund is to be formed by raising capital from international markets and a modest sales levy on each barrel of oil consumed. The terms of lending would range from 12-20 years and the interest rates would be 4-5 per cent.

An Asian Reinsurance Corporation was launched in Bangkok in May 1979. Each of the eight members have subscribed $500,000 to the share capital of the Corporation which expected to become the "Lloyd's Bank" for Asia and the Pacific. The founding members were Afghanistan, Bangladesh, China, India, the Philippines, South Korea, Sri Lanka, and Thailand.[14]

(ii) Sub-regionalism: The importance of ASEAN

Among the sub-regional organisations in the ESCAP region ASEAN has made a remarkable impact in the region both in the economic and political spheres. It has achieved tremendous growth since its launching in 1967. In the early 1970's China, the Soviet Union, and Ho Chi Minh's Vietnam traded verbal attacks with ASEAN. But by 1978 their stance towards ASEAN had undergone a remarkable transformation.

In 1971 a United Nations official at the ESCAP referred to ASEAN as a "joke" because it pretended to be a strong regional organisation but did not even have a secretariat or a set of operational programmes with any degree of visibility. Yet today ESCAP has an ASEAN unit inside its International Trade Division and is the executing agency for a formal dialogue between ASEAN and the United Nations. The present level of international recognition for and prominence of ASEAN has opened the way for talk of "ASEANisation" as the scenario for Asian regional cooperation. It is worthwhile, therefore, to examine how ASEAN has been able to affect both the style and the content of the functioning of international organizations in Asia.

Prior to ASEAN, Asian international organisations developed in seclusion from one another. They struggled to maintain themselves by seeking funds mostly from a single non-Asian source. Politico-military integration set-ups moved towards closure and technical bodies barely managed to survive. What was lacking was a cohesive spirit based on a clear convincing rationale and ability to influence the formation of non-governmental international organisations. ASEAN achieved its breakthrough because of *a*) a sub-regional approach, *b*) proliferation of non-governmental ASEAN association (a sort of moral persuasion rather than a collusive course of imposition of policies in the private sector; *c*) caucus solidarity to influence and control the outcome of plenary sessions of other Asian international organisations; *d*) placement of ASEAN nationals at vital personnel sectors manning ESCAP and other organisations; *e*) locations to attract majority of the headquarters of Asian international organisations; *f*) quick resolution of political conflicts among its members; *g*) neo-functionalism, with political support given to technocrats, who designed a clearing union, a trade bloc, and a system of allocating petroleum and rice to member countries in short supply at reduced rates and industrial complementation.[15]

Some of the latest projects of intra-ASEAN cooperation as of December 1979 are listed below to highlight the progress of ASEAN:

1) The ASEAN Preferential Trading Agreement (PTA) covering 2,327 items by the end of the year has to have higher tariff cuts on the preferential rates than the then 10 per cent tariff cuts.

2) Two ASEAN area projects—the Malaysian Project costing about $171.5 million and the Indonesian project costing about $313 million—were scheduled for commencement of production in 1984 and 1982 respectively.

3) Thailand has been given sanction for a rock-salt soda ash project.

4) The Philippine proposal for substitution of a compound fertiliser project in place of super-phosphate project also has been sanctioned.

5) ASEAN sea-bed project is scheduled to be completed in 1981 and it will link all ASEAN countries through an underwater cable network.

6) Establishment of ASEAN emergency rice reserve of 50,000 tonnes is mooted.

7) On the security front the Premier of Singapore, Lee Kuan Yew, is on record as voicing in the first week of May 1979 the possibility of some mutual security pact among agreements and token force in Thailand for the ASEAN countries. According to Lee, this is possible in view of the fluid and sensitive situation persisting in Indo-China and competition between China and the Soviet Union for a hold over Southeast Asia with Vietnam butting in as a middle power.[16]

Apart from the projections made by ESCAP a number of studies have been undertaken or are in progress regarding the prospects for regional economic cooperation in Southeast Asia, South Asia, and the Pacific. These studies (mostly by economists) project future trends of trade and point out the role which trade expansion can play in the development of the region. However these studies do not necessarily have much impact on the policy-making organs of the countries concerned. This is because political considerations play a major role both in short and long-term economic policy-making.

It is important to remember in this context that Asia continues to be a major arena for the conflict between the United States and its Western allies and the Communist countries. It was this conflict that was the basis for the establishment of the Baghdad Pact in 1955 which later became the Central Treaty Organisation (CENTO). Similarly the Southeast Asian Treaty Organisation (SEATO) was set up to "contain" Chinese expansionism in Southeast Asia. Both organisations began to stress economic and technological cooperation as their original rationale became less meaningful as a result of the Sino-Soviet split and the introduction of a bilateral approach in American policy towards Asia after the decline of "monolithic communism."

The winding up of SEATO in 1977 and of CENTO in 1979 is an indication of the desire of former American allies to dissociate themselves from too close a link with the major world powers. This is clear from the fact that Turkey, Iran, and Pakistan continue to lay stress on the RCD (Regional Cooperation for Development) although recent political developments in the region have given a further set-back to this effort.

At the same time another major trend in the Pacific region should not be overlooked. This is the attempt by highly industrialised countries of the Pacific (United States, Canada, Japan, and Australia) to come together and evolve common trade and development policies. This development has been talked of for several years and a good deal of thinking seems to have gone into it. Its concrete manifestation are unlikely to be seen in the form of an organisational framework in the near future. On the other hand, it is likely to influence the policies of member countries towards the association of developing countries such as ESCAP and ASEAN. The role which transnational corporations can play in the determination of these policies remains to be seen.

(*iii*) *Findings*

It will be noticed that the ESCAP countries, like the ECLA countries, had realised the futility of trying to further economic integration at the continental level in the absence of an adequate infrastructure. The stress laid on the building up of trade promotion facilities, the furtherance of commodity associations and communities, and other measures decided at the ESCAP's conference of August 1978 is an indication of this trend. At the same time, the important role played by ASEAN in the development of a major sector of the Asian region is an indication of the pragmatic role which can be played by a sub-regional organisation of like-minded countries at approximately the same level of development. However, some other tasks listed by us in the last paragraph of Chapter Eight still require the attention of the ESCAP member-countries.

REFERENCES

1 Edward S. Milenky, "Latin America's Multilateral Diplomacy: Integration, Disintegration and Interdependence," *International Affairs* (January 1977), p. 79. For an earlier account of the Andean Pact, see pp. 141-45.

2 *Comercio Exterior*, March 1979, pp. 116, 118.

3 Milenky, n. 1, p. 78.

4 Gordon Mace, "The Andean Group at the Ten Year Mark," *International Perspective* (September-October/November-December 1979).

5 *Comercio Exterior*, February 1978, pp. 84-6.

6 Ibid., May 1978, p. 232 and August 1978, p. 353.

7 Ibid., February 1978, pp. 84-5.

8 Ibid., August 1979, pp. 287-9.

9 Milenky, n. 1, pp. 83-6.

10 Ibid., pp. 90-2.

11 *Commercio Exterior*, November 1975, p. 436.

12 Ibid., October 1979, pp. 386-90.

13 *Times of India*, 24 August 1978.

14 *Asian Recorder*, 1979, pp. 15029-30 and also *Asian Recorder*, 1980, p. 15365.

15 See Michael Haas, "ASEANisation of Asian International Relations," *Asia Pacific Community* (Fall 1979), pp. 72-85, for a detailed discussion of the role of ASEAN.

16 *Asian Recorder*, 1979, p. 14924.

CHAPTER X

CONCLUSION

Developments in Latin America and Asia during the past few years indicate that the serious world situation has been aggravated by the lack of solidarity of the developing countries on a regional as well as on an international basis.

In the first place, the 1973 oil crisis has shown no signs of abating. It has hit developing countries far worse than it did the industrialised ones; yet the former have made little or no effort to combine to face this common threat.

According to the Willy Brandt Commission for a North-South dialogue, a colossal amount of $450 billion or more is being spent every year on arms, as against a meagre sum of $20 billion or so being spent on development, the world over. The Commission put forth a balanced set of recommendations urging a more equitable distribution of the world's wealth on the basis of a concept of global responsibility for economic and social development.

Third World unity in the economic sphere continues to be an issue. The Havana Declaration of the Non-Aligned States issued in September 1979, was full rhetoric, pledging solidarity and a common front against military and political alliances and blocs, opposition to spheres of influence and balance of power politics, and the threat to sovereignty over natural resources on the part of the developing countries. It urged the immediate dismantling of foreign military bases and installations in the Indian Ocean. The United Nations Industrial Development Organization (UNIDO) conference held in January 1980 in New Delhi concluded without an agreement between the Group of 77 and the industrialised countries. The appeals to the rich nations at the conference for concessions were described by one UNIDO delegate as "talking to the deaf."

In Latin America, there was a trend towards more fundamental changes. The fall of Salvador Allende in 1973 had been followed by a strengthening of military regimes in Brazil and Argentina. The success of the Brazilian regime in its economic development programme, and the continued domination of the military in Argentina, Chile, Peru, and many smaller countries had been a hallmark of the 1970's. The fall of the liberal regimes in the early sixties had been succeeded by an authoritarian era. An indication of the reduced power of the United States in the region was the pressure brought to bear by the Latin Americans on the US to surrender the Canal Zone to the Republic of Panama. A revised treaty was signed in 1978, one of the major achievements of President Carter's early years. The new regime in Nicaragua, which succeeded the fall of the Somoza dictatorship, seemed to be poised to provide for economic change, and received strong economic support from other Latin American countries. At the same time, there was instability in the Central American countries of Honduras, Guatemala, and El Salvador, which was said to have been instigated by Cuba.

In Asia the Soviet intervention in Afghanistan in December 1979 worsened the situation. The Soviet Union (which a few years ago had proposed the Brezhnev Doctrine for an Asian collective security pact) had now intervened in a buffer state which was also a member of the non-aligned movement. India initiated a series of talks with her neighbouring countries and the Soviet Union in order to ease the situation.

The attempt of a united and resurgent Vietnam to woo ASEAN did not make headway. China, Thailand, and the United States felt it necessary to reduce the influence of Vietnam in Southeast Asia, which in their view had already had disastrous effects in Kampuchea.

What kind of economic restructuring is feasible in a situation where the Cold War seems to have been revived, and the possibility of a nuclear war cannot be excluded, where the poverty of Third World countries as a whole is disguised by pockets of affluence and boom conditions in some of them, and where the demand for concessions from the industrialised countries has elicited little or no response?

We started the study of Latin American integration with an

examination of the international framework and the background of integration in Latin America at the end of the Second World War. Due to the high level of skills of its people, the infrastructure which still survived the devastation of the war, and the vast sums of money pumped into its economy by Marshall Plan Aid, Western Europe made a rapid recovery from the devastation of the Second World War and moved towards economic integration on the traditional pattern of trade expansion based on a common market. This approach received support from the United States and enabled the multinationals to establish themselves on the European industrial scene.

Both ECLA and ECAFE (now ESCAP) tried to work towards an international economic community somewhat on the lines of the EEC. The Latin American Free Trade Area, which was set up by the Treaty of Montevideo in 1960, was more an aspiration than a reality. The fact that the integration movement was sought to be concretised in the form of a free trade area in its early stages was due to the West European example. However, in the course of building up this model the Latin Americans did not give enough importance, as we have seen in Chapter Seven, to the lack of infrastructure, communication facilities, and to a comparable economic base. They preferred integration at a continental (i.e. Latin American) level rather than at a subregional level, where it would have been economically viable. The financing of integration raised problems of increasing dependency on the US. Most of the international financing agencies, with the possible exception of the Inter-American Development Bank, were not free from pressures. For example, US support was forthcoming in Central America on the understanding that US business interests would be protected.

During the 1970's there was a change in approach in Latin America. In the first place the stress shifted from LAFTA to subregional integration (mainly the Andean Pact). Secondly, economic self-reliance began to emerge as an instrument for subregional integration. This arose due to the importance given by the Andean Pact to the adoption of a common code in regard to foreign investment. Thirdly, the Latin American countries worked together in order to evolve a common economic policy towards countries outside the region through SELA (the

Latin American Economic System). SELA was a successor to CECLA, which had originated in an attempt to work out common policies in UN conferences. It took up new programmes on a voluntary basis, sponsored new organisations to carry out programmes initiated by it, and promoted the formation of Latin American multinational corporations.

SELA was particularly significant because its leadership was with the oil-rich countries of Mexico, Venezuela, and Peru. Thus there was a possibility of resource mobilisation from within the region rather than from outside. As against the traditional European model of custom unions and common markets, SELA was based firmly on the nation-state as the unit of operation.

In Asia growth of ASEAN was spectacular during the 1970's. All member countries seemed to have a common approach to economic development based on free enterprise, promoted by a fairly centralised nation state.

Some of the basic elements of the New International Economic Order (NIEO) were adopted by ASEAN for its common progress as guidelines:

1) Generalised system of preferences for raw materials and manufactured goods;

2) reinsurance pools to conserve foreign exchange, especially during transactions among member countries;

3) commodity price stabilisation schemes, in order to provide protection from the vicissitudes of global price fluctuations;

4) productivity improvements, marketing assistance, funds for research and development capabilities of Third World and production projects;

5) transfer of technology; and

6) giving importance to the needs of land-locked countries.[1]

Two of the main conclusions we reached while assessing the integration movement upto the early seventies were the need for (a) subregional integration and (b) dependence on internal resources and ideologies rather than on "imitation" and blind acceptance of foreign resources. The Lima objectives stressed the importance of collective self-reliance and redeployment of resources as against global interdependence and market equilibrium.

Economic integration has gone through different phases governed by different theoretical considerations and approaches which have been discussed earlier in this study. The dominant considerations that influenced the early movement towards integration were (1) the traditional customs union theory, and (2) the Prebisch thesis, arguing for gains to be derived by the peripheral countries. The market approach and the integrated development approach both laid great stress on trade. Internal factors of growth tended to be neglected or ignored. By way of overcoming the deficiencies in the integration process, great stress at present is laid on self-reliance at the inter-regional level and collective self-reliance at the intra-regional level. This outlook is a welcome new phase.

Collective self-reliance is possible between certain groups of countries having (a) common economic interests, and (b) sufficient political motivation to join their efforts together systematically and durably, so as to reduce the perennial dependence relations that enslaves them to the centre of the world order. Such regional collective self-reliance demands that there should be

1) progressive integration of internal economies and gradual reduction of ties with the centre. This means the eventual disappearance of the dual economy and the emergence of a self-centred economy of member countries;

2) determined efforts by the economies of the region to become self-reliant and planned economies;

3) a focus on the sphere of production to evolve a regional division of labour and a new international division of labour; and

4) priority to be placed on the basic needs of the people and on improving their standard of living collectively.

Development strategies need not be identical, otherwise ultimate political unification into one State would become an absolute necessity.

Thus regional collective self-reliance proposes a radical change in outward influence and inward control without completely replacing outward-directed by inward-directed development. Its success would lie not in pursuing a comprehensive range of objectives, but in achieving specific results and need-oriented objectives at the earliest opportunity.

The production of goods and services at a regional level would be designed both for enhancing the availability of goods and services and for strengthening the bargaining power of the countries concerned. The stress would be on the minimum material needs like food, clothing, footwear, materials for low-cost housing and popular consumer durables like watches, pens, and radio receivers. In such a programme, the stress would be on investment in human resources and on distribution along with production.

The financing of the new approach to economic integration would have to be carefully worked out to avoid undue dependence on any one source, whether it be the World Bank and other dollar sources, or the OPEC currencies. Both of these approaches would subject the economies of the countries to fluctuations.

An Asian Clearing Union with the Asian Monetary Unit (AMU) as the unit of account already exists for some of the ESCAP countries. This eliminates reliance on foreign exchange for intra-regional trade. This experience of ESCAP can be a useful pointer to other developing countries involved in collective self-reliance.

In order to reduce the hold of the multinational corporations on the transfer of technology, it is necessary to evolve and enforce a code of conduct for the multinationals. Such a code should be evolved by the regional bodies as the international code has been delayed.

The experience of OPEC could be adapted in order to form a producer's forum to stabilise prices and diversify exports, and a purchaser's forum to control prices of imports. The success of OPEC cannot be repeated because other commodities are not in such great demand as oil. However, some progress can be made in this direction.

Finally, it is necessary for Third World countries to cooperate on a regional basis for the establishment of a new information order to counteract the influence of the world media, and make the Third World community a reality.[2]

In our review of developments in Latin American and Asia during the 1970's in Chapters Seven and Eight we have seen that both regions have taken strides towards the rectification of defects in the functioning of regional organisations and solutions to some of the problems which faced them in the early 1970's appeared to be within reach. The pragmatic approach in regard to project planning and the building up of the infrastructure has been accepted by several Latin American organisations. The growth of SELA, as a major force for furthering development and integrating the economies of the area at the continental level, and the emergence of the Andean Pact as an example of sub-regional integration, laying stress on a common approach to foreign investment, are important pointers in this regard. The development of regional groupings for the exploitation of natural resources around the Rio de la Plata and the Amazon river have also made some progress.

In the ASEAN region there has also been a pragmatic effort based on a common approach to economic problems of member countries. It is remarkable that these five countries, which had little contact with one another just after the Second World War, now seem to have developed a sense of community and the organisation has begun to play a role as a catalyst in the affairs of ESCAP. There are even proposals for them to develop a sense of solidarity and build up a security system at a political and military level against a possible threat to the region.

The concept of integration with which Latin America began was somewhat oriented to the evolution of a self-reliant approach, the object being to reduce dependence on the US economy. This approach, however, gave way to a static approach to integration based on the Western European model. The dynamic aspects of integration based on economies of scale, accumulation of capital, infrastructure building, and technological progress—all of which were expected to give an impetus to public investment and higher rates of growth—tended to be ignored. Latin America initiated and actively participated in the common efforts of Third World countries for economic development. It is now evident that regional groupings can be a viable policy of international trade and development provided the dynamic effects of growth are allowed to operate.

There is however an important caution to be introduced here. Third World countries benefiting from rapid economic development do not necessarily solve their political and economic problems, unless stress is laid on the distribution of the gains of integrated development as discussed in this chapter.

Even the originator of much of the thinking of the Third World in this area, Raul Prebisch, has recognised in recent years that the theory of growth was "our great mistake, a great mistake that lasted for many years. We thought that an acceleration of the rate of growth would solve all problems. Now we know that does not happen." In an interview in December 1978 he argued that the laws of the market, even with powerful trade unions and mass involvement in politics, cannot solve the problem. This can be done only by "a complete transformation of the system" which "presupposes a change in the power structure either through a democratic process or through violence." He points out that the high consumption patterns of the elites in the centre and the periphery are closely interlinked and there is a great wastage of capital because of imitation of consumption styles in the centre by the periphery. The consumption society can function smoothly only when a country "agrees to submit to certain limits on the distribution of income in the process of industrialisation and democratisation and allows the higher income surplus to be transferred to the means of production . . . ."[3]

While agreeing broadly with this view, it should be noted that a confrontation between the Third World countries and the industrialised countries is not necessary. Third World countries should stop running after high technology. If there are areas where sophisticated technology is inevitable, they can be reserved for international corporations with a time limit, as was done by the Andean Group of countries. Other areas, concerned with the fulfilment of basic needs, can be developed with local or regional capital, resources, and know-how.

If Latin America and Asian countries were to follow the dynamic aspects of integration they would avoid some of the worst dangers of development which may face them due to the revolution of rising expectations.

The stress should not be on the mere setting up of new institutions, but on making them responsive to people's needs and delinking the developmental process in the Third World countries from the vested interests, both national and international, so that "man" becomes the centre of development.

REFERENCES

1 Michael Haas, "ASEANisation of Asian International Relations," *Asia Pacific Community* (Fall 1979), pp. 72-85.

2 For a detailed study on collective self-reliance and on project approach see Edgardo A. Floto, "Economic Integration and Collective Self-reliance," *Economic Integration and Third World Collective Self-Reliance* (Third World Occasional Paper No. 4; Switzerland: Third World Forum, 1979), and also the Preface by Ismail-Sabri Abdalla in the same book.

3 See interview with Raul Prebisch by Altaf Gauhar in Arusha, Tanzania, December 1978, in "North-South Dialogue," *Third World Quarterly* (January 1980), pp. 14-20.

TABLE I

Country Profile of Latin America

(total and per capita by region and country, 1976)

Regions and Countries	*Population*		*Area*	*Density*	*Gross Domestic Product 1976*	
	Total 1976	*Average annual rate of growth*				
	in thousand	*percentage*	*km²*	*inhabitants per km²*	*total millions of $US*	*per capita $US*
	(1)	(2)	(3)	(4)	(5)	(6)
LAFTA	**278,960**	**2.8**	**19,309,635**	**14**	**354,334**	**1,270**
Argentina	257,20	1.3	2,766,889	9	47,420	1,844
Brazil	109,180	2.8	8,511,965	13	144,615	1,325
Chile	10,450	1.8	756,945	14	11,234	1,075
Mexico	62,330	3.5	1,972,547	32	79,139	1,270
Paraguay	2,780	2.8	406,752	7	1,699	611
Uruguay	2,800	1.2	176,215	16	3,693	1,319
Andean Group	**65,700**	**3.0**	**4,718,322**	**14**	**66,534**	**1,013**
Bolivia	5,790	2.7	1,098,581	5	2,406	415
Colombia	24,330	2.9	1,138,914	21	14,795	608
Ecuador	7,310	3.5	283,561	26	4,955	678
Peru	15,910	3.1	1,285,216	12	13,359	840
Venezuela	12,360	3.2	912,050	14	31,019	2,510

	(1)	(2)	(3)	(4)	(5)	(6)
CACM	**17,460**	**2.9**	**422,718**	**41**	**11,930**	**683**
Costa Rica	2,020	2.6	50,700	40	2,345	1,161
El Salvador	4,120	3.2	21,041	196	2,186	531
Guatemala	6,260	2.9	108,889	57	4,363	697
Honduras	2,830	3.8	112,088	25	1,201	424
Nicaragua	2,230	3.3	130,000	17	1,835	823
Caribbean Community	**4,876**	**1.5**	**257,480**	**19**	**6,649**	**1,364**
Barbados	250	0.7	431	580	379	1,516
Belize	144	3.1	22,965	6	109	757
Guyana	780	1.8	214,969	4	438	561
Jamaica	2,070	1.6	10,991	188	3,045	1,471
Trinidad and Tobago	1,100	1.1	5,128	214	2,392	2,174
Eastern Caribbean Common Market	**532**	**1.0**	**2,996**	**178**	**286**	**538**
Antigua	71	1.4	442	161	37	509
Dominica	76	1.1	751	101	34	420
Grenada	96	0.4	344	279	59	614
Monsterrat St. Kitts-Nevis	13	1.4	98	133	13	1,036
Anguilla	66	0.5	357	185	41	587
St. Lucia	110	1.2	616	179	65	598
St. Vincent	100	1.2	388	258	37	339

Source: UNCTAD, *Handbook of International Trade and Development Statistics, 1979.* Table No. 6.1A, p. 474.

TABLE II.A

Foreign Trade: Exports F.O.B.

(Total value of exports in current prices from Latin America, millions of US dollars)

Countries	*1960*	*1965*	*1970*	*1975*
World[1]	128,000	186,400	312,500	873,600
LAFTA	**7,280**	**9,384**	**12,350**	**30,440**
Argentina	1,079	1,493	1,773	2,961
Brazil	1,269	1,596	2,739	8,670
Mexico	763	1,120	1,281	2,859
Paraguay	27	57	64	176
Uruguay	129	191	233	384
Venezuela	2,432	2,744	2,850	9,540
Andean Group	**1,582**	**2,183**	**6,260**	**15,390**
Bolivia	51	110	190	529
Chile	490	688	1.234	1,661
Colombia	465	539	727	1,465
Ecuador	145	180	210	897
Peru	431	666	1,044	1,297
CACM	**439**	**760**	**1,110**	**2,300**
Costa Rica	86	112	231	493
El Salvador	117	189	228	515
Guatemala	117	188	298	624
Honduras	63	127	172	293
Nicaragua	56	144	175	375

[1] Excluding trade with one another of the following countries: People's Republic of China, Mongolia, Democratic People's Republic of Korea, and Democratic Republic of Vietnam.

Note: World and regional totals include countries and territories not listed separately and estimates when full data is not available. Totals have been adjusted, where necessary to approximate Exports f.o.b.

Source: United Nations, *Handbook of Internotional Trade and Development Statistics, 1972*, Table Nos. 1.1, pp. 3 and 5; UNCTAD, *Handbook of International Trade and Development Statistics, Supplement 1977*, Table Nos. 1.1 and 1.2, p. 4.

TABLE II.B

Foreign Trade: Imports C.I.F.

(in current prices of Latin America)
(millions of US dollars)

Countries	*1960*	*1965*	*1970*	*1975*
World[1]	**135,500**	**197,500**	**328,700**	**907,200**
LAFTA	**6,940**	**7,429**	**11,630**	**37,930**
Argentina	1,249	1,199	1,694	3,947
Brazil	1,462	1,096	2,849	13,692
Mexico	1,187	1,560	2,327	6,580
Paraguay	32	47	64	186
Uruguay	244	150	231	557
Venezuela	1,060	1,297	1,640	5,327
Andean Group	**1,561**	**2,080**	**4,470**	**12,960**
Bolivia	69	134	159	558
Chile	500	604	931	1,776
Colombia	519	454	843	1,495
Ecuador	100	169	274	824
Peru	373	719	619	2,984
CACM	**510**	**889**	**1,230**	**2,950**
Costa Rica	110	178	317	694
El Salvador	122	201	214	601
Guatemala	138	228	284	733
Honduras	72	122	221	404
Nicaragua	72	160	198	517

[1] Excluding trade with one another of the following countries: People's Republic of China, Mongolia, Democratic People's Republic of Korea, and Democratic Republic of Vietnam.

Note: World and regional totals include countries and territories not listed separately and estimate when full data is not available. Totals have been adjusted, where necessary to approximate import c.i.f.

Source: United Nations, *Handbook of International Trade and Development Statistics, 1972,* Table No. 1.2, pp. 11, 13. UNCTAD, *Handbook of International Trade and Development Statistics, Supplement 1977,* Tables 1.1 and 1.2, p. 5.

TABLE II.C

Network of Exports of Latin America
(millions of US dollars)

Year	World[1]	EC. CL. I[2]	USA	Western Europe[3]	Latin America[4]	Developing Africa	Developing Asia
1960	8,590	6,750	3,600	2,730	680	61	61
1965	11,060	7,990	3,530	3,630	1,080	91	115
1970	15,040	10,980	4,440	4,990	1,700	87	213

[1] Includes special category exports, ships stores and bunkers and other exports of minor importance whose destinations could not be determined. United States special category exports are included in total exports (by destination as well as in exports) by commodity class to the world as a whole, but are excluded from the detailed commodity class by destination data. Excluding trade of Socialist Countries of Asia with one another.

[2] United States, Canada, Western Europe, South Africa, Japan, Australia, and New Zealand.

[3] Including Turkey and Yugoslavia.

[4] Consists only of the twenty Republics.

Source: United Nations, *Handbook of International Trade and Development Statistics, 1972,* Table 3.1, pp. 54-5.

TABLE II.D

India-LAFTA Trade, 1965-1970

Country	*1965*	*1966*	*1967*	*1968*	*1969*	*1970*
			Exports in million US $ FOB			
Argentina	246.6	254.5	283.7	338.1	364.3	398.4
Bolivia	3.5	7.7	9.9	13.9	14.0	12.5
Brazil	201.7	187.7	161.2	193.1	241.4	305.8
Colombia	20.0	31.9	23.1	34.2	54.7	69.4
Chile	56.4	60.0	84.3	91.8	94.4	148.1
Ecuador	13.4	13.0	14.5	16.4	16.1	31.2
Mexico	44.0	64.3	57.2	62.2	86.7	121.0
Paraguay	17.6	19.9	15.6	16.2	18.9	31.1
Peru	62.2	60.4	40.0	50.5	57.5	65.8
Uruguay	16.0	26.9	17.1	18.9	30.6	32.9
Venezuela	160.8	149.5	145.1	165.1	168.3	129.4
Total	**842.2**	**875.8**	**851.7**	**1,000.4**	**1,146.9**	**1,345.6**
			Imports in million US $ CIF			
Argentina	289.4	252.3	253.6	275.3	365.9	385.9
Bolivia	14.0	15.2	17.6	18.9	24.5	31.5
Brazil	273.0	238.0	226.5	276.7	296.0	282.1
Colombia	39.3	57.9	37.9	48.0	75.3	69.4
Chile	137.5	166.5	185.6	178.1	207.3	216.5
Ecuador	19.5	14.9	28.9	20.6	20.6	31.7

Mexico	30.0	34.9	38.6	42.9	51.9	62.5
Paraguay	13.9	15.1	17.2	16.9	17.1	17.6
Peru	88.0	100.2	104.1	107.8	106.3	108.8
Uruguay	45.1	57.3	46.9	42.0	58.2	88.5
Venezuela	36.2	35.0	38.7	47.1	61.5	52.7
Total	**985.9**	**987.3**	**995.6**	**1074.3**	**1284.6**	**1347.2**

Source: John W. Sloan, "LAFTA in the 1960's: Obstacles to Progress," *International Development Review*, no. 1, 1972, p. 18.

TABLE II.E

World Trade: Index Numbers by Regions and Country

I. Unit Value (Price) Index
1953 = 100

Country	*1938*	*1948*	*1952*	*1954*	*1955*	*1956*	*1957*	*1958*	*1959*	*1960*
					Exports					
Argentina	—	—	103	85	87	81	78	74	73	78
Brazil	—	59	105	*117*	92	89	87	79	64	63
Chile	31	68	98	89	97	*112*	87	77	86	89
Colombia	21	66	97	*120*	106	107	107	90	76	77
Costa Rica	—	—	—	114	102	*116*	109	98	—	—
Ecuador	17	71	98	*126*	111	112	110	115	—	—
Nicaragua	—	63	100	*127*	108	112	101	87	75	76
Peru	—	—	*119*	108	105	111	108	92	—	—
					II. Volume Index					
Argentina	—	—	59	108	94	103	111	120	122	*123*
Brazil	—	*133*	85	100	109	111	103	99	115	*120*
Chile	139	154	151	*168*	158	153	159	156	*181*	163
Colombia	64	74	82	92	92	83	79	83	*100*	95
Costa Rica	—	—	—	93	99	72	95	*120*	—	—
Ecuador	73	86	110	109	110	112	129	*132*	—	—
Nicaragua	—	58	96	113	158	123	140	156	*192*	130
Peru	—	—	97	105	123	130	*147*	121	117	—

Source: United Nations, *Statistical Yearbook*, p. 431.

TABLE II.F

Leading Export Commodities of Underdeveloped Nations

(based on 1967 trade data)

Country	*Number of leading export commodities*	*Export of leading commodities as per cent of total exports*	*Leading export commodities*
Argentina	4	61	Meat, wheat, corn, wool
Bolivia	1	63	Tin
Brazil	4	58	Coffee, iron ore, cotton, cocoa
Chile	3	85	Copper, iron ore, nitrates
Colombia	2	69	Coffee, oil
Costa Rica*	2	60	Coffee, bananas
Dominican Republic	5	91	Sugar, coffee, cocoa, bauxite, tobacco
Ecuador*	3	84	Bananas, coffee, cocoa
Guatemala*	4	69	Coffee, cotton, banana, sugar
Haiti*	3	68	Coffee, sugar, sisal
Honduras*	3	67	Bananas, coffee, wood
Jamaica*	4	75	Alumina, bauxite, sugar, bananas
Nicaragua	5	69	Cotton, coffee, meat, cotton seed, sugar
Paraguay	6	77	Meat, wood, cotton, quebracho, tobacco, oilseeds
Peru	6	78	Copper, fishmeal, cotton, silver, lead, sugar
Uruguay	3	84	Wool, meat, hides
Venezuela	2	98	Oil, iron ore

Source: Harry Magdoff, *The Age of Imperialism: The Economics of U.S. Foreign Policy* (New York, 1969), pp. 99-100 (*based on* International Monetary Fund, *International Financial Statistics*, July 1968).

Note: Statistics are for 1967, except for those marked with asterisks, which are for 1966 or the latest year for which reports are available).

SELECT BIBLIOGRAPHY

Books

Aggarwal, M.R., *Regional Economic Co-operation in South Asia*, New Delhi, 1979.

Anderson, Charles W., *Politics and Economic Change in Latin America: The Governing of Restless Nations*, Princeton, N.J., 1967.

Andic, F., et al, *A Theory of Economic Integration for Developing Countries*, London, 1971.

Astiz, Carlos Alberto, ed., *Latin American International Politics: Ambitions, Capabilities and the National Interest of Mexico, Brazil and Argentina*, Notre Dame, 1969.

Baerresen, Donald, Martin Carnoy and Joseph Grunwald, *Latin American Trade Patterns*, Washington D.C., 1965.

Bailey, Norman A., *Latin American in World Politics*, New York, 1967.

Balassa, Bela, *The Theory of Economic Integration*, Homewood, Ill., 1961.

Beaulac, Willard L., *A Diplomat Looks at Aid to Latin America*, Carbondale, Ill., 1970.

Berle, Adolf A., *Latin America—Diplomacy and Reality*, New York, 1962.

Blachman, Morris J. and Ronald G. Hellman, ed., *Terms of Conflict: Ideology in Latin American Politics*, Philadelphia, 1977.

Blasher, Coll, *The Hovering Giant: U.S. Responses to Revolutionary Change in Latin America*, Pittsburg, 1976.

Broide, Julio, *Banco Interamericano de Desarrollo, sus antecedentes y creacion*, Washington, D.C., 1961.

Business International Corporation, *LAFTA, Key to Latin America's 200 Million Consumers*, New York, 1966.

Cale, Edward G., *LAFTA: Progress, Problems, Prospects*, Washington, D.C., 1969.

Cardosa, Fernando Henrique and Enzo Falletto, *Dependency and Development in Latin America*, trans. by M.M. Urquidi, Berkeley, 1979.

Chilcote, Ronald H. and Joel C. Edelstein, *Latin America: The Struggle with Dependency and Beyond*, Cambridge, 1974.

Cochrane, James D., *The Politics of Regional Integration: The Central American Case*, New Orleans, 1969.

Cornell-Smith, Gordon, *The Inter-American System*, London, 1966.

———, *The United States and Latin America: An Historical Analysis of Inter-American Relations*, New York, 1974.

Cotler, Julio and Richard R. Fagen, ed., *Latin America and the United States: The Changing Political Realities*, Stanford, 1974.

Davis, Harold Eugene, J.J. Finan, and F. Taylor Peck, ed., *Latin American Diplomatic History*, Baton Rouge, 1977.

Dell, Sidney, *Trade Blocs and Common Markets*, New York, 1963.

———, *A Latin American Common Market ?* London, 1967.

Demas, William G., *Carribean Integration and Development*, Jamaica, 1976.

Development Problems in Latin America: An Analysis by the U.N. Economic Commission for Latin America, Austin, 1970.

Dewitt, R.Peter, Jr., *The Inter-American Development Bank and Political Influence with special reference to Costa Rica*, New York, 1977.

Dreier, John C., ed., *The Alliance for Progress: Problems and Perspectives*, Baltimore, 1962.

Duncan, W. Raymond, *Latin American Politics of Developmental Approach*, New York, 1976.

Einaudi, Luigi R., *Latin America in the 1970s*, Santa Monica, 1972.

Eisenhower, Milton, *The Wine is Bitter: The United States and Latin America*, Garden City, N.Y., 1963.

Ellis, Howard S., ed., *Economic Development for Latin America*, New York, 1961.

Fagen, Richard R., ed., *Capitalism and the State in U.S.—Latin American Relations*, Stanford, Calif., 1979.

Fenwick, Charles G., *The Inter-American Regional System*, New York, 1949.

Fontaine, Robert W. and James D. Theberge, *Latin America's New Internationalism: The End of Hemispheric Isolation*, New York, 1976.

Friedeberg, A.S., *United Nations Conference on Trade and Development of 1964: The Theory of the Peripheral Economy at the Centre of International Political Discussions*, Rotterdam, 1968.

Galbraith, J.K., *The New Industrial State*, New York, 1967.

Gerassi, John, *The Great Fear: The Reconquest of Latin America by Latin Americans*, New York, 1963.

_______, *The Great Fear in Latin America*, New York, 1966.

Ghai, Dharam, *El Comercio estatalyla integracion economica regional entre paises en desarrollo*, New York, 1973.

Grant, Margaret, ed., *South-Asia Pacific Crisis*, New York, 1964.

Gray, Richard B., ed., *Latin America and the United States in the 1970s*, Ithaca, 1971.

Gregg, Robert W., ed., *International Organisation in the Western Hemisphere*, Syracuse, N.Y., 1969.

Grunwald, Joseph and Miguel S. Wionczek, *Latin American Economic Integration and the United States*, Washington, D.C., 1971.

Gunnemann, Jon P., ed., *The Nation-State and Transnational Corporations in Conflict, with special reference to Latin America*, New York, 1975.

Gunther, John, *Inside South America*, New York, 1966.

Gupta, Sisir, *India and Regional Integration in Asia*, Bombay, 1964.

Haas, Ernst B., *The Uniting of Europe: Political, Social and Economic Forces 1950-57*, London, 1958.

Haas, Ernst, B. and Philippe C. Schmitter, *The Politics of Economics in Latin American Regionalism: The Latin American Free Trade Area after Four Years of Operation*, Denver, 1965.

Hacia la Integracion Acelerada de America Latina, Mexico, 1965.

Hansen, Roger D., *Central America: Regional Integration and Economic Development* (National Planning Association Studies in Development Progress, No. 1), Washington, D.C., 1967.

Hasan, Parvez, Regional Plan Harmonization: A Case Study of RCD, Karachi, January 1968, mimeographed.

Hayter, Teresa, *Aid as Imperialism*, Harmondsworth, 1971.

Hellman, Richard G. and H. John Rosenbaum, eds., *Latin America: The Search for a New International Role*, New York, 1975.

Herrera, Felipe, *Nacionalismo Latinoamericano*, Santiago de Chile, 1967.

Hilton, Ronald, ed., *The Movement Toward Latin American Unity*, New York, 1969.

Hirschman, Albert O., ed., *Latin American Issues: Essays and Comments*, New York, 1961.

Hodgson, Jaqueline Lou, "An Evaluation of the Prebisch Thesis," Doctoral Dissertation, Department of Economics, University of Wisconsin, 1965-66.

Horowitz, Irving Louis, et al., eds., *Latin American Radicalism: A Document Report on Left and Nationalist Movements*, New York, 1969.

Inter-American Development Bank, *The Inter-American Development Bank and the Economic Integration of Latin America*, Washington, D.C., 1969.

Inter-American Institute of International Legal Studies, *Instruments Relating to the Economic Integration of Latin America*, Dobbs Ferry, New York, 1968.

International Conferences of American States: First Supplement 1933-40, Washington, D.C., 1940.

International Conferences of American States: Second Supplement 1942-54, Washington, D.C., 1958.

Jacob, P.E. and Toscano, *The Integration of Political Communities*, Philadelphia, 1964.

Jaguaribe, Helio, et. al., *La Dependencia Politico-Economica de America Latina*, Mexico, 1970.

_______, *Political Development: A General Theory and a Latin American Case Study*, New York, 1973.

Jansen, G.H., *Non-Alignment and the Afro-Asian States*, New York, 1966.

Johnson, J. John, *Political Change in Latin America: The Emergence of the Middle Sectors*, Stanford, 1959.

Kahnert, F., P. Richards, E. Stoutjesdijk and P. Thomopoulos, *Economic Integration Among Developing Countries*, Paris, 1965.

Kantor, Harry, *The Ideology and Programme of the Peruvian Aprista Movement*, Berkeley, Calif., 1953.

Karnes, Thomas L., *The Failure of Union: Central America 1824-1960*, Chapel Hill, 1961.

Kojima, Kiyoshi, ed., *Pacific Trade and Development*, Tokyo, 1968.

Konig, Wolfgang, *Mexico y la integracion economica de America Latina*, Buenos Aires, 1973.

Krause, Walter and F. John Mathis, *Latin America and Economic Integration: Regional Planning for Development*, Iowa City, 1970.

Lagos, Gustavo, *International Stratification and Underdeveloped Countries*, Chapel Hill, 1963.

________, ed., *La Integration Latinoamericana: Situacion y Perspectivas*, Buenos Aires, 1965.

________, *Instituciones y Desarrollo Politico de America Latina*, Buenos Aires, 1966.

Lagos, Gustavo and Horacio H. Godoy, *Revolution of Being: A Latin American View of the Future*, New York, 1977.

Lekachman, Robert, ed., *National Policy for Economic Welfare at Home and Abroad*, New York, 1961.

Lipset, Seymour Martin and Solari, eds., *Elites in Latin America*, London, 1967.

Madariaga, Salvador de., *The Rise of the Spanish American Empire*, London, 1947.

Mariategui, Jose Carlos, "*Siete Ensayos de Interpretacions de la Realidad Puruana*, La Habana, 1963.

Maritano, Nino, *A Latin American Economic Community: History Policies and Problems*, Notre Dame, 1970.

Martinez-Piedra, Alberto, *Socio-Economic Change in Latin America*, Washington, D.C., 1970.

McClelland, Donald H., *The Central American Common Market: Economic Policies, Economic Growth and Choices for the Future*, New York, 1972.

Mora, Jose A., *From Panama to Punta del Este: Past Experience and Future Prospects*, Washington, D.C., n.d.

Morawetz, David, *The Andean Group: A Case Study of Economic Integration among Developing Countries*, Cambridge, 1974.

Myrdal, Gunnar, *Economic Theory and Underdeveloped Regions*, London, 1957.

Naoroji, Dadabhai, *Poverty and Un-British Rule in India*, Delhi, 1962.

Nehemkis, Peter, *Latin America: Myth and Reality*, New York, 1964.

Nisbet, Charles T., ed., *Latin America: Problems in Economic Development*, New York, 1969.

Nye, Joseph S., Jr.. ed., *International Regionalism: Readings*, Boston, 1968.

Okita, Saburo, *Essays in Japan and Asia*, Tokyo, 1970.

Oliveira-Campos, Roberto de, *Reflections on Latin American Development*, Austin, 1967.

Pendle, George, *A History of Latin America*, Harmondsworth, Middlesex, 1965.

Perloff, Harvey S., *Alliance for Progress: A Social Invention in the Making*, Baltimore, 1969.

Petras, James, and Maurice Zeitlin, eds., *Latin America: Reform or Revolution*? New York, 1968.

Pike, Fredrick B., *The United States and the Andean Republics: Peru, Bolivia, and Ecuador*, Cambridge, Mass., 1977.

Prebisch, Raul, *Change and Development, Latin America's Great Task Report submitted to the IDB*, New York, 1971.

______, *The Economic Development of Latin America and its Principal Problems*, New York, 1950.

______, *Towards a Dynamic Development Policy for Latin America*, UN Publication 64 II G4, New York, 1964.

Rhodes, Robert I., ed., *Imperialism and Underdevelopment: A Reader*, New York, 1970.

Robertson, A.H., *European Institutions: Cooperation, Integration, Unification*, New York, 1966.

Robson, P., ed., *International Economic Integration*, Harmondsworth, 1971.

Rockeffeler Report on the Americas, Chicago, 1969.

Rogers, William D., *The Twilight Struggle: The Alliance for Progress and the Politics of Development in Latin America*, New York, 1967.

Rowe, J.W.F., *Primary Commodities in International Trade*,

Cambridge, 1965.

Santamaria, Carlos Sanz de, *Some Reflections on Latin American Integration*, Washington, D.C., n.d.

Schmitter, Philippe C. and Ernst B. Haas, *Mexico and Latin American Economic Integration*, Berkeley, 1964.

Shapiro, Samuel, ed., *Integration of Man and Society in Latin America*, Notre Dame, 1967.

Sindhwani, Trilok N., *Economic Feasibility of an Asian Common Market: A Study of the ESCAP Region*, New Delhi, 1975.

Singh, Lalita Prasad, *The Politics of Economic Cooperation in Asia: A Study of Asian International Organization*, Columbia, 1966.

Sunkel, Osvaldo, ed., *Integracion Politica y Economica: El Proceso Europeo y el Problema Latinoamericano*, Santiago de Chile, 1970.

Swansborough, Robert H., *The Embattled Collossus: Economic Nationalism and United States Investors to Latin America*, Gainesville, Fla., 1976.

Tambs, Lewis A., ed., *United States Policy toward Latin America: Antecedents and Alternatives*, Temple, Arizona, 1976.

Third World Forum, *Economic Integration and Third World Collective Self-Reliance*, Third World Occasional Paper No. 4, 1979.

Torre, Haya de la, *El antiimperialismo yel APRA*, Santiago, 1936

Urquidi, Victor, *Free Trade and Economic Integration in Latin America: The Evolution of a Common Market Policy*, Berkeley, 1962.

Vandenberg, Arthur H., Jr., ed., *The Private Papers of Senator Vandenberg*, Cambridge, Mass., 1952.

Veliz, Claudio, ed., *Obstacles to Change in Latin America*, London, 1965.

_______, *The Politics of Conformity in Latin America*, London, 1967.

_______, *Latin America and the Caribbean: A Handbook of Documents*, New York, 1968.

Vodarsik, Dennis J., "Building The Latin American Community: The Meaning and Politics of Latin American Integration," Ph. D. Dissertation, Georgetown University,

Department of Government, 1969.

Wagner, R. Harrison, *U.S. Policy toward Latin America: A Study in Domestic and International Politics*, Standord, 1970.

Whitaker, Arthur P., *The United States and the Southern Cone: Argentina, Uruguay, and Chile*, Cambridge, 1977.

_______, *The Western Hemisphere Idea*, Ithaca, 1954.

White, John, *Regional Development Banks: A Study of Institutional Style*, London, 1970.

Wiarda, Howard J. and F. Kline Harvey, *Latin American Politics and Development*, Boston, 1979.

Wightman, David, *Toward Economic Cooperation in Asia: The United Nations Economic Commission for Asia and the Far East*, New Haven, 1963.

Wionczek, Miguel S., ed., *Latin American Economic Integration: Experiences and Prospects*, New York, 1966.

_______, ed., *Economic Cooperation in Latin America, Africa and Asia: A Handbook of Documents*, Cambridge, Mass., 1969.

Wynia, Gary W., *The Politics of Latin American Development*, New York, 1978.

ARTICLES

Aguilar, M. Alonso, "El Capitalismo Opulente de John Kenneth Galbraith," *Problemas del Desarrollo* (October-December 1969), pp. 113-40.

Antonio, Murga F., "Dependency: A Latin American View," *NACLA Newsletter*, Vol. IV, No. 10 (New York : North American Congress on Latin America) (February 1971), pp. 1-13.

Arndt, H.W. "Latin America turns to the Pacific," *International Development Review*, No. 1 (1971), pp. 41-3.

Axline, W. Andrew, "Integration and Development in the Commonwealth Carribean: The politics of regional negotiations," *International Organization*, Autumn 1978, pp. 953-74.

Baer, Werner, "The Economics of Prebisch and ECLA," *Economic Development and Cultural Change*, no. 2, 1962.

Baltra, Alberto Cortes, "El Pacto Andino y el Capital Extranjero," *Problemas del Desarrollo*, October-December

1970, pp. 69-71.

Bath, C. Richard and Dilmus D. James, "Dependency analysis Latin America: Some criticisms, some suggestions," *Latin American Research Review*, Vol. 11, No. 3, pp. 3-54.

Bhagwati, Jagdish, et al., "Trade Expansion and Economic Cooperation among Developing Countries : Report by an Expert Committee appointed by the Secretary-General of UNCTAD" (UN Document TD/B/68), reprinted in *Journal of Common Market Studies* (*JCMS*), September 1967, pp. 88-115.

Bodenheimer, Suzanne, "La Crisis del movimiento social democrata en America Latina," *Estudios Internationals*, January-March 1979, pp. 551-3.

Bond, Robert D., "Regionalism in Latin America: Prospects for the Latin American economic system (SELA)," *International Organization*, Spring 1978, pp. 401-24.

Brewster, Harelock and Clive Y. Thomas, "El liberalismo economico y el concepto de integracion economica," *Foro Internacional*, April-June 1969, pp. 406-19.

Cochrane, James D., "US Attitudes toward Central American Integration," *Inter-American Economic Affairs*, Autumn 1964, pp. 33-50.

Denham, Robert Edwin, "The Role of the US as an External Actor in the Integration of Latin America," *JCMS*, March 1969.

Dobosiewicz, Z., "Economic integration in Latin America," *Studies on the Developing Countries*, No. 4, 1974, pp. 86-116.

Escobar, Richard Lagos, "Latin America and the International Economy," *Journal of Interamerican Studies*, February 1976, pp. 100-14.

Fagen, Richard R., "The Carter Administration and Latin America: Business as Usual," *Foreign Affairs*, No. 3, 1979, pp. 652-69.

Fenwick, Charles G., "The Ninth International Conference of American States," *American Journal of International Law*, July 1968, p. 573.

Flanders, M. June, "The Economics of Prebisch and ECLA: A Comment," *EDCC*, April 1964, p. 312.

———, "Prebisch on Protectionism: An Evaluation," *The Economic Journal*, No. 294, June 1964, pp. 323-4.

Frankenhoff, Charles A., S.J., "The Prebisch Thesis: A Theory of Industrialism for Latin America," *Journal of Inter-American Studies* (*JIAS*), April 1962, p. 181.

Gauhar, Altaf, "North-South Dialogue: An interview with Raul Prebisch," *Third World Quarterly*, January 1980, pp. 14-20.

Gregg, Robert W., "The UN Regional Economic Commissions and Integration in the Underdeveloped Regions," *International Organization*, Spring 1966, pp. 208-32.

Haas, Ernst B., "The Uniting of Europe and the Uniting of Latin America," *JCMS*, 1966-67, pp. 315-43.

Haas, Michael, "ASEANisation of Asian International Relations," *Asia Pacific Community*, Fall 1979, pp. 72-85.

Herrera, Felipe, "The UN Regional Economic Commission and Integration in the Underdeveloped Regions," *International Organization*, Spring 1966, pp. 219-20.

Islam, Nurul, "RCD, Pakistan, Iran and Turkey," *JCMS*, March 1967, pp. 283-301.

Javits, Jacob K., "Last Chance a Common Market," *Foreign Affairs*, April 1967, p. 454.

Kitamura, Hiroshi, "Economic Development and Regional Planning in South-East Asia," *Economic Bulletin for Asia and the Far East*, September 1969, pp. 1-8.

Lagos, Gustavo, "The Political Role of Regional Economic Organizations in Latin America," *JCMS*, June 1968, p. 291.

Laredo, Iris Mabel, "Posicion de Los Estados Unidos Frente a la Integracion de America Latina: Afirmaciones of Tendcucias," *Revista de la Integracion*, November 1968, pp. 59-60.

Lleras, "The Alliance for Progress: Aims, Distortions, Obsta-Cles," *Foreign Affairs*, October 1963, pp. 25-37.

Lowenthal, Abraham F., "The United States and Latin America: Ending the Hegemonistic Presumption," *Foreign Affairs*, October 1976, pp. 199-213.

Lowenthal, Abraham F. and G. Traverton, "La formulacion de politicas norteamericandas Lacia America Latina: algunas proposiciones especulativas," *Foro Internacional*, April-June 1979, pp. 600-17.

Mace, Gordon, "The Andean Group at the Ten Year Mark," *International Perspective*, September-October/November-December 1979.

Mamalakis, Markos J., "Minerals, Multinationals and foreign

investment in Latin America," *Journal of Latin American Studies*, November 1977, pp. 316-36.

Martz, Mary Jeanne Read, "SELA: The Latin American economic system," Ploughing the seas?" *Inter-American Economic Affairs*, Spring 1979, pp. 33-64.

Milenky, Edward S., "Latin America's Multilateral Diplomacy: Integration, Disintegration and Independence," *International Affairs*, January 1977, p. 79.

Mitchell, Christopher, "Common Market: The Future of a Commitment: Punta del Este and After," *Inter-American Economic Affairs*, Winter 1967, pp. 73-87.

________, "The Role of Technocrats in Latin American Integration," *Inter-American Economic Affairs*, Summer 1967, pp. 13-20.

Nye, Joseph S., "United States Policy toward Regional Organization," *International Organization*, Summer 1969, pp. 728-32.

Odell, Peter R,, "Economic Integration and Special Patterns of Economic Development in Latin America," *JCMS*, March 1968, pp. 267-8.

Orantes, Isaac Cohen, "Funcionalismo integracion centroamericana," *Foro Internacional*, October-December 1968.

Petras, James and Moris Moiley, "Foreign aid and U.S. Chilean relations, 1964-1974," *Social Praxis*, nos. 3-4, 1974, pp. 161-78.

Pollock, David H., "Pearson and UNCTAD: A Comparison," *International Development Review*, 1970, no. 4, pp. 14-21.

Prebisch, Raul, "International Trade and Payments in an Era of Coexistence: Commercial Policy in the Underdeveloped Countries," *American Economic Review*, May 1959.

________, 'Interpretacao do Processo de Desenvolvimento Economico," *Revista Brasileisa de Economia*, March 1951, pp. 7-117.

________, "Joint Responsibilities for Latin American Progress," *Foreign Affairs*, July 1961, pp. 622-33.

Reinton, Per Olav, "Elementos Cognoscitivos y Valorativos en los Programas Latinoamericanos de integracion," *Revista de la Integracion*, November 1970, pp. 154-64.

________, "The Legitimacy of Latin American Integration," *America Latina*, October-December 1969, pp. 3-23.

Saez, S. Raul, "The Nine Wise Men and the Alliance for Progress," *International Organization*, Winter 1968, pp. 257-8.

Sanjuan, Pedro A., "To see ourselves as others see us: some Latin American perspectives on US policy," *Washington Quarterly*, Spring 1979, pp. 60-7.

Santos, Theotonio Dos, "Crisis de la Teoria del Desarollo y las Relaciones de Dependencia en America Latina," *Boletin de CESCO*, October-November 1968, pp. 26-9.

Schmitter, Philipps, "Central American Integration: Spillover, Spill-Around or Encapsulation?" *JCMS*, September 1970 pp. 47-8.

Segal, Aaron, "The Integration of Developing Countries: Some Thoughts on East Africa and Central America," *JCMS*, March 1967, pp. 267-9.

Sepulveda, Cesar, "Reflexiones Sobre la Alianza para el Progresso," *Foro Internacional*, July-September 1967, pp. 67-79.

Stavenhagen, Rodolfo, "The Future of Latin America : Between Underdevelopment and Revolution," *Latin American Perspectives*, no. 1, 1974.

Stepan, Alfred, "The U.S. and Latin America: Vital Interests and the Instruments," *Foreign Affairs*, no. 3, 1979, pp. 659-92.

Stoneham, P.E., "Inter-regional Trade Cooperation in Development Asia," *JCMS*, December 1967, pp. 197-210.

"The Andean Subregional Integration Movement," *Peruvian Foreign Trade News* (Lima), September 1969.

Toledo, Mario Monteforte, "La Integracion Centroamericana," *Problemas del Desarrollo*, October-December 1970, pp. 40-60.

_______, "Los intelectuales y la integracion Centroamericana," *Revista Mexicana de Socialogia* October-December 1967, pp. 844-5.

Torres-Rivas, Edelberto, "Desarrollo, integration y dependencia an Centroamerica," *Estudios Internacionales*, January-March 1970.

Walker, Thomas W., "El Papel de la democracia cristiana en la integracion de America Latina," *Foro Internacional*, July-September 1970, pp. 77-91.

Wionczek, Miguel S., "The Rise and the Decline of Latin American Economic Integration," *JCMS*, September 1970, pp. 53-9.

JOURNALS

ADB Annual Report.
American Economic Review.
Economic Bulletin for Asia and the Far East.
Economic Development and Cultural Change.
Far Eastern Economic Review.
Inter-American Economic Affairs.
International Conciliation.
International Development Review.
International Organization.
Journal of Common Market Studies.
Journal of Inter-American Studies.
UN Economic Survey of Asia and the Far East.

INDEX